DIANAWORLD

DIANAWORLD

AN OBSESSION

EDWARD WHITE

W. W. NORTON & COMPANY

Independent Publishers Since 1923

For information about permission to reproduce selections
from this book, write to Permissions, W. W. Norton & Company, Inc.,
500 Fifth Avenue, New York, NY 10110

For information about special discounts for bulk purchases,
please contact W. W. Norton Special Sales at
specialsales@wwnorton.com or 800-233-4830

Manufacturing by Sheridan
Book design by Brooke Koven
Production manager: Anna Oler

ISBN: 978-1-324-02156-8

W. W. Norton & Company, Inc.
500 Fifth Avenue, New York, NY 10110
www.wwnorton.com

W. W. Norton & Company Ltd.
15 Carlisle Street, London W1D 3BS

1 2 3 4 5 6 7 8 9 0

CONTENTS

DIANAWORLD

INTRODUCTION

O F THE VARIOUS titles that Diana Spencer collected during her life, it is the unofficial one of "the People's Princess" that has most come to encapsulate her reputation. The origins of the term are contested. Many have claimed that Tony Blair's spin doctor, the shrewd, calculating Alastair Campbell, invented it. Others have said it derived from Anthony Holden, a royal biographer and translator of ancient Greek poetry and Italian opera. Julie Burchill, a republican iconoclast perhaps best known for her writing about pop music, asserts that it was in fact she who bestowed the title upon Diana in a laudatory article about the princess published in 1992.

That credit for Diana's definitive sobriquet has been attributed to—and claimed by—such diverse figures is entirely fitting. In the half century of her existence as a public entity, Diana's mythology has been molded, burnished, and appropriated by an enormous cast of people. When her former personal protection officer Ken Wharfe published his reminiscences of Diana in 2017, he suggested that one of his motivations for doing so was that his old boss "has increasingly been written out of history." It was a tendentious claim then, provably false now. Of late, Diana has acquired a resurgent topicality. Key parts of her reputation—her rejection of deference, her questioning of institutional authority, her bridling against *the way things are*—seem very in keeping with the current age. Moreover, an audience of young adults, many not born until after her death, have "rediscovered" her through numerous television, film, and theatrical productions, reacting to the chapters of her life as though tuning in to breaking news events. The complication here is that so much of the fictionalized Diana is slathered in mythology—some belonging to Diana alone, some to an endless roll call of predecessors and antecedents, stretching back centuries.

This book is about those layers of mythology and the people connected to them. It is less a biography of Diana, more the story of a cultural obsession told via an exploration of "Dianaworld," the sprawling, ever-evolving precinct of her various lives—public and private, real and imagined. It is a place inhabited by era-defining statesmen as well as the most marginal figures in our society; of legendary performers as well as outsider artists; of priests, poets, and drag queens. It features not only "Dianaists"—her supporters and advocates—but also her critics and adversaries.

Each chapter of the book addresses Diana's connection with different communities, groups, and individuals who have, in some way or other, shaped her singular reputation. The dominant focus is Diana's relationship with Britishness, especially the English component of that identity. Yet, as Dianaworld is a global community, the Diana fixations of hundreds of millions of people beyond the United Kingdom are also covered in depth. Unlike conventional biographies of Diana, this book devotes much space to examining how she has touched ordinary people, most of whom never met her but consider her a vital presence in their lives. These include those who have written about her; those who have made her the subject of their unfulfilled dreams; those who have styled themselves on her; those who have satirized her; those who run fan clubs in her memory; those who cling to fantastical conspiracy theories about her life and death.

What follows is at least as much about the princess's people as it is the People's Princess. The voices of those people are harvested from myriad sources rarely, if ever, used in books about Diana, the royal family, or the monarchy. These include oral history interviews from the capacious archives of the British Library and written submissions to the Mass Observation social research project, in which the thoughts and feelings of anonymous members of the British public capture the details of everyday life—as well as their responses to notable national events, including Diana's wedding in 1981 and her funeral in 1997. An even more intimate record of such moments comes from the Great Diary Project archive at Bishopsgate Institute in London, a marvelous collection of many thousands of diaries donated from people across the UK. These resources are augmented by original interviews conducted by the author with people in Britain and beyond, all of whom report sharing a distinct connection with Diana.

As a result, the Diana excavated in these pages is a woman of mythological complexity and far-reaching significance. Frequently, she is a "cut-and-shut" cultural figure. Typically, cut-and-shut refers to the practice of welding together different parts of two cars to make a single new vehicle. From a distance, the result can look thoroughly successful; it is only on close inspection that the incongruities and potential instabilities reveal themselves. In Diana's case, she has often been the locus of very different, perhaps antithetical, identities: ancient and modern, royalist and republican, nationalist and internationalist. On a personal level, Diana could be every bit as contradictory: beguiling and frustrating, admirable and infuriating, weirdly clueless and astonishingly astute. She appeared damaged, vulnerable, and pained by the life she led. Yet her enormous capacity for risk-taking exacerbated almost every difficulty she encountered as a member of the royal family. It sometimes seems that she felt a problem was never being truly addressed unless done so through the most extreme course of action. This aspect of Diana—the woman who existed away from the public gaze—will be charted in the subsequent pages. But the numerous mythological and imaginary Dianas will always be the chief concern. There will be stories of Diana clones, Diana in the afterlife,

Diana transposed to cultures far removed from her own, and many other speculative versions of the princess past, present, and future.

Of course, so much of our collective Diana obsession is rooted in the myth and magic of the British monarchy. This book rejects the pervasive idea that the lives of those who inhabit that enduring institution should only be of concern to ardent royalists. The royal family has always been central to political and cultural life in Great Britain; the connections between Britishness and the monarchy are manifold, deep, and complex. Yet a notion persists that to examine the experiences of royalty or to give serious consideration to the royal family's relationship with the general public should be the preserve of House-of-Windsor fanatics or, at the very least, those firmly in favor of a hereditary head of state. A case in point: on 10 December 1992, the day after it was announced that the Prince and Princess of Wales were to separate, the *Liverpool Echo* canvassed twenty-two locals for their opinions on the news. There was much opprobrium for Charles. One man said the prince should have his backside publicly spanked, though where and by whom he didn't divulge. Others said that their political opinions precluded them from having a take on the announcement or any of its potential ramifications. "I'm a republican," said one person. "I really don't care what happens." One might think this a quintessentially British attitude: when confronted by something important that you fundamentally oppose, whatever you do, don't make a fuss; just ignore it. Much British republicanism is expressed as a variation on this theme. Not only is the monarchy outmoded and unjust, runs the logic, it is a childish frivolity of interest only to the weak-minded. Anything to do with kings, queens, orbs, scepters, and all the rest of it is beneath serious attention. But the monarchy is too enmeshed with the vital realities of British life—and too ingrained within our collective imagination—for it to be ignored simply on the grounds that it ought to be abolished.

In modern times, nothing better carries the argument than the phenomenon of Dianaworld. The princess and the universe that has woven itself around her allow us to examine so many aspects of life in modern Britain, and a good deal of the rest of the planet.

❧ 1 ❧

Blood Family

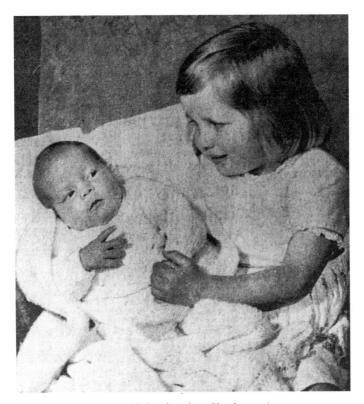

Diana with her brother Charles, 1964.

As reproduced on page three of the *Lynn News & Advertiser*, the image was splotchy and indistinct, but the paper's editor swore that this posed photograph of a toddler and her younger sibling captured something essential about the teenager the world was coming to know as Lady Diana Spencer. "Even at the tender age of two," ran the spurious caption, "Lady Diana's fondness for young children was evident, as she shows here, cuddling her newly-born brother."

It was March 1981, just a few weeks after Diana's engagement to the Prince of Wales had been officially announced, and newspapers around the world were full of this stuff: fluff based on the scantiest of facts, rehearsing the foundations of Diana's mythology: her love of children, her boundless capacity for empathy, her fairytale devotion to her dashing prince. But the *Lynn News & Advertiser* had more authority than most on the early life of the future princess. Based just a few miles down the road from Sandringham, the giant royal estate that was home to Diana's august family for most of her childhood, the paper had documented key moments in the Spencers' lives for nearly thirty years.

To some, Diana would always be "Lady Di" rather than Princess Diana. And though she hated her name being abbreviated— one of innumerable small liberties taken by journalists to stake a claim on her public image—this is largely true of Diana herself, for whom the Spencer family name and titles were a source of great pride. Being a Spencer in the last quarter of the twentieth century gave Diana a rare position, a chance to trill up and down the social scale in a way that wasn't available to her parents' generation. In the decades since she journeyed from ancestral pile to front page of *The Sun* and the *National Enquirer*, so much of her identity has been interpreted through the lens of her Spencerness—sometimes it helps give us clues as to the person Diana was, but just as often it heaps cliché and trope upon her mythological pyre. It appeals both to modern ideas about understanding the self through psychoanalysis and genetics, as well as to the medieval irrationality upon which British nobility rests. Being a Spencer is alternately cast as a source of Diana's agency, and of her victimhood; it is supposedly what condemned her to a life of emotional upheaval but also provided her with the innate strength to lock horns with the monarchy in the way that has secured her legend.

WHEN DIANA Frances Spencer was born, her family had been a mighty social presence for half a millennium. According to lore, the Spencer name can be traced to an ally of William the Conqueror, but it was in the Tudor period when the Spencers really thrived, turning their fortune as landowners and sheep farmers into titles, grand estates, and royal favor. By the late nineteenth century, the Spencers were among the brightest stars in the firmament of British nobility. When the extreme turbulence of the twentieth century sent some aristocratic clans into a tailspin, the Spencers held firm.

In 1954, the thirty-year-old Viscount Althorp, John Spencer—heir to the Spencer earldom, better known as Johnnie—married the Honourable Frances Roche, the eighteen-year-old daughter of Maurice Roche, 4th Baron Fermoy, and Lady Ruth Fermoy, in a ceremony at Westminster Abbey. In recent years, Johnnie had served as equerry to King George VI and later to Elizabeth II, the new sovereign whose attendance at the wedding made the occasion worldwide news. In his sermon, the Bishop of Norwich explicitly tied the nuptials to Elizabeth's coronation, which had taken place at the abbey the previous year. Just as Elizabeth had made a sacred commitment to her country, said Bishop Herbert, so this marriage should be considered an act of patriotic devotion, "an addition to the home life of your country, on which, above all others, our national life depends." It was an emphatic iteration of aristocratic identity. Love, companionship, and fidelity were all well and good, but God, Queen, and Country were the unbreakable bonds.

The Roches, too, had exceptionally strong royal connections. Frances's mother, Lady Fermoy, was both a close friend of, and lady-in-waiting to, the Queen Mother, while Lord Fermoy had been a member of George VI's shooting party at Sandringham, in Norfolk, the day before the king died in 1952. The Roches had long been tenants of the Windsors on those very same grounds, living at Park House, where Frances had been born on 20 January 1936, the same day that King George V passed away. After Lord Fermoy died suddenly in 1955, it was here that Johnnie and Frances made their marital home. With its ten bedrooms and spacious grounds, Park House was an idyllic setting in which to raise the children that Johnnie and Frances welcomed into the world: Sarah came first in 1955, followed by Jane in 1957; a boy, John, who lived only ten hours, in 1960, a year before the arrival of Diana in 1961. The family was completed in 1964 with the birth of Charles, who, as the only surviving male, was destined to inherit the Spencer earldom and the seat in the House of Lords that came with it. Of the Spencer siblings, Diana was the only one not to have royalty among her godparents.

According to reports from the time, Diana wasn't present at her brother's christening—she'd fallen down a dozen stone steps the day before and was nursing a bump on her head—but she would encounter royalty regularly in the coming years: Princes Andrew and Edward occasionally came to use the pool at Park House, and now and then the Spencer children were invited to the queen's residence at Sandringham. A commonly told story is that of Diana's first meeting, at age five, with her future husband, when Prince Charles, then seventeen, found his mother playing hide-and-seek with the little girl from down the road. However, in newspaper reports from just before the wedding, using quotes supposedly direct from Diana, it was said that she was eleven or twelve at the time of her first meeting with Elizabeth. It might be that the hide-and-seek story is apocryphal, or perhaps this encounter was deemed inappropriately informal for inclusion in the official history of Lady Diana's connection with the Windsors. There's also the chance that Diana had simply grown up so accustomed to contact with the world's most famous family that looking for Her Majesty tucked behind the curtains or wedged inside the armoire wasn't quite as memorable an experience for her as it would have been for the rest of us.

On the surface, Johnnie and Frances were a model postwar aristocratic couple. Yet the years of Diana's childhood was a time when even the grandest families felt the hot breath of progress blowing down their necks. Members of their class had once been regarded as inherently dignified and admirable; in the 1960s, their flaws and foibles became fodder for mass entertainment. Upper-class twits and patrician authority figures were mocked on stage, on screen, and on the page. Scandals concerning toffs caught with their pants round their ankles or their fingers in the till became a staple of an increasingly undeferential popular culture. Divorce among the establishment generated particular attention.

At the outbreak of the First World War, just one in every four hundred and fifty British marriages ended in divorce. In the subsequent fifty years, dissolving a marriage became easier and less stigmatized, but it was still necessary for one party to be provably at fault, a situation which trapped many in miserable relationships. In the 1960s, divorce became a touchstone social issue, and it proved most captivating to the public when it involved the highborn. The most memorable case was that of the Duke and Duchess of Argyll, who divorced in 1963 amid scandalous revelations of infidelity and spousal abuse. In such cases, the lofty ideals of the aristocratic marriage, the very foundations on which the centuries-old hereditary system was built, were revealed to be a sham: the upper class, it turned out, was at least as flawed and fallible as everyone else; the Spencers were no exception.

In 1967, the BBC broadcast several documentaries about the state of modern marriage, including one titled *The Stresses of Divorce*. The program featured a young model named Sandra Paul who had taken what was considered the startling decision of walking out on her aristocratic husband, Robin Douglas-Home, Johnnie's cousin.

The documentary's interviews with Paul and Douglas-Home made for unforgettable television that doubled as a notable moment in British social history—a Spencer family tradition that Diana, her brother, and her youngest son have all furthered. In her quiet voice, Paul explains how she refused to tolerate Douglas-Home's selfishness and galivanting; unmentioned in the program are his numerous purported affairs, including with Princess Margaret. To maintain her self-respect and regain her autonomy, Paul had pursued divorce, despite her husband's fierce resistance to what he felt was a public humiliation. "I had to be ruthless in order to be free," she says, the kind of statement that could have come from Diana's lips thirty years later.

It is intriguing to wonder whether Frances watched *The Stresses of Divorce* when it aired, as at that very moment she was making her own attempt to break out of domestic misery. Having married very young, Frances endured great unhappiness in her marriage, experiencing the death of her newborn son, John, and a few months later a miscarriage during a pregnancy that only she knew about. As an adult, Diana seemingly confirmed rumors that her father physically abused her mother. "I remember seeing my father slap my mother across the face," she once confided to a friend; "I was hiding behind the door and Mummy was crying." As Frances reached thirty, she drifted ever further from her husband and fell in love with Peter Shand Kydd, the heir to a fortune built on wallpaper manufacturing. Johnnie was disbelieving when Frances announced her intention to leave him, as was her mother, aghast that Frances wanted to turn her back on her social status and remove the children from close proximity to the royal family. Frances gained the reputation of "a bolter" who chose her new man over her children. It's closer to the truth to say that Johnnie used his wealth and social heft to make sure that Frances was unable to take the children with her. In court, Ruth Fermoy sided with the viscount, painting her daughter as an inadequate mother. Ultimately, it was ordered that the children should stay with Johnnie, with Frances given access on certain weekends and during the school holidays. Diana recalled the memory of seeing her mother driving away from Park House as deeply scarring. Both she and her brother, Charles, recalled the unhappiness of being separated from their mother and the anxiety caused by being shuttled from one parent to the other.

The Spencers' divorce was finalized in 1969, the year in which Parliament approved the Divorce Reform Act, a socially transformative piece of legislation that introduced the no-fault divorce. In 1969, 51,000 marriages were dissolved in the UK. Twelve years later in 1981, the year of Diana's wedding, that figure had all but trebled to 145,000. Diana herself noted the way in which society was irrevocably altered by the surge in divorces during the 1970s, saying that by the time she reached her teens, so many of her schoolmates had divorced parents, her situation ceased to be unusual. Of course, those cases encompass tales of liberation as well as upset. But Diana's origin story—her telling of the rupture in her parents' marriage—was part of the fairytale story that wrapped itself around her from the moment she became a media fixture. It established her as an emblem of an increasingly common rite of passage among British people from all class backgrounds and the tendency to map a sense of self-identity onto the psychological scars of childhood.

The Great Diary Project—an archive of diaries written and donated by members of the British public—contains decades' worth of diaries by a man from the west of England who had lived through most of the twentieth century. In his expansive, often sad, sometimes anguished, diary entries during the final weeks of Diana's life, he ruminates on illness and dying, loneliness, the meaning of existence, and the lasting damage of unhappy childhoods. He wrote that he felt close to tears when news of Diana's death came; "poor Di, so human, so lovable." A couple of days later he thought about what he could learn from Diana's life as he contemplated his own death. If he won the lottery before that day came, he said he would establish a "Society of Deprived Children for anyone over the age of eighteen." As we will see, Diana's ability to connect with people has often been located in her Spencerness, a kind of demotic genius that supposedly redounds through generations of one remarkable family. Ironically, it might be that Diana's crucial point of identification with the public was the moment when the Spencers were ripped apart.

In her thirties, Diana suggested that Frances's departure was just one in a series of wounding rejections she had endured, starting with the moment of her birth. Her parents, she believed, were so desperate for a male heir following the harrowing death of baby John the previous year, that they looked on her, a third daughter, as an inconvenience. Yet she also insisted, "I was my father's favourite, there's no doubt about that." It's fitting, in a way, that Diana expressed such contradictory feelings about something as fundamental as whether she was shunned by her parents from her first breath. As often as she claimed to have been harmed, affronted, and let down by her various relatives over the years, she remained intensely proud of being a Spencer; it was the foundation of her idea of who she was, as both a private person and a public figure.

Much of Diana's upbringing was plainly conventional for a child of her background. For a time she was schooled at home by a governess before attending Silfield School in nearby King's Lynn, moving to Riddlesworth Hall, also in Norfolk, when she was nine. Her secondary education was pursued as a boarder at West Heath Girls' School in Kent. It was here that Diana learned she had become Lady Diana at the age of thirteen, when Johnnie inherited the title of Earl Spencer upon the death of his father in 1975. Diana, who had already been given the nickname "Duch" by her classmates on account of her grand bearing, was delighted about her elevation. In addition to the titles, Johnnie also inherited the Spencer properties, the fulcrum of which was Althorp, the gigantic stately home and thirteen-thousand-acre estate that has been the Spencer seat ever since the sixteenth century. Diana described moving there as a "terrible wrench," at least partly because thirteen months later Johnnie married again, another parental betrayal in Diana's eyes. His second bride was Raine McCorquodale, the ex-wife of the Earl of Dartmouth and daughter of Barbara Cartland, whose sugary romance novels Diana adored. Like her mother, Raine was an extraordinary personality, a steel girder beneath a cocoon of baroque femininity. Toward the end of her life, Diana seemingly developed an appreciation for Raine's tenacity and flair for self-preservation, but initially the Spencer siblings loathed their step-mother: "Acid Raine," they called her. Such was their animosity, Johnnie didn't tell them about the wedding until after it had taken place, for which Diana, now fifteen, hit him in the face as punishment. Her father's second marriage piled a further layer on Diana's adolescent disaffection and her feelings of neglect and rejection, all of which was central to the story she told us about herself, and the place she occupies in the collective imagination as a forever-wounded child in tragic search of healing.

The current Earl Spencer, Diana's brother, has spoken of the "good Spencers" myth that has surrounded his family for centuries, the notion that the Spencers are praiseworthy, "modest do-gooders." But the family's more recent past has developed a rival myth of sadness and tragedy, in which Diana has become the central figure. Lady Margaret Douglas-Home, the mother of Robin whose divorce was featured in *The Stresses of Divorce*, grew up at Althorp as the daughter of the 6th Earl Spencer and sister of Jack Spencer, Johnnie's father. While her upbringing was full of the material comforts and privileges that all Spencer children enjoy, it was smothered in sadness: her mother died giving birth to her, a fact that the rest of the family never seemed to forgive her for, and which caused her father to collapse in on himself. In her memoirs, Margaret sketches her childhood in gothic tones: To escape the pervading melancholy, she used the vastness of Althorp as a portal to a world of her imagination, climbing onto the roof for spells of lonely daydreaming. By the age of thirteen, her elder siblings had flown the nest, leaving just her and her "distant . . . wretched . . . broken" father rattling around one of the great stately homes of England or, as she puts it, "an elderly, solitary man living on memories, and a solitary child; no one in between." The introduction to Margaret's memoir is written by Diana's brother, Charles, who could almost be describing his and Diana's early years when he writes of Margaret's childhood as defined by "the sadness of her motherless state, with her broken Father tragically looming in the background." Diana recalled times after her parents' split when she would lie in bed listening to her brother crying at night for his absent mother; she wanted to comfort him but was too afraid of the dark to get out of bed.

Charles Spencer has noted the pall of sadness that flowed from Margaret's generation, an inheritance as real as any of the Spencer property that was handed down from earl to viscount. Of his grandfather, Margaret's brother, he says, "I genuinely believe that the death of his mother at such an impressionable age, combined with the undiagnosed depression that his father slipped into, impacted hugely on him," turning him into the brooding, distant adult who raised Johnnie. In a brief remembrance of his boyhood, Johnnie echoed the tone of his aunt Margaret's recollections, unable to shake off a sense of loneliness and gloom that swirled within the family. He, too, reached for some fantastical means of imaginative reinvention—redolent of the fairytale narrative that envelops Diana. After receiving his last present from Father Christmas at the age of six, Johnnie says he "moved into the chill world of the grownups. But, like [Lewis Carroll's] Alice, I could escape. In my case it was into the Park at Althorp." When Johnnie inherited the earldom and began selling off prized artworks and carpeting the polished floors, Charles speculates that he did so as "revenge for not feeling loved as a child." And, although there are those who remember Johnnie differently, Diana was adamant that her father was never capable of giving her the demonstrative love that she craved in the vulnerable years following her parents' divorce. Charles has also publicly discussed—and in considerable detail—the scarring experiences of his childhood at home and school. One might say that the next link in the chain is Prince Harry, whose tale of an unhappy upbringing includes many elements of earlier Spencer childhoods: a messy divorce that captured—and entertained—the watching public, the painful absence of one parent, and a lack of attentive, tactile parenting from another.

The sadness of Margaret's childhood echoed in the lives of her own children. In her son, we catch a glimpse of a family trait that bloomed in Diana: living with one's heart on one's sleeve. In *The Stresses of Divorce*, Robin Douglas-Home at times appears the very picture of wounded masculine pride and upper-class contempt, complaining of the "leering little clerks in solicitors' offices" who arranged his divorce; he seems disbelieving of this new world in

A family gathering to mark the golden wedding anniversary of the 7th Earl Spencer and Countess Spencer, March 1969. From left to right: Richard Wake-Walker, Lady Anne Wake-Walker (Diana's aunt, daughter of the Earl and Countess), Elizabeth Wake-Walker, Christopher Wake-Walker, Earl Spencer, Countess Spencer, Sarah Spencer, Viscount Althorp (John Spencer, Diana's father), Jane Spencer. Diana stands next to her brother Charles in the front row.

which a chap can be defied by his wife and dictated to by men from the suburbs wearing off-the-rack suits. But he also communicates vulnerability in a way that was considered remarkable for the era, especially among British men, crying without self-consciousness as he talks of his emotional pain. When Douglas-Home sheds his first tear, the picture cuts to the interviewer, Alan Whicker, who makes a point of looking away, perhaps as a show of empathy for his interviewee, or by way of apology that we the audience should have to watch something so pitiful as a grown man blubbering, or perhaps because he finds the whole thing so awkward and unusual that he doesn't know what else to do. As the picture cuts back, Douglas-Home blows his nose and lights up a cigarette, his cheeks still wet. He vows never to remarry. "I just don't want to be destroyed. Again." A year and a half later Douglas-Home took his own life at the age of thirty-six.

From almost the moment Diana became a renowned national figure, her own emotional expressiveness was a source of fascination and confusion. "Lady Diana wept openly," announced the front page of *The Sun* on 21 February 1981, reporting Diana's response to the death of a horse. Continued on page seven, the report returned to Diana's crying in four separate paragraphs, three of which evoked the image of tears rolling down her cheeks. Other national newspapers carried similar articles. That she made no effort to hide her upset, not even by wiping the tears from her face, clearly confounded what was expected of someone poised to be the nation's next queen. In a 1984 book titled *Dear Princess*, which provides answers to children's questions for Diana, the authors tell one little boy that the royal family does not like to express emotion in front of others and for that reason "Diana probably regrets kissing Prince Charles goodbye in public, the first time he went away after they were engaged, because everyone could see she was crying."

Of all the things in her life that Diana might well have regretted, it seems unlikely that shedding a tear when she was upset would be one of them. In *The Sloane Ranger Handbook* (1982), a largely satirical look at what it meant to be young, idle, and rich in the vicinity of

London's upper-class haven of Sloane Square, Diana was identified as the gold standard—the "Supersloane"—not only because she embodied "the Old Guard instincts" but because she was "more in touch with her emotions" than was traditionally common among her peers: "She cried, she blushed, she *swore*. . . . She kissed people. Suddenly it was no longer COOL to be cool."

So established has the "sad Spencer" myth become that Frances's biographers asserted that "it seems as if there is a curse on her family," making one wonder, "Are the Spencers set to become a kind of British version of the Kennedys?" Rather than translating the Spencer story into that distinctively American idiom (always a temptation for those interpreting Diana), it is also possible to see the recent chapters of the family story as part of several home-grown narratives. One of those is the tale of upper-class decline, in which aristocratic lives are scoured for tales of hardship, unhappiness, and dysfunction, mirroring the relative social demise of those who had once been regarded as preeminent. Arguably, being posh and filthy rich was more fashionable in the Thatcher years of the 1980s than it had been since the era of the Bright Young People in the 1920s. But alongside tales of glamour and excess there was a tendency to depict the social elite as somewhat pitiful, afflicted by the modern world's inverted snobbery,* as well as the conditions of their background: emotional stuntedness, excessive consumption, and purposelessness. By the early 1990s, the Spencer story told to the public encompassed pretty much all of this. A 1994 edition of *Tatler* that featured a lengthy piece about Diana's misery contending with childhood demons and a failed marriage also ran "From Silver Spoon to Silver Spoon," an article detailing how those "born with every advantage that affluence and aristocracy can afford are more likely to succumb to the latest tidal wave of heroin washing up on our shores." Among the article's stories of ruin and loss was

---

* In 2017, Earl Spencer said that when writing a history of the Battle of Blenheim he'd had to push aside the prejudice of "those who believed someone from my background was too stupid to talk, let alone write."

that of Lady Alethea Savile, ex-girlfriend of James Gilbey, one of Diana's close male friends.* Within this context, Diana was identified as both a paradigmatic member of the dysfunctional upper classes and a bridge between them and the rest of the population: someone who had experienced familial misery and wasn't afraid to show it, casting off the old-fashioned ways in the process.

DIANA MAY have strayed from certain ingrained stereotypes, yet aristocracy remains aristocracy: it is still a precinct for myth, legend, and archaic notions of heritage. Lady Colin Campbell's 1992 study, *Diana in Private: The Princess Nobody Knows*, is absorbing, less for what it tells us about its subject, more for what it reveals about its author's worldview. Amid frequent name-dropping, Campbell insists there is nothing in the world she loathes more than a snob, though she has no compunction in describing Park House as a "comfortable, ten-bedroomed house, which is often called large and rambling by people who have never had access to really big houses." She also uses words such as "blood," "bloodline," and "breeding" more than seems possible for a biography written at the end of the twentieth century. Within the first few pages, she suggests that Diana's boldness might have been shaped by her mother's influence. Sensible enough: An authorized biography of Frances describes how, as a young girl, she enjoyed practicing ballet steps on the Park House roof. The young Frances was "brave to the point of foolhardiness," say the authors Max Riddington and Gavan Naden, something that could easily have been said of Diana, who spent her life diving into the shallow end of the pool, sometimes literally. But Campbell locates these things in the context of Diana's "Burke blood," an Irish heritage on one side of

---

* A few years earlier, Charles Spencer had appeared on the popular breakfast show *Good Morning Britain* where he pushed back on the idea that Oxford was full of mixed-up sybarites, following the death of his Oxford contemporary, Olivia Channon, who died of an accidental heroin overdose.

Frances's family, that supposedly bequeathed a fiery, irrepressible "Irish temperament" to mother and daughter.

As Campbell shows us, Diana, the modern individual on the psychoanalyst's couch, shares space with a Diana who is perceived through mystical notions of "breeding" or "blood," something between a genetic inheritance and an ineffable cosmic force that frequently stretches historical and scientific credulity. One Spencer family member told the biographer Sarah Bradford that Spencers are "very difficult and complicated," and that the Queen Mother was astonished at the unruliness of Spencer women, a trait upheld by Diana. But Bradford doesn't limit the Spencer reference points to close relatives—a grandmother, mother, or sister, perhaps. Rather, she cites Georgiana Cavendish, Duchess of Devonshire, and Sarah Churchill, Duchess of Marlborough, as examples of Diana's "headstrong" forbears through whom we can comprehend her essential being—her essential Spencerness—despite the former not being a direct antecedent of Diana's and the latter being born all the way back in 1660. Nevertheless, Bradford is confident that "the blood of these distant ancestors meant that Diana was never going to be the mousy little girl some people thought—or perhaps hoped—that she would be." The idea of an irreducible Spencerness tumbling down the centuries was evident in the marketing campaign for *The Duchess*, a 2008 film about Georgiana, Duchess of Devonshire, promotional materials for which featured a photo of Diana alongside Keira Knightley in character as Georgiana and a trailer which cited the two women as "related by ancestry and united by destiny."

Blood and breeding as an explanation of Diana's magic comes even from those who profess themselves to be thoroughly modern people with no time for old-fashioned fallacies about class identity. Mary Clarke worked as a nanny for Diana and her siblings at Park House and believed that although "there were supposedly different classes in life, I had, nonetheless, never regarded one as any better than another." But Clarke's convictions appear to have abandoned her on meeting Diana's Spencer grandmother. "As soon as

I met her I realized the difference generated by breeding . . . that indefinable quality that is bred into an aristocratic family that has existed for generations" and which those on the outside can never replicate; "Diana has inherited many of her qualities." Somehow Diana's special ancient stock and rarefied upbringing allowed her to be incomparably normal. Patrick Jephson served as Diana's equerry in the late 1980s and early 1990s and has written one of the most thoughtful and textured accounts of the princess. Yet even he indulges in medieval cant about bloodlines, declaring that "the advantage of hereditary leaders is that, wherever they are and whatever they wear, they usually carry the genetic badge of office that marked their ancestors for greatness." Thus, the current occupants of Buckingham Palace are able to "quell a mob with a single Hanoverian glare."

There are numerous tales of Diana waving away her background, dismissing her name, rank, and heredity as so much arcane silliness. Yet Diana was exceptionally proud of her heritage, not simply the family bonds between close relatives, but everything entailed in being a Spencer, centuries of inherited specialness which supposedly was the very thing that allowed her to relate to everyone. "Whenever things got too much for her," says Diana's friend Rosa Monckton, "she would say to herself: 'Diana, remember you're a Spencer' (she was far prouder of this than of being royal). . . . She had the manners of a true aristocrat, and instantly made people at ease." Elsa Bowker was one of several people close to Diana to confirm that the princess took great strength from her Spencer heritage. "When I came here, I had my title. I don't need your title," Diana told Prince Charles when they argued about the prospect of divorce.

But how do we reconcile these readings of Diana as an exemplar of aristocratic breeding with her reputation for being, as she put it once, "closer to people at the bottom than to people at the top"? Her father believed his daughter's most beguiling qualities— her demotic instincts, her lack of interest in status (obsession with being a titled Spencer notwithstanding), her supposed girl-next-door ordinariness—came straight from the Spencer stable. "They are just there," he said, "they are hereditary." Others have claimed that Diana's common touch came from her mother's side of the family tree. Bafflingly, Campbell's biography would have us believe that Lady Fermoy's interest in music had something to do with it. Whether the credit belongs to the Spencers, the Roches, or the Burkes, the explanation is basically the same: Diana was unencumbered by class identity, snobbery, or elitism of any kind precisely because she was so thoroughly, *truly*, aristocratic.

A more satisfying answer is that Diana entered the royal family at a precise historical moment when the cultural worlds of Britain's various class communities drifted close enough together to allow Diana access to a dress-up box of different identities, moving up and down the social ladder as no royal had ever done—or been able to do—before. She expressed her purported classlessness through her experience of childhood turmoil, her love of pop music, soap operas, and Hollywood. In certain circumstances, she could also do it via her vocal cords. A famous example of how important accent and dialect were in defining social status in twentieth-century Britain is Nancy Mitford's 1955 essay which playfully outlined the vocabulary that distinguished upper-class (U) from middle-class (Non-U) people. "Glasses" was Non-U, for example, whereas "spectacles" was U. Supposedly, one's class background would always shine through; no matter how hard a social climber tried to come off posh, they'd always slip up somewhere along the line, using "toilet" when they should have said "lavatory." The kicker was that U words were often the same as those used by the working class, making the business of passing as one's social superior loaded with peril. A much easier task was to use language to go the other way, the kind of verbal slumming that Diana and many of her aristocratic peers took up once the cultural transformations of the 1960s had begun.

When Roy Strong, former director of the Victoria and Albert Museum, first met Diana not long after her wedding, he was moved to note in his diary that she was like "Eliza Doolittle at the embassy ball. . . . Her accent is really rather awful considering that she is an earl's daughter. Not an upper-class drawl at all but rather tuneless and, dare I say it, a bit common, as though it were the fashion to learn to talk down." In a way, it was—though this might have seemed abominable to a man like Strong who comes from an unambiguously Non-U background and has spent his adult life trying to sound as U as possible.* On a similar theme, when a columnist for the *Cambridge Daily News* pondered the confusing swirl of new class identities in the 1980s, he noted that "upper-class youth has been trying to pass itself off as working-class for ages. Consider the Princess of Wales's accent." Many years later, Strong thought the coarsening of British culture that he detected in Diana's glottal stop had gotten so bad that the 2010s were "the golden age of the trashocracy, where the Queen is on the B-List and David Beckham is on the A-list." Irrespective of the truth of the statement—and Beckham himself would probably contest it: he is an unshakable monarchist who queued thirteen hours to see Elizabeth II lying in state—if one were to search for a cultural figure who bridged the gap between those two, the *true* Posh and Becks, Diana would be as good a candidate as any.

Strong was far from the only person to invoke Eliza Doolittle (probably the heroine of *My Fair Lady* if you're U, *Pygmalion* if you're Non-U) in relation to Diana. The princess herself apparently made the link because of her "lack of formal education"—though she was, of course, given an extremely expensive formal education, including a stint at a Swiss finishing school. When in Covent Garden flower market early one morning, she burst into "Wouldn't It Be Loverly." This, at least, is what the journalist and biographer

---

* Today, Diana's sons' accents are variously praised and criticized for not being in the cut-glass style of their father's. The linguist Dr. Geoff Lindsey has a You-Tube channel on which he compares William and Harry's speech with that of the king's. Lindsey ascribes the rising intonation that differentiates the princes' speech from that of the king's to the effect of postwar social trends that lessened the prestige of being upper class.

Andrew Morton told us in a book he wrote on the princess that was published in 1990. But within two years, when Diana was pouring her heart out to him about the pain she absorbed as a child of a broken home, she explained that it would be ridiculous to compare herself to a Cockney flower girl: she was, after all, a Spencer.

THE RAREFIED quality attributed to Spencer hemoglobin hasn't stopped the rest of the world from trying to claim Diana as their own flesh and blood. Over the years, headlines have been created by the discovery of extremely distant, sometimes debatable, links between Diana and other public figures including Oliver Cromwell, Audrey Hepburn, Humphrey Bogart, the Marquis de Sade, George Washington, Harriet Beecher Stowe, Winston Churchill, Arthur Scargill, Herman Goering, and Colin Powell. When Glenn Close's link to Diana was revealed on PBS's *Finding Your Roots*, the show's YouTube page was littered with comments from users struck by the strong family resemblance that they were certain had made its way down from the one set of great-great-great-great-great-great-great-grandparents that the two women have in common. Others expressed envy that Close could claim such a dazzling distant relative. Diana is not only the People's Princess, but the World's Eighth Cousin.

On her home soil, there is far less interest in the Diana diaspora. As Diana was introduced to the British public, the comment on her illustrious ancestors was matched by the attention paid to her impeccable Britishness—or, more often, her impeccable (southern) Englishness, something that might be best expressed as Anglo-Britishness. "A sprig of a family tree that had roots spreading deep into the history of England" is how she was described in a hastily published biography of her in 1981, the book beginning with the Spencer and Windsor family trees laid out side by side. Of central importance was her connection to a seventeenth-century royal dynasty, the "royal Stuart blood" which flowed in her because of her five lines of descent from Charles II.* "More royal than the royals" is something that's still routinely said about Diana, though it doesn't make a great deal of sense; you can't move for royal branches in the Windsor family tree. What's really meant by this is that Diana is "more British than the royals," still questionable, but a notion that's always been fundamental to her public image. The celebration of Diana's unadulterated Britishness revealed an unease about the German heritage of the Windsor family that lingered throughout the twentieth century. Elizabeth II, of course, was a direct descendent of Queen Victoria who herself was a Hanoverian, the German dynasty that took the British crown in 1714. When Victoria married her German husband, Prince Albert, in 1840, the House of Saxe-Coburg and Gotha was established, the name by which the royal family was known until it was changed to Windsor during the First World War, to distance itself from Germany. But the name change never entirely removed the memory of the family's origins.

In the two hundred years before the creation of the House of Windsor, it was customary for British royals to marry royalty from elsewhere in Europe. Queen Victoria's offspring were so enmeshed in continental dynasties that she became known as the "grandmother of Europe." But by the 1970s, when Prince Charles came to look for a bride, Europe's monarchies had either vanished or diminished, making it increasingly likely that Charles would marry British. This, combined with the fact that the empire was now a withered husk, meant that the House of Windsor became more of a symbol of an inward-looking Britishness than ever before—despite being widely regarded as a bunch of Germans in disguise. In 1992, the historian Michael Billig noted this dichotomy in his analysis of interviews with sixty-three British families on the subject of the royals. As Billig outlines in his book *Talking of the Royal Family*, the issue of Windsor foreignness came up repeatedly in the interviews, which were conducted on his behalf by Marie Kennedy. "Mixed blood,"

---

* The fact that the Stuart dynasty was Scottish, not English, in origin seems to have often been ignored in the London-based media.

remarked one woman, who pointed out the German, Greek, and Danish ancestry in the Windsor past; "you can't really say they're an English Royal Family." Diana proved the exception, her heart pumping pints of royal blood around her regal body. Hugh Montgomery-Massingberd, author of numerous books on the royals and a former editor of *Burke's Peerage*, had it worked out down to decimal points. According to him, Diana's thoroughbred breeding means that William will be the "most 'British' sovereign since James I with 58.8 percent British blood," a remarkably low figure considering that both of William's parents were bred, born, and raised in Britain, as were three of his four grandparents. In her research on how Diana was regarded around the time of her death, the folklorist Marion Bowman recorded a conversation she had with a Druid who was adamant that Diana's marriage to Charles had been engineered by the Windsors in order to restore "the ancient British royal bloodline," as Diana was, so the Druid believed, descended from the rulers of the era of Camelot, and in her son William—whose middle name is Arthur—the country will have a "new King Arthur for the new millennium." If, to many British people, Diana represented Britishness reborn, to at least part of the population, she was also the salvation of an ancient heritage; her arrival had at last wrested back the throne from foreign hands.

Nobody has captured this sentiment more emphatically than Julie Burchill, the bestselling author and Diana biographer. Burchill's contempt for the monarchy and the Windsors is surpassed only by her adoration of Diana, whom she sees as an agent of Anglo-Saxon creative destruction implanted within the heart of the "dirty great foreign con" that is the royal family. Her biography of Diana is one of the strangest books ever written about her, but also one of the most enlightening: it reveals a strain of thought that hums in the background of so much coverage of Diana but is rarely articulated so explicitly or entertainingly. She begins by sketching a Disney-style fantasy in which members of Diana's purported family of ultra-distant relatives—Louisa May Alcott, Graham Greene, Bismarck—hover around her at the moment of her birth, like the fairy godmothers in *Sleeping Beauty*, each magically passing on to her one of their traits. But Burchill is very clear as to Diana's true identity: "a beautiful Anglo-Saxon virgin captured and forcibly wed to a swarthy Graeco-German." Non-English inbreeding accounts for the family's grotesque physical unattractiveness, but Diana is English sex on legs: "flirtatious and gawky, like a colt not yet inclined to bolt. She was so *ENGLISH* and how very sexy that word is . . . *Inn*—the dark deep interior—*glishhh*—the lush glide to a lip-smacking finish." At one point Burchill cheers urban Britain's social diversity, its "power-dressed girls of various hue and heritage whose only interest in ethnicity was the 'city' bit"—but she cannot let go of the Windsors' original sin of not being, in her mind, authentically British. The Spencers, on the other hand, are equated as the true soul of England, an ancient, class-straddling family whose "surliness seemed bred in the bone," and who "relied on sheep, land and marriage for money; very much the working-class way." For several centuries before Diana arrived, "The country belonged more to her people," that is, the Spencers, "and by extension to all of us English commoners," than it did to any of the outsiders who occupied the throne.

Burchill's biography was only published after its subject's death, but had she read it, Diana would very likely have enjoyed the panegyric on the Spencers' Englishness almost as much as the digs at the Windsors' ethnicity. "The Germans," Diana called them; the Austrian-born Princess Michael was "the Führer." Prince Philip she called "Stavros" on account of his part-Greek heritage, and presumably a reference to the character of a Greek kebab shop owner created by the comedian Harry Enfield in the 1980s. It wasn't meant viciously and was in line with jokes that millions of other Britons have told about the royals over the years. It does, however, reflect Diana's awareness of and pride in her own identity. Once her sons were born, she was firmly of the mind that her responsibility was to shape them as new types of Windsors, providing a new style of kingship, one that was much more "English," as she saw it.

Key to this was deciding where the boys were to be educated, something that occupied the attentions of rather a lot of people in the late eighties and early nineties. Lady Colin Campbell found space in her biography to express concern that Diana had settled on Sedbergh, a boarding school in Cumbria. "It is my favourite boys' school. . . . I should hate to see it ruined by Prince William's presence," which would make it "the most fashionable place for the sons of snobs." Charles, apparently, wanted William and Harry to go to his alma mater, Gordonstoun, though his old headmaster, John Kempe, disagreed and publicly urged that the princes be educated at a state comprehensive, an idea that formed the premise of a British children's TV program called *Palace Hill*. Diana rejected all these suggestions and insisted the boys be sent to board at Eton College, famous for producing centuries of charming, affable, upper-class chaps with the bulletproof self-confidence needed to run the country and—when there was such a thing—the empire. Eton was traditionally where Spencer males were educated, including Diana's father and her brother, the latter having been a classmate of ex–prime minister Boris Johnson and a near contemporary of David Cameron.* When Diana spoke of raising princes who were in touch with "the man on the street," she meant by making them more like the men in her family. The Englishness that Diana wanted to instill in her children was aristocratic rather than royal, informed more by her experience of inherited wealth, status, and privilege than by their father's experience of the same. Historians have argued that the reign of the Windsors' German ancestors shifted the royals to a plane beyond class, their dual status as sovereign and model bourgeois family combining with their foreignness to isolate them from the norms of aristocratic life. If that was ever the case, it is also the case that Diana pinned the family closer to the class system than at any time in the modern era, making her

---

* Other old Etonians include James Colthurst, the aristocrat who conducted the secret interviews with Diana that formed the basis of Andrew Morton's *Diana: Her True Story.*

sons more typical of the English upper classes than her ex-husband has ever been.

As VISCOUNT Althorp, Charles Spencer gained a reputation for personifying the sort of unpleasant things that Eton, Oxford, and a title can do to a young man of means. "Champagne Charlie" the tabloids caricatured him; a cad and a bounder who consorted with "chinless wonders with too much money," as the DJ Tony Blackburn fulminated during his BBC Radio London show in 1984. Blackburn alleged that Spencer and others had behaved like obnoxious oafs at a fashionable London restaurant where the viscount had gone to celebrate his twentieth birthday with a group of friends, some of whom insulted and threw objects at other diners. "Althorp did come up to me and apologise," said Blackburn, "but quite honestly I thought the affair was quite disgusting."

Spencer's depiction in the press frustrated him: "I am not a Hooray Henry," he told a journalist in 1987. "I am staggered that the image could have survived so long. . . . the worthwhile things I've done have all but been ignored." Given that he was only twenty-two at the time, there perhaps wasn't a great litany of achievements worthy of newspaper coverage. He stressed his commitment to fulfilling his aristocratic duty: "I want to maintain and, if possible, improve my family's house and estate when it comes to me," he said. It seems fair to say that he's done just that. Much more than his father ever did, Charles Spencer has a deep passion for Althorp, its history, and the stories of those who have inhabited it across the centuries. He has written engrossing volumes about Althorp, the Spencers, and the Stuart kings from which his kin famously descended. His book *The White Ship* tells the true story of a ship-wreck in 1120 that sparked a struggle for political power, not usually a topic that would appear on frothy breakfast television shows, yet Earl Spencer nabbed a spot on Lorraine Kelly's program on ITV to publicize it, along with a chat about Harry and Meghan, memories of his sister, how his father inspires him to make sure that the general public always "feel that they are welcome guests" when they visit the family grounds, and Tim the Peacock, Althorp's "famous resident," who has a formidable social media presence. In 2024, Charles Spencer published *A Very Private School*, an affecting memoir of his dreadfully unhappy time at Maidwell Hall boarding school, during which he experienced some horrific abuse. The book will quite probably become a definitive modern account of so-called boarding school syndrome, what one author terms "the psychological trauma of the 'privileged' child" who is packed off to be educated at an elite institution at a young age. It also adds a further chapter to the story of the Spencers as a family afflicted by sadness but blessed by emotional honesty. On the home page of the Althorp estate's official website, there are advertisements for the book accompanied by photographs of Earl Spencer posing with it in various locations in Althorp House, cementing the link between his material inheritance and his emotional one.

The Spencers are as close to being the people's aristocrats as it's possible to get—and Diana remains at the center of it all. The earl's relationship with his sister, their centuries of Spencer ancestors, and the bricks and mortar that have housed them, are entwined even on his X profile—@cspencer1508, the year the Althorp estate came into Spencer possession. At the time of writing, his posts begin with a pinned statement, an admission from a *Times* journalist that it was wrong of her to state that he had refused Diana a home at the time of her divorce, and that he had in fact offered her numerous Spencer properties including Wormleighton Manor, which has been in Spencer hands even longer than Althorp. The rest of the page is a fast-cut montage of the family's epic past: Spencer children at a fancy-dress party in 1902; Johnnie in military uniform during the Second World War; a coin from the reign of Emperor Carausius found in the Althorp soil. In 2021, several websites reported as "news" the fact that Spencer had posted a photograph of the island in the Althorp grounds where Diana is buried. A few hundred yards from the gravesite is a summer house that was bought by a Spencer forebear in 1901, now dedicated to Diana's memory. Inscribed upon its walls are lines from the eulogy her brother gave at Westminster Abbey, that remarkable public rebuke to the Windsors in which he praised his sister's "natural nobility," and pledged that Diana's vision of how her boys should be molded into men would be protected by "we, your blood family." Spencer's words caused a thunderous wave of applause to spread from the streets of London all the way up the nave of the abbey, though the public's interpretation of his words—as captured by the Great Diary Project—is fascinatingly varied. Some recalled nothing but loving praise of his sister, others thought it a patriotic condemnation of the news media, but some heard a Spencer pecking at the cuckoos in the nest. "It was as if he was tracing his lineage against Hanoverian and Greek houses," wrote one man, from the very pocket of Northamptonshire where the Spencers have dominated for five hundred years.

The elastic properties of Spencer blood are no less evident today than they were at the time of Diana's emergence as a public figure. In his memoir, Prince Harry recounts a time when he took an HIV test in front of the world's media. As a needle punctured the end of his finger, he pondered his so-called "blue blood. . . . My family always said it was blue because we were special. . . . Watching the nurse channel my blood into a test tube, I thought: Red, just like everyone else's." Overcome by the visceral proof of his ordinariness, he seems on the verge of beseeching, "If you prick us, do we not bleed?" Instead, he begins a new paragraph: "I turned to Rihanna and we chatted. . . ." It is an episode steeped in the Diana Spencer experience: dedicated royal, ordinary person, global celebrity, and humble humanitarian, all at once, any hint of contradiction be damned. Like his mother, Harry traverses the edifice of social rank with the dexterity of Spiderman. A true Spencer, he declares himself appalled by class distinction yet baulks at dropping his titles. He tells us the distaste he felt when he once read a snarky newspaper story that speculated he might have been dating a model. "The snobbery, the classism," thunders Prince Harry, Duke of Sussex, "was nauseating."

2

The Rat Pack

The nineteen-year-old Lady Diana Spencer encounters the news
media, November 1980.

OR MUCH OF 1980, Diana led a strange existence: drifting and uneventful yet teetering on something epically life changing that scared her as much as it thrilled her. Since leaving school at the age of sixteen without any academic qualifications, she had spent a few months at finishing school, taken a cookery course, and done part-time stints as a children's dance instructor, a nanny, an assistant at a private nursery, and a domestic cleaner for her sisters and their friends. On turning eighteen, she used a chunk of inheritance money from her mother's side of the family to buy her own flat in London where she hosted dinner parties for her fellow Sloane Rangers. Life seems to have been perfectly agreeable, but nothing in it tallied with what Diana later told numerous people was her long-standing conviction that she was different from those around her and felt destined for an elevated existence, married to a great man with whom she would realize her romantic fantasy of a domestic life that was salving, fulfilling, and extraordinary.

Then in the summer of 1980, she spent the weekend at the Sussex home of the de Pass family along with several other guests, including Prince Charles who, aged thirty-one and very much in want of a wife, was the world's most eligible bachelor. He had previously met Diana at Althorp in 1977, back when he was courting her eldest sister, Sarah, and had apparently thought the youngest Spencer girl jolly and sweet-natured. Two and a half years later, Diana gave him a full display of Diananess—a flirtatious assault of openhearted charm and compassion that seduced countless others during the thirty-six years of her life—and she rocketed to the top of his list of potential brides. As they sat next to each other on a haystack in a ploughed field, Diana earnestly told him how moved she had been when watching him at the funeral of his beloved great-uncle Dickie—Lord Mountbatten—several months earlier. "It was the most tragic thing," she told Charles; "you should be with somebody to look after you." Charles was smitten. "He was all over me for the rest of the evening, followed me around, everything," said Diana more than a decade later. "I was flattered, but it was very puzzling." Was she really perplexed by the effect she had on him? Recollections vary, but some who knew Diana in her teens believe she had set her sights on becoming the Princess of Wales a long time before she made it so.

From a modern, outside perspective, the next few months of courtship don't look particularly serious; Charles and Diana are known to have spent time together only a handful of times. Yet by the autumn, there was a feeling within the Palace that Diana was The One. Fleet Street—London's newspaper trade—picked up the scent. In the pages of the London tabloids, Diana was a fantabulous concoction: a delightful, ordinary girl, who was also born royalty and angelic in the way that only the invented women of romantic fiction could be. Then on 16 November, the *Sunday Mirror* made a front-page splash with a story claiming that Diana had twice sneaked aboard the royal train late at night for secret liaisons with Prince Charles as he travelled around the country. In the report, a Mrs. Camilla Parker Bowles, "close friend and confidante" to the prince, was named as an aide in the clandestine meetings; years later it was suggested that Camilla was in fact the woman who went aboard the train, not Diana at all.

The Palace has always maintained that the scoop was a smutty fabrication from the fetid depths of gutter journalism. Diana stuck to the same line and was reportedly mortified by the story, its imputations, and the speculation it invited about the most intimate aspects of her private life. Irrespective of its veracity, the story contained many of the features that would define her relationship with the so-called Rat Pack, the group of Fleet Street reporters dedicated to covering the royals. It had the furtive intrusion into royal privacy, anonymous sources, and the accusation that Diana and the other royals were not quite the people they presented themselves to be. The stories also sketched warring visions of Diana: a chaste Victorian maiden and a modern young woman; a respectable girl of decorum and dignity and a scheming rebel whose behavior needed to be watched. In short, the parameters for the next two decades of Diana on the page were now set in place.

DIANA DID her best to be a Londoner, but hers was a royal London life, an experience of the city by proxy. Not for her the Londoner's privilege of disappearing in plain sight, ignoring everyone in the vicinity while they ignore you back. Michael Palin saw her once in L'Escargot, the oldest French restaurant in town, and recorded the occasion in his diary in a way that suggests he—and surely others—were looking intently, while she pretended in vain not to feel their eyes: "She holds her head and shoulders in a hunched, protective curve, as if not wanting to draw attention to herself." Some chance: Diana was watched just about everywhere by just about everyone.

Snooping on royalty has been a London pastime for centuries. George III was reportedly furious when a property developer built homes overlooking the grounds of Buckingham Palace, advertising them as an unrivalled spot from which to ogle the royal family as they went about their daily lives. Two hundred years later, an inventive west London real estate agent made the papers when he tried something similar, marketing a basement flat's subterranean location as a prime spot from which to watch Charles and Diana helicopter in and out of Kensington Palace. In an oral history interview from 2003, Londoner Betty Judge gave happy recollections of family excursions in the 1930s when her parents took her to peer through the railings of 145 Piccadilly, the house where the future queen and her sister were raised, watching Princesses Elizabeth and Margaret playing in the garden, as though the girls were either, depending on one's perspective, ultraprivileged residents of the world's most magnificent gated community, or panda cubs in London Zoo. Judge said she never gave Diana the same treatment—she had no time for Diana and declined to talk about her—but plenty of others did. Another Londoner, Ian

Jackman, travelled with a group of fellow Diana enthusiasts to Windsor Castle one Easter, knowing their idol was spending the holiday there. According to Jackman, Diana caught sight of the little group outside the castle's private quarters and began playing peekaboo with them, comically popping her head back and forth from behind the curtains.

That moment of performance in front of distant spectators brings to mind Diana's introduction to Fleet Street. The journalist James Whitaker had a rather storied past with the Spencer sisters. In 1977, Sarah Spencer had been courting Prince Charles when Whitaker published an article, under the pseudonym Jeremy Slazenger, that quoted Sarah saying to him that she would never marry someone she wasn't in love with "whether he was the dustman or the King of England." This was apparently enough for Charles to discount Sarah as a possible bride, but Whitaker remained on good enough terms with the Spencers to merit an invitation to Jane's wedding in 1978. "You're the wicked Mr. Whitaker, aren't you?" said the sixteen-year-old Diana when she introduced herself, a hint at her irrepressible attraction to potential hazards, gentlemen of the press included.

Months later, in January 1979, Diana and Sarah were invited to Sandringham for a shooting weekend by Prince Charles. As usual Whitaker was on Charles's trail, hoping to spot a future Princess of Wales. From a distance, Whitaker scrutinized the royals and their guests through his binoculars. He saw nothing much to excite him at the time and imagined that Diana might be a possible bride for Andrew rather than Charles. But, as he told one of Diana's biographers, he remembered the occasion for the conspicuous way that Diana had returned his gaze, yanking the prince's binoculars across his neck so that she could watch those who were watching her. Whitaker was in pursuit of Charles again in September 1980—this time on a fishing trip on the River Dee in Scotland—when he realized that the heir to the throne was accompanied by a young lady: it was Diana, who this time darted behind a tree, her insistence on not being photographed a clear signal that there was something serious developing between her and Charles. Whitaker was frustrated by her evasion, but delighted by the unusual fashion in which Diana kept an eye on her pursuer—a deliberate performance of wary observation—by taking out her compact mirror to watch Whitaker in its reflection. "What a cunning lady," he thought to himself, recognizing a fellow player of the game. "You had to be a real professional to think of using a mirror to watch us watching her."

With his outsize personality, toothsome grin, and plummy foghorn voice—he was once likened to "a retired brigadier addressing a pair of deaf daughters"—it would be easy to imagine James Whitaker unserious, a pastiche of a particular type of Englishness. "Nice toffs in three-piece suits with three-piece names to match," is how the former tabloid hack Sharon Marshall summed up the royal reporters she encountered during the Diana years. In many ways, Whitaker was the apotheosis of the breed. Yet he was also a born newspaperman, as tenacious as he was ebullient, a character who couldn't have existed at *Bild*, the *New York Post*, or anywhere other than a London tabloid at the end of the twentieth century.

He entered journalism in the 1960s, when deference still reigned. "One was very reverential in those days," in which royal reporting was conducted among champagne and smoked salmon, "and it was all extremely civilized." Everything changed at the very end of the decade when Rupert Murdoch swooped in from Australia and bought the *News of the World* and *The Sun*. Murdoch revolutionized the British newspaper business with a diet of sex, celebrity, and a brusque questioning of the establishment, especially the monarchy, an institution he loathed. In 1978 one of Murdoch's columnists on *The Sun* openly informed the royal family that the era of unchallenged deference was over: "Admiration is no longer automatic and there is no reason why it should be."

At this time, Charles was on the cusp of thirty, and it was his search for a wife that led to a style of royal reporting much closer to the best and worst of Fleet Street tradition. "James and I pioneered covering the royals as a full-time occupation in the aggressive style that is now the normal practice," says Arthur Edwards, Whitaker's photographer partner at *The Sun*. "We were the founding fathers of the Royal Rat Pack." Whitaker claimed to have been surprised by how unguarded and forthcoming Diana was in her early dealings with journalists, something he thought could only lead to trouble for her and the country—or so he told fellow journalists after the Waleses' marriage had blown up. "Look Diana," he supposedly told her a few weeks before she and Charles got engaged, "you mustn't go on talking. If I ask you a question you mustn't answer it." He might have preferred it that way, too. In Diana he found the perfect subject for his aptitude for watching. His greatest Diana scoops were based on him silently looking at her from a distance, such as the time in 1985 that he stared at her for six hours while she relaxed aboard a yacht in the Mediterranean; from studying her behavior and the total lack of interaction between her and Charles, he deduced that something was dreadfully wrong in their marriage. He named this as his greatest revelation in all his years covering Diana—six hours in which *nothing* happened, other than him not letting her out of his sight.

Whitaker was far from the only brilliant Rat Pack hack who struck gold with Diana time and again, but none of them relished it in quite the way he did. He preferred his Diana distant and uncommunicative; he enjoyed the challenge of solving the silent clues. When the American writer Peter Lefcourt came to London in the early nineties to research the habits of the Rat Pack, Whitaker invited him to his home and, with characteristic bonhomie, spoke at length about how he kept tabs on the princess. "He had this whole, almost command post of royal watching," Lefcourt recalled thirty years later. "Friends and spies everywhere; tracking her like a military operation." Whitaker favored a different metaphor. "I would always regard myself as master of fox hounds," he said in 1993, explaining how he pursued Diana and Charles's other love interests. "It was a certain amount of sport. . . . Up to a point they would enjoy the thrill of the chase." *Up to a point.* For him, though, the fun was boundless.

*   *   *

AT THE time of his early stalking of Diana, Whitaker worked for the *Daily Star,* a new title dedicated to "Tits, bums, QPR, and roll-your-own fags," in the purported words of its editor in chief, or "all the nudes fit to print," as others described it.* It would seem unnatural territory for a man who presented himself as being almost as grand as any aristocratic duke, though he wasn't any less out of place at the *Daily Mirror,* the left-wing, working-class paper for which he worked from 1982. Arthur Edwards, who remained at *The Sun* long after Whitaker's departure, recalls the time Whitaker saw him eating in a greasy spoon in a rough-and-ready London neighborhood: "Fuck me, Arthur," Whitaker exclaimed, "it's enough that we have to write for them. We don't have to eat with them as well."

It wasn't just his—somewhat exaggerated—shire Tory demeanor that made Whitaker stick out like a "big fat tomato," to use the nickname William and Harry bestowed upon him; some of the moral and social assumptions in his writing about Diana belonged to the Edwardian era. Revisiting the royal-train story in 1992, he asserted that the British public of 1980 "wanted its future Queen to be a virgin bride," and having "charmed everyone with her freshness, her innocence . . . her unquestionable virtue," the discovery that Diana may have had sex outside marriage "would have destroyed [her] credibility with a trusting and adoring public," though he cited no evidence to support an assertion that sounds more redolent of the Britain of 1880 than 1980. It's worth bearing in mind that forty-four years earlier, the *Daily Mirror* had pushed back on the commonplace notion that the British people would not have "accepted" Edward VIII marrying the twice-divorced American, Wallis Simpson. An editorial claimed the paper had elicited opinions from its readers and "Not one per

---

* QPR, short for Queen's Park Rangers, an unglamorous London soccer team. "Fag" is British slang for cigarette.

cent of the letters received criticise the King in his choice of Mrs Simpson." It seems likely that something similar would have been true of Diana and the question of her "virtue."

Whitaker also concluded that Diana's flatmates should be believed when they insisted that Diana was not the mystery woman who had boarded the train, because they were "well brought-up girls who were not used to evasion." "Well brought-up" was a common adjective in his work; it appears to have meant "privately educated and not working class"—that is, unlike almost everyone who read his reporting. Such primness was especially conspicuous from a reporter whose greatest hits included taking surreptitious photos of Diana while she was several months pregnant and wearing a bikini. For some scoops he cited "friends" of Diana's as his source; other times there were "aides" or "Palace insiders" but, as with all other royal watchers, it's not always clear how well sourced his sources were. There was, however, a common perception that he was unusually close to the Windsors, perhaps partly because he suggested as much in his numerous appearances in the daytime TV slots dedicated to royal news and gossip. The notion of Whitaker being unusually well-connected and unerringly well-informed was trumpeted by his employers. After Diana's engagement to Charles was announced, the *Daily Star* lauded him as "the man who ALWAYS knew" that the couple were destined to marry. For a time, at least, he did have a solid link to the Spencers. Among the many stories that he broke about Diana was the first public allegation that she suffered from an eating disorder, which he published in the *Daily Mirror* in 1982. He later claimed that his key source for the story had been Diana's sister Sarah. There were occasions when he didn't need an inside track, relying instead on his eyes, ears, and his dueling sensibilities of traditional English gentleman and tabloid hound. This was when he was at his funniest, intentionally or otherwise. He once threw shade on Joan Collins for having "wormed her way" into a function in Florida that Diana was attending. Whitaker played the pantomime dame, sniffing at Collins for festooning herself with diamonds, while admiring her chutzpah, recognizing a pair of elbows as sharp as his own.

His tabloid persona, like Diana's, consisted of overlapping layers of the archaic and the contemporary, much like London's ahistorical skyline where twenty-first-century towers of steel and glass loom above Georgian mansions and 1960s concrete blocks. When interviewed by Ali G—the comedy character played by Sacha Baron Cohen—at the turn of the century, he said that the media had paid far too much attention to the sadly departed Diana, though it was his own enthusiastic participation in the frenzy that allowed him to carve out a public profile as a walking English anachronism, a posh throwback living as a modern pop culture celebrity, giving etiquette advice on Russell Brand's radio show and losing one's love handles on *Celebrity Fit Club*. His clunking incongruities speak to the peculiar space that Diana occupied on Fleet Street, whose coverage flitted antically between populist and elitist, censorious and salacious, courtly and creepy. Her own inconstancy was a central fact of her existence—but it was nothing compared to the whirligig of emotion that she propelled among the men running the nation's biggest newspapers, for whom she became both an object of fascination and a focus for their insecurities about their place in the world.

While upscale publications such as *Vogue, Debrett's,* and *Tatler* saw the pre-wedding Diana in light of her royal and aristocratic relationships, the "Lady Di" persona depicted in *The Sun* and the *Daily Mirror* was a unique variation on recently established Fleet Street character types. In the early eighties tabloids, she was presented as the posh girl next door who had won the golden ticket, perhaps a Sloane Ranger reboot of Viv Nicholson, the young working-class woman who in 1961 won a fortune on the football pools and instantly became a new tabloid archetype that is still a strong presence in British popular culture to this day.* Not that

---

* As with Diana, Nicholson's dream turned nightmarish. The money soon went, leaving her with unwanted notoriety and a life spent grappling with the sad consequences of unimaginable good fortune.

traditional images of royalty didn't shine through; James Whitaker's reporting is cast-iron proof that they did. But in the liminal cultural space that she occupied, Diana was the point of fusion of discrete traditions.

A good example is the famous photograph of her posing outside the Young England Kindergarten where she worked before marrying Prince Charles, her first posed photograph for the press. In an effort to shoo away the photographers who followed her across the city and were now amassed outside her place of work, Diana agreed to pose for a few photographs with two of the children whose parents were happy for it to go ahead. In the imagery

Diana poses for the cameras, September 1980.

created by the characteristic tilt of Diana's head, her mournful eyes, and the children she held close to her, scholars have identified an evocation of Victorian femininity or even an echo of Renaissance depictions of the Annunciation of the Virgin Mary. Yet from the waist down, with the sun streaming through her lightweight skirt to create a silhouette of her legs, this image of Diana echoes the aesthetics of a backlit photo of Ulla Lindström in an unbuttoned white shirt that appeared in *The Sun* in 1969, now sometimes cited as the first Page Three picture, a regular feature showcasing full-page photos of nearly naked young women. It is a cut-and-shut image of Diana, in much the same way that Whitaker was a cut-and-shut reporter, all "ma'am as in ham" one minute and "three-in-a-bed romp" the next.

The tendency to bounce images of Diana off decidedly non-royal images of women was a recurring theme on Fleet Street. In 1985, Whitaker wrote a front-page article for the *Daily Mirror* about a photograph of Diana that resembled the legendary picture of Marilyn Monroe's dress billowing around her thighs. The very last tabloid scoop to mark Diana's lifetime was "THE KISS," as the headline in the *Sunday Mirror* labelled the grainy image of Diana on a yacht in the Mediterranean kissing her new boyfriend, Dodi Fayed, the son of the billionaire Mohamed Al-Fayed. Fleet Street veterans would recall this as a low-resolution redux of the moment in 1962 when Elizabeth Taylor was photographed kissing Richard Burton aboard a yacht off the coast of Italy, a seminal moment in the development of modern celebrity culture.

THE YEAR after Britain gained its new Princess of Wales, *The Sun* acquired a new editor: the cartoonishly obnoxious Kelvin MacKenzie, under whose leadership Britain's best-selling paper became gleefully bigoted and phenomenally successful, selling as many as 4.3 million copies per day by 1988. Under the new editor, *The Sun* deployed the royal family as a key weapon in its circulation battle with the *Daily Mirror*. To the consternation of Harry Arnold,

Whitaker's friendly rival at *The Sun*, MacKenzie instructed him to bring him a new royal story for each Monday's front cover: "Don't worry if it's not true," he told Arnold—especially if it was about Diana, who was to be used by MacKenzie for much more than a slew of great photos and juicy gossip.

MacKenzie embraced Murdoch's antiestablishment schtick but added a turbo-charged Anglo-British jingoism that contained within it anti-European xenophobia. That combination put *The Sun* in a very odd position in relation to the royal family. On the one hand, the monarchy was to be revered as the great symbol of British patriotism; on the other, the royals represented overweening elitism, edged with their Germanness. To his staff, MacKenzie, as Diana did, referred to the Windsors as "the Germans"; photographing them was "whacking the Germans." It betrayed not only cynicism about the royal family but about the nation they were meant to embody. Britain gone to the dogs, shafted at every turn by scheming Europeans—especially the French and the Germans—were constant themes of MacKenzie's *Sun*. He belonged to a generation born during or shortly after the Second World War who felt stung by British decline and Germany's remarkable transformation following the defeat of Nazism. When it suited him, he was happy to denounce Diana as an out-of-control harpy who was besmirching the Crown. But as the natural English Rose who had married into the stuffy old Windsors, she was also a gorgeous Anglo-British hero who put the Germans to shame.

A run of stories from a seven-day stretch in April 1987 gives a strong flavor of how Diana fit into MacKenzie's neuroses regarding Britain, Germany, and the royals. First, an editorial taunted the queen with the apparent insinuation that she had secretly allowed her cousin Katherine Bowes-Lyon—"sad Kate" *The Sun* called her—to languish in a mental hospital for forty-six years. The following day's edition rejoiced that "no-nonsense American experts" had hailed "booming Britain" and its "remarkable recovery" over that of West Germany's. The day after that, Diana's compassion was championed when it was reported that she would shake the hands of a number of people with AIDS, followed by the next day's front page that declared "THE SUN INVADES GERMANY!" in retaliation over some negative reporting in the German press about the behavior of British tourists in Spain. Alongside photographs of *Sun* journalists in military uniform, there was a pledge to "give those Krauts a lesson to remember." It was obviously a joke, but it still reveals the extent of MacKenzie's thin-skinned fixation. Such was the commitment to the gag that the article ran to page four, which featured an invasion map, directly opposite which was a story about how "Dazzling Di" had recently met British soldiers and "quick-marched her way into everyone's hearts." The photos of her, wearing a white Sgt. Pepper–style suit, made her look like some angelic standard bearer of MacKenzie's invasion force.

Halfway through the "annus horribilis"—Elizabeth II's description of 1992, the year in which Windsor Castle burned down, and the marriages of Charles and Diana and Prince Andrew and Sarah Ferguson publicly imploded—Andrew Morton's notorious biography of Diana, full of details of her extreme unhappiness, was serialized in *The Sun* and *The Sunday Times*, another Murdoch title. In response, the *Daily Mirror* initially attempted to frame itself as both a loyal servant of the monarchy and Diana's biggest fan, labelling *Diana: Her True Story* as a sordid work of fiction. It railed against the Murdoch papers—those "republicans down the road"—who by publicizing Morton's book, were exploiting the Palace's noble tradition of not commenting on gossip, rumor, and lies. "This newspaper is not prepared to see the monarchy crack up because it will not fight back." No mention was made of all the delving into royal private lives that Whitaker and his *Daily Mirror* colleagues had committed themselves to for the last decade. Instead, it accused Murdoch of leading an outrageous campaign to traduce the royal family and destabilize the monarchy. The *Daily Mirror*, of course, was run by its own self-interested plutocrat, Robert Maxwell. A Jewish Czech immigrant who was ostensibly left-wing, Maxwell shared Murdoch's sense of being an outsider among the

English public schoolboys who dominated the British establishment, though unlike Murdoch he spent most of his adult life trying to gain their acceptance rather than making them look foolish. Four years later, when Diana lost her title of Her Royal Highness in divorce proceedings, the *Daily Mirror*, now edited by former Murdoch protégé Piers Morgan (who had his own obsession with sticking it to the Germans—and his own issues with the royals), loudly proclaimed a campaign to reunite the so-called Queen of Hearts with her HRH.* "Last night," read one front page, "the Queen and other senior royals were said to be amazed" that the paper had received thousands of furious letters from readers, 69,245 of whom had so far signed a petition, and that the paper was giving away bumper stickers to press Diana's claim.

But before any of that, in April 1992, two months before Morton's incendiary bomb was dropped, MacKenzie offered a jocular portent of the humiliations that were about to rain down when he put a nude watercolor of Diana and Sarah Ferguson, the Duchess of York, on his paper's front page, one of a series of naked images of the royal family painted by the artist Don Grant. The accompanying report clanged with brazen disingenuity, quoting one Conservative MP who was aghast that there were no laws to prevent "this kind of humiliation of our Royal Family." The photographer Arthur Edwards declared them "outrageous," before adding that they weren't even anatomically accurate: "I have seen Diana in a bikini and the artist has done her a favor and made her too slim round the middle." There were nostalgic flashes to a time long before the Windsors, when pamphleteers and caricaturists ridiculed and insulted royalty in graphic, scatological fashion. But really this was classic Kelvin MacKenzie: a mixture of confected moral outrage, seaside postcard bawdiness, and gleeful taunting of those in high places. He was whacking them all—the Germans, Diana, the whole bloody lot of them.

---

* The "Queen of Hearts" nickname had stuck ever since Diana had referred to herself as such in a BBC interview the previous year.

*　　*　　*

"DIANA HAD a hypnotic effect, not just on the tabloids but all newspapers," says Richard Kay, a *Daily Mail* journalist who held the unwieldy position of being both a member of the Rat Pack and a friend of Diana's during her final years. The obsession, Kay says, went both ways: "She took an unhealthy interest in the press pack," and found their attention "fascinating and ghastly. . . . She became fascinated by why the media was obsessed about the most trivial things, like what she wore to the gym, what car she was driving, how her hair looked on a certain day." He recalls the occasion in 1989 when even Diana's trip to the dentist made front-page news.

The extent to which she was victim or collaborator in this saturation coverage is a question that lingers. There were plenty of times when she leaked stories to journalists that burnished her image as a betrayed wife, a selfless public servant, and a devoted mother. Seemingly, even in that first photo of her outside the Young England Kindergarten, it was Diana's idea to include children in the shot. Despite her fury at having her privacy encroached upon by photographers—especially by the aggressive, profane paparazzi—she was sometimes keen for photographs to be taken of her, even when on holiday with her children. In conversation with Tina Brown, Diana intimated that this kind of behavior was a necessary evil: "what's the alternative! To just sit there and have them make your image for you?" Surely, she never did that. Maybe some of the fascination with her press coverage was born of the various traditions she was fitted into, the numerous mythical iterations of herself that were not in her control. But she was also adept at engaging with the press in a highly calculated way, one that could encourage a false feeling of closeness; it is noticeable how many Rat Packers publicly declare having had a unique bond with the Princess of Wales.

The photographer Tim Graham was one of those. In the introduction to a book of his photographs of Diana, he is described as having a "profound spiritual contact" with Diana: "Tim Graham stirs the Princess of Wales to her depths." In his memoir of 1993, James Whitaker's former photographic partner, Arthur Edwards, went for the less colorful, but still rather grandiose claim of being Diana's "favourite newspaperman" and "closer to the royal family than any journalist or photographer has ever been." Given that his book was published in the wake of Andrew Morton's biography (the key source for which was Diana herself), and that Diana was at this time known to be giving stories directly to Richard Kay, Edwards's assertion of unprecedented intimacy was clearly contestable. But self-delusion was a key part of the Fleet Street approach to reporting on Diana. The fantasy version of her they put on the page coexisted with a fantasy version of their own relationship with her. Edwards's memoir begins with an exchange between him and Diana in 1992, shortly before the Waleses' separation was announced. It's meant to reassure the reader of his privileged inside track. More than anything, it exhibits Diana's flair for creating an atmosphere of intimacy where none existed. As he asked the princess about her plans for the coming year, Diana—exploiting the power of the unsaid—drip-fed the suggestion of a story, revealing next to nothing, but giving the sense that something momentous had been shared. Severally, Edwards describes the method Diana employed to do this: "Looking me straight in the eye, as if willing me to realize what was about to happen"; "watching my reaction to see if she was getting the message across"; "Instead of an answer, she looked into my eyes and smiled."

Being an "early discloser" was part of Diana's disarming way of moving through the world. Many a time, she told a member of the public some surprisingly private detail about her life within seconds of meeting them. Clive James—who wrote that hyperventilating introduction to Tim Graham's book—related something similar when he first met Diana, at an event at the Cannes Film Festival. Having turned him to jelly by telling him how much she enjoyed his TV series, Diana reeled him into her confidence when she glanced across the room and saw Robert Maxwell. "Ooh. There's that odious man Maxwell over there. Don't want to meet *him* again. Yuck." Immediately, James felt he had been let behind the velvet rope. "She had just handed me a story that would have embarrassed the bejesus out of the Royal Family. . . . For the air of complicity she had generated between us in so brief a time, the best word I can think of is 'cahoots.'" When she scouted around for Fleet Street allies in the early 1990s, she floated tidbits to Richard Kay at social occasions. "The temptation would have been immense for me to have gone back to my office, written down everything she had told me and presented it as a world exclusive," says Kay. But he also knew that had he done that "the phone would never have rung again." *Cahoots.*

Between 1992 and 1995, Diana did more than share knowing glances or indiscreet remarks. To Andrew Morton, she told the story of her unhappy life, albeit repeatedly denying that she had been at all involved with the book. To Martin Bashir, the journalist on the BBC's current affairs program *Panorama*, she went much further. In an explosive interview at Kensington Palace in November 1995—one that Diana arranged in secret, without the knowledge of the royal family or even her own staff—she spoke on camera to Bashir about her dismal marriage and what she thought was a Palace conspiracy to silence her and remove her from public life. Her relationships with these journalists were purely of convenience. When she heard that Morton was following up his first huge hit about her with a second volume covering the new post-separation life she was building for herself, she moaned to friends that he had surely made enough money from her by now. Another time, she mimed vomiting when on the phone to a journalist she was supposedly friendly with, but apparently couldn't stand the sight of.

The ambiguity that existed in her relationship with the Rat Pack was absent from her feelings about the paparazzi whom she viscerally loathed. Physical intimidation and verbal abuse were among the favored methods of certain photographers who tried to provoke her into giving them a good shot; Charles Spencer has spoken of one paparazzo who told Diana that he would "hound her until the day she died, and then he would urinate on her grave."

As so often with Diana's situation within the royal family, the nature of her experience was broadly in keeping with previous generations; it was the scale and intensity that differed. The first paparazzo to get under the Windsor skin was Ray Bellisario, a British photographer, who made himself an enemy of the Palace for having the temerity to take lots of candid photographs of the royals in public, something that had never been done before, but was in step with a slowly emerging new attitude to tabloid reporting that entered Fleet Street from the start of Elizabeth II's reign. Bellisario was also notable because he resented being known as a paparazzo. Away from the royal snaps that earned him money, he had documented famine, natural disasters, and industrial accidents. He may be the archetype of the paparazzo with a conscience, a character type played by Dominic West in the 1997 feature film *Diana & Me*. The movie tells the story of an Australian woman named Diana Spencer (Toni Collette) who wins a competition to meet her namesake and idol, but ends up falling in love with Rob Naylor, the odious London paparazzo portrayed by West, who turns out to be a Dianaist himself, a humanitarian who has photographed war and extreme poverty, and is privately disgusted by the shallow celebrity culture from which he earns a living. The film was effectively torpedoed when Diana died: the producers reshot a few sequences, but nobody was interested in watching a film about the relentless pursuit of Diana which ends with a paparazzo living happily ever after.

There isn't even a trace of Naylor and Bellisario in *Dicing with Di*, the account that Glenn Harvey and Mark Saunders wrote of their career as "Di-chasers," papping Diana around the world. Published in 1996, the book is two hundred pages of braggadocio and trolling. Instead of photojournalists with a yearning to expose the truth, Harvey and Saunders present themselves as Kodak pirates, highwaymen with telephoto lenses. They boast about their ingenuity and mock many of those they encounter for their stupidity, their arrogance, their vanity, their dishonesty, their looks, and—this being Britain—their accents. Upper-class Englishwomen, for example, "look and sound like horses. Even Diana, who is exceptionally beautiful, has a voice that begins to grate on you after three words." They are also limitlessly proud of the anger and upset they triggered in Diana: "While she was jumping walls, running down fire escapes, putting towels over her head and threatening us with tennis rackets she was literally putting money in our hands!"

Jayne Fincher, the only female photographer among the Rat Pack, is another of those members of the press who claims to have shared something special with Diana. "I often felt that when she gazed into my camera lens, her look was different from the ones she directed at my male colleagues," reckons Fincher. "Her expression was more relaxed and vulnerable with me." In his memoir, Arthur Edwards creates that familiar split-screen image of Diana, splicing a demure Victorian lady with that of a post-sexual-revolution bit of alright. At times, she is "a magical human being" and "the nearest thing to an angel on earth," selflessly tending to the sick and wounded. But there are moments when his typewriter appears to have been commandeered by a daydreaming Benny Hill, such as when describing the time Diana climbed a ladder to gather conkers—the seeds of horse chestnut trees that are used in a popular children's game—sending a large crowd of male onlookers wild with desire. "They gathered around," says Edwards, "gazing upwards, pretending to offer advice, but secretly enjoying the royal peep show. The more Diana strained to grab conkers, the more the thin fabric of her tee-shirt stretched against her figure, revealing that she had not bothered to wear a bra. . . . Knowing she was turning the men on, she giggled but finished her task. Then she slowly descended the ladder, thrilling the assembled staff with her feline grace." He swears it's all true—or so his sources tell him. But it sounds like fantasy, the kind of thing you'd find in a bawdy British comedy film from the 1970s or an invented letter in a tabloid advice column. On a separate occasion, his attempt to upskirt the princess at an official royal engagement was thwarted—but *The Sun* managed to turn it into a story anyway under the headline "KEEP YOUR EYES OFF MY THIGHS."

*   *   *

WITH DIANA on the scene, watching royalty gained unprecedented intensity. Entirely new publications emerged to cater for audiences who desired close-up coverage. First published in May 1980, and still going today, *Majesty* magazine was launched as a repository for the vast number of high-quality color photographs of the royal family that had no outlet. Prince Charles graced its first cover, but that autumn, to quote the magazine's website, "Lady Diana Spencer arrived on the scene, stimulating a global interest in royal matters that shows no sign of abating." A similar publication, *Royalty*, also emerged to capitalize on the fever-pitch frenzy that surrounded Diana. While *Majesty* was the brainchild of two Austrian entrepreneurs, *Royalty* was founded by Bob Houston, the Glaswegian son of a steelworker who had made his name as a pioneering editor of the music weekly *Melody Maker* in the swinging sixties, following which he edited the official publication of the National Union of Miners.

Both *Royalty* and *Majesty* slaked a public thirst for more Diana, closeup, in vibrant color, and high definition, but did so in a deferential, adoring manner. Yet no matter how advanced the technology or the sharpness of the pictures it took, there were limits to how far the press could venture inside the Waleses' marriage. To some extent, the gaps were filled with what might best be described as fan fiction. Most notably, there was the abundance of copy-and-paste articles that clogged Fleet Street titles at regular points of the year. Around the time of Diana's birthday, for instance, there were articles that remarked at how the shy teenager of 1980 had blossomed into a confident woman, who was now completely on top of her royal role. After 1986, when rumors began to swirl that Charles and Diana's marriage was under strain, numerous erroneous reports had the couple sailing through the storm, their bond stronger than ever. Less frequent, but just as patently false, were articles published around the time of the Queen Mother's birthday which revealed how Her Majesty—then the most venerated of all the Windsors—had guided Diana through the timidity and anxiety of her early years. Other fixtures in the fictional Windsor universe included artists' impressions of private moments. The *Sunday Mirror* had the deeply weird "Tales from the Nursery," a cartoon strip about Charles and Diana's experience as parents, which spun a fantasy of the prince and princess loved-up in domestic bliss, William a cherubic scamp, and Harry the permanently sleeping baby upon whom they all dote. In one especially far-fetched edition, the queen and Diana natter away on the phone like old friends. The morning after William was born, the *Daily Mirror* attempted to transport us into the scene of Diana's labor via a sketch of the delivery room showing doctors, a midwife, and Charles standing around Diana, all of them smiling beatifically.

Of course, press interest didn't only take readers into Diana's life, it put her into our lives, too. Almost as soon as she had been identified in the British press as Charles's latest squeeze, newspapers and magazines around the globe were afflicted with the early symptoms of Dianamania. The author John Pearson surveyed the European coverage of Diana shortly before and after her wedding and concluded that the way in which she was portrayed was distinctly different from country to country. French publications focused on Diana's clothes and diet; Italians depicted her as a "suffering royal holy mother" at the center of endless domestic strife; German papers concentrated on Diana's efforts to be the ultimate *hausfrau*. It sounds a little pat, but numerous stories that made their way to Fleet Street do support Pearson's scheme. A fortnight before the engagement, for example, Diana was upset by a report in Germany that quoted her as saying that it was her mission in life to provide Charles with a brood of "sweet babies" and that she knew "the latest scientific methods of deciding which sex of baby to have."

British newspapers expressed incredulity that such impertinence and intrusion could be performed against the royal family, providing them with a convenient justification for then printing the very things they claimed were beyond the pale. The notion that the foreign news media has not historically treated the Windsors with the deference of their British peers is true, of course. Diana's former press secretary, Dickie Arbiter, points out that before Charles and Diana, the British press felt inhibited about reporting marital strife within the royal family, but in the first fifteen years of Elizabeth II's reign, French newspapers published seventy-three reports that Queen Elizabeth and Prince Philip were to divorce, sixty-three that she was about to abdicate, and ninety-two stories about a new pregnancy. But even in the post-Murdoch era when Fleet Street—and other parts of the British media—took a newly aggressive and excitable approach to royal reporting, the idea persisted that non-British journalists were conspicuously abysmal in their treatment of Diana. Diana's old local newspaper, the *Lynn News & Advertiser*, declared itself appalled at the conduct of the European news media regarding west Norfolk's favorite daughter: "Happily our national and provincial Press, by and large, steered clear of such reckless journalism."

Local news may have not indulged in the sharp practices that characterized the tabloids on Fleet Street or the paparazzi, but their coverage of Diana was barely less obsessive. In February 1985—to pick one example out of hundreds—Diana made a visit to a nursing home in Oxford whereupon she was overheard mentioning to a volunteer manicurist that she had a habit of biting her fingernails. In the coming days, this stunning revelation was reported across the UK. The *Liverpool Echo*, one of the most prominent local newspapers in the land, stuck it on the front page, while BBC Radio Manchester spun a news item around it. Nobody mentioned that the princess's bitten fingernails had already made the news, back in 1981 when sharp-eyed observers of her engagement photos noted tell-tale signs as Diana showed off her famous sapphire ring; there was never any such thing as an "old" Diana news story, an attitude that certain Fleet Street publications maintain to this day. Over the next decade, journalists would reprise the theme of Diana's troubled relationship with keratin as though it were a profound insight into some aspect of her identity. "The Princess of Wales might seem perfect," revealed the *Reading Evening Post* in 1994, like it had the next Watergate on its hands, "but . . . she is a nail-biter."

Just as Fleet Street had its Diana perennials, so local editors possessed their own store of templates whenever they wanted a bit more of the People's Princess in their pages. When Diana was pregnant, double-page spreads were produced about local expectant mothers with the same due date; when a juicy new book about her was published, a reporter was sent to trawl nearby bookshops to see what the locals made of it. Inevitably, whenever Diana cut a ribbon or unveiled a plaque, papers from the surrounding area squeezed every drop of coverage from the event, the story splashed across multiple pages with gushing prose about her radiant charms and interviews with those who had given her flowers, spoken to her, and—a strikingly common feature—dared to kiss her ungloved hand. But even when she had been nowhere near the local area, she still made the papers. The *Newcastle Evening Chronicle*, for instance, deemed it newsworthy that an employee at a local wine bar once completed a ten-week course at the same cookery school where Diana had, at a different time, taken lessons as a teenager. But very often no connection to the local area was deemed necessary for a Diana story. A paper in Dundee once reported the moment when, in London, a gust of wind had blown Diana's car door shut, a chilling turn of events which could have—*but didn't*—hurt her fingers. In Aberdeen, a subeditor headlined a write-up of Diana's visit to the National Children's Orchestra, hundreds of miles away in the south of England, as "Di's Confession," because she had remarked that music "was not her strongest point" when at school.

The consequence of all this coverage—at a time when local newspapers held a much greater prominence in provincial British life than they do today—was to make Diana seem like a local as well as a national figure. More than Diana, the People's Princess, or Diana, Queen of Hearts, in the last twenty years of the twentieth century she was "Diana the Inescapable." To a woman who spoke to the *Birmingham Mail*, Diana's ubiquity was a blessing, providing her life with "a little bit of meaning." But the familiarity could also breed contempt or, at the very least, compassion fatigue. Mass Observation—the social research project that records the thoughts and feelings of myriad anonymous Britons on a variety of topics—received a mountain of testimonies about the day Diana died. One participant wrote that when her mother realized the British media had responded to Diana's death by slathering her image across TV, radio, and the press, she fumed that even in death Diana's presence was total—or words to that effect. "Bloody cowing rotten lousy stinking bloody lousy Princess bloody cowing sodding Diana's dead and they've took everything off for the cow."

∽ 3 ∼

Will the Real Diana Please Sit Down

Princess Diana at a polo match in Cirencester,
England, August 1983.

WHEN BUCKINGHAM PALACE announced on 24 February 1981 that the Prince of Wales was officially engaged to Lady Diana Spencer, it ended years of tedious speculation about when and to whom Charles would marry, and set in motion months of rising excitement about the magical day on the horizon—a fairytale distraction from the thicket of social and economic ills that plagued Britain at the time. Amidst the happy talk, however, were murmurs of concern, generally quieted by an exercise in national self-delusion that this obviously ill-suited couple had a gainful future. The yawning age gap seemed all the bigger considering how little the bride and groom knew each other: the thirty-two-year-old Charles, a young fogey if ever there was one, and his teenage fiancée had courted for only a few months. A giant red flag was waved in the happy couple's television interview when they were asked whether they were in love. "Of course," said Diana, blushing and pulling a face that looked like coyness or possibly doubt, quite probably both. Charles, forever playing the philosopher prince, at first replied in the affirmative, before choosing to query the premise of the question: "Whatever 'in love' means." But just about everyone in Britain—including, to some extent, Charles and Diana themselves—chose to ignore all available evidence and dusted off the bunting in anticipation of a midweek public holiday.

Leading up to the big day, there was much speculation about what Diana's dress would look like. Its creators—David and Elizabeth Emanuel, almost as young and gauche as the bride—had endured a stressful time keeping their design secret, going so far as placing strands of decoy material in the rubbish to throw scavenging, scoop-hungry reporters off the scent. Their job was made all the harder by repeated alterations necessitated by Diana's alarming weight loss, a result of a sustained bulimic episode triggered by the pressures of her strange new circumstances, and the dawning realization that Charles's heart still belonged to his old flame, Camilla Parker Bowles.

On the day of the wedding, Diana journeyed through London in a horse-drawn carriage, evocative of Caroline of Brunswick if you knew your royal history, and Cinderella if you didn't. Shortly before 11 a.m., she stepped out of the carriage to reveal the dress, a vast creation of silk taffeta and lace with an extravagant, almost comical, twenty-five-foot train. If the Mass Observation reports are anything to go by, the public's initial response was not over-whelmingly favorable. "The bride's dress proved to be a let down to all the women around me," wrote one woman. "Remarks such as 'Fancy having off-white,' and 'what a lot of creases' were very pronounced." Another correspondent noted that in the week fol-lowing the wedding they had numerous conversations about "the dishevelled state of 'The Dress.'" In Rose Joseph's workroom, there were more important concerns than whether or not she liked the design. Joseph worked for Ellis Bridals in London, and the com-pany had two hundred customers already signed up, sight unseen, for a replica of whatever it was that Diana would be wearing. From the moment the dress appeared on television, she was sketching frantically, cutting material as Diana was saying her vows.

A thousand miles away, the Canadian artist André Durand watched the ceremony alongside a gaggle of fishermen, crowded around a TV on a beach in Portugal. He, too, was riveted by the spectacle, its gaudy upper-crust ostentation, and the pileup of mythological lore and historical allusion, all of which coalesced in the bride's gigantic dress. Inspired, he created *A Mystic Marriage*, the first of his many paintings of Diana. He has depicted her in some of her best-known outfits, in historical attire, and nude. In each case, her appearance is used as a way of likening her to a fic-tional, mythological, or religious figure—from Pulcinella to the goddess Fortuna. In *A Mystic Marriage*, Diana appears like a cross between Botticelli's Venus and a young Miss Havisham, emerging from the waves utterly swamped by her wedding dress, just as she was in real life, literally and metaphorically. The gown she wore that day was an eruption of cultural fantasies—both her own and those of the 750 million others looking on. With Diana, it was ever thus.

NEVER HAS anyone been so often seen yet so rarely heard as Diana, Princess of Wales. The writer James Lees-Milne was one of many who tuned into her *Panorama* interview in November 1995 certain that this was the first time they had ever heard her speak. "I imagined she would be like a silly little debutante," Lees-Milne confided to his diary, noting how "adult and articulate" she sounded, with a "low, croaky voice." Other than the condescension, what's strange about Lees-Milne's observation is that in earlier diary entries he recorded his visit to see the Duchess of Devonshire at Chatsworth in 1992, during which he sat near to Diana at dinner one evening. You'd imagine that he'd have heard her speak then—unless this was one of those occasions when Diana would refuse to engage with dinner companions. "She just wouldn't respond," an anonymous friend told the biographer Sally Bedell Smith of the times when Diana would shut down in social situations—"the most difficult woman in the world." Or, perhaps, like Roy Strong, Lees-Milne was so disappointed by her accent that he blacked out the sound of her voice altogether.

The fact that the world's most recognizable face had the least recognizable voice was handy for impressionists. Jan Ravens imitated Diana for the television show *Spitting Image* and said that it was only after Diana did a high-profile broadcast interview with Alastair Burnet in 1985 that there was any need for accuracy: before then the public hadn't a clue what the princess sounded like. Even in 1991 Kate Robbins, a fellow *Spitting Image* alum, said that impersonating Diana for the royal-family satire *Pallas* was pretty straightforward as her voice was still unknown to most of her compatriots. "Just make her nicely spoken and a little bit dizzy" was her rule of thumb.

In her muteness, however, Diana was thought to be remarkably articulate. Her eyes were considered especially eloquent, interpreted variously as reservoirs of pain and beacons of compassion, defiant, playful, and seductive. "I remember those eyes," says Manolo Blahnik, one of Diana's favored shoe designers, "sometimes downcast, curious, but full of wonder and mischievousness." No matter her age or her circumstances, "those eyes" would always give Diana away. A few weeks before the wedding, the *Daily Mirror* published a grainy black-and-white photograph of a group of young girls, pupils at Riddlesworth Hall, Diana's old prep school, singing hymns on Parents' Day, ten years earlier. "Can YOU Spot Lady Di?" the headline challenged its readers. The giveaway, the paper said, was the way that nine-year-old Diana was looking at the camera: "She peers guardedly. . . . Her slightly nervous expression, anointed with shyness," in the manner that a decade hence, "photographers know so well."

The use of the word "anointed" is peculiar, though indicative of the quasi-religious tone of writing about Diana at various points in her life. Still, it can't be denied: the little girl darting a glance at the camera in 1971 is instantly recognizable as the woman spilling her guts to Martin Bashir on *Panorama* in 1995, her eyes ringed with thick black ovals of kohl. Her addiction to eyeliner exasperated her makeup artist Barbara Daly, who told her that her eyes were already prominent enough. Diana ignored the advice and kept her pencil at hand, often applying it herself before appearing in front of the camera. Such deliberate exaggeration was one of several ways in which she appeared reminiscent of a silent-film star, nonverbal but always apparently communicating through appearance and body language. Professor Therese Davis has pointed out intriguing similarities between what she describes as Diana's "facial performance" on *Panorama* and the array of facial expressions performed by Falconetti playing the lead role in *The Passion of Joan of Arc* (1928), a silent classic of French cinema. Of course, there's no suggestion that Diana was ever consciously influenced by this or any other silent film. Nevertheless, the parallels underline how unusual and effective was Diana's use of her face and body as a nonspeaking voice that held her audience rapt.

The profundity of the superficial has always been a key consideration of royalty, especially in the age of mass media. "Dress is a trifling matter," Queen Victoria once told her son, the future Edward VII. "But it gives also the outward sign from which people in general can and often do judge upon the *inward* state of mind and feeling of a person." Diana seems to have lived by this credo, supported by the unshakable belief of so many others that she used her hair, makeup, and clothing as an elaborate semaphore, signaling to us everything which she didn't, or couldn't, say aloud. *Vanity Fair* was influential in creating the mythological canon of the various iterations of Diana—charting the sea-changes in her emotional and psychological development as the soap opera of her life began its latest episode—all of which the magazine identified in Diana's physical appearance. In 1985, then-editor Tina Brown described the princess's "shoulder pads and frosted bearskin hairdo" as an "extraordinary physical transformation from mouse to movie star" that transmitted an identical inner change. Four years later, Joan Juliet Buck scrutinized Diana's calculated, self-possessed appearance down to the "veins along the top of each foot" that were "the same blue-green as [her] dress." She was "dedicated Di" now, whose wardrobe of "collarless suits and plain coatdresses in various colors shows remarkable restraint," the hallmark of the unique public servant she had become. A steely, vengeful Diana was depicted in 1993. Her eyes were no longer sorrowful, plaintive, or shy as earlier coverage of Diana had told us, but "commanding," her "nose expressive of powerful will." Four years later, this Napoleonic Diana was exiled to her Elba: "Diana Reborn" was photographed for the magazine by Mario Testino as a multi-millionaire minimalist and "postmodern icon."

To some, however, this constantly evolving language of appearance wasn't a form of genius but an infuriating defect. In Diana's first iteration as a public figure, her wardrobe was hailed by *The Official Sloane Ranger Handbook* as the ultimate Sloane Ranger look:

ruffled shirts with ribbons and piecrust collars, baggy sweaters, and straights skirts. It was a backward-looking aesthetic, redolent of not only a time before the youth rebellions of the 1960s, but those of the 1920s, too. In a sense, this put the Sloanes on a similar footing to some of their more adventurous peers: Britain in the 1980s was a place of dedicated sartorial nostalgia, exemplified by Vivienne Westwood's influential 1981 collection, Pirate. Inspired by the fashions of the eighteenth century, Westwood's designs were a key influence on the New Romantic movement, but when they went on sale at the World's End, the boutique on the King's Road that Westwood co-owned with the former Sex Pistols manager Malcolm McLaren, the Diana effect sullied the collection's legacy—at least, that's how McLaren remembered it. "A terrible thing happened," he recalled many years later: "we opened the store and Diana Spencer came in; she was the first customer. . . . I thought, 'Oh my God, we're ruined! . . . I've lost all credibility.'" Thanks to Diana, he said, the clothes "got into the wrong hands," selling to "every would-be, wannabe Diana Spencer on the Fulham Road." Neither McLaren nor Westwood thought Diana in the least bit stylish, just a dreary fashion victim. Far from being a trendsetter, Westwood told *Woman and Home* magazine in 1995, the princess was "someone ruled by the trends." She had particular disdain for Diana's shoes, "those horrible little pumps that are neither one thing nor the other. It's as though her clothes are supposed to tell you that she's both a feminist and sexy at the same time." To many of Diana's biggest fans, this was precisely what she was dressing to say. But to Westwood—a pioneer of the punk aesthetic and one of the most influential British designers of the last century—Diana's changing appearance was a vast catalogue of bourgeois conformity, a betrayal of the royal responsibility to project magnificence— "something I call civilisation"—and all because she was "too busy trying to be middle-class." It's a reminder that Diana's enormous popularity never translated into anything we could call "cool," that quality of cultural edge—or aching, petty elitism, depending on how you look at it.

* * *

DESPITE HER twenty-first-century reputation as a style icon, during Diana's lifetime it was far from universally acknowledged that she had a flair for dressing. Though she appeared nine times on Eleanor Lambert's famous best-dressed lists, for instance, she was also named on the worst-dressed lists compiled by the fashion critic Richard Blackwell. According to many of those who helped to curate her appearance, Diana never even had any particular interest in clothes. Rather, it was felt that she possessed an instinct for performance and presentation, one which the fashion critic Colin McDowell puts down to breeding and upbringing: "What the nobility tend to possess," he claims, "is not fashion sense, but style." Maybe. Yet it's also the case that there are plenty of members of the upper class who have no more style than the rest of us, just the illusion of it conjured from old houses and ancient titles. In any case, it is certainly true that Diana's entrée to the fashion world came thanks to her social background. In the 1970s, both her sisters landed jobs at British *Vogue*, Sarah as an assistant for the magazine's editor, Beatrix Miller, while Jane served in a similar role for the beauty editor, Felicity Clark. It was Clark who marked Diana as one to watch, "a gawky fourteen-year-old," who was "very pretty and had those lovely eyes." In the late seventies, Clark attempted to photograph her for a feature on "up-and-coming beauties." As Clark recalls it, that plan was thwarted when Diana fell ill, but a further opportunity presented itself in 1981, when Diana was photographed as one of three aristocratic young women whom *Vogue* deemed worthy of public notice, the others being the Honourable Louisa Napier and the Countess of Halifax.

Diana arrived fizzing with excitement about being photographed. "She was a jeans and T-shirt sort of girl, with not a lot of clothes in her wardrobe . . . [who] hadn't thought a great deal about fashion," and was "rather thrilled" when she saw the rack of designer garments that had been picked out for her, including a pink blouse by the Emanuels. It was a coincidence that the photographs taken by Lord Snowdon—the celebrity photographer who had been Princess Margaret's first husband—appeared in the February 1981 edition, at the very moment when the engagement was announced. For the next several years *Vogue* staff, especially fashion editor Anna Harvey, mentored and shepherded Diana in her clothing choices. In acting as Diana's fashion counsel, Harvey and her colleagues were performing a type of national service. When *Vogue* published its December 1984 edition devoted to "The Englishwoman," Snowdon's latest portrait of Diana was used as the gold standard, the "world's best-known and most romantic example."

Among the designers that Anna Harvey paired Diana with was Frederick Fox, a legendary milliner, who at one point was designing hats for eight royal women simultaneously: "God," he once recalled of handling his regal clientele, "it was a nightmare trying to keep them all apart." Fox's first Windsor client was Princess Alexandra in the mid-1960s, before Hardy Amies—one of Elizabeth II's most trusted dressmakers—invited him to make hats for the queen. At first, he had no access to Elizabeth, meaning that the first six hats he designed for her were made with only a postage stamp for reference. It was no great hindrance: Elizabeth approved of the designs, and Fox made hundreds of hats for her across thirty-five years, becoming an expert in the convoluted etiquette involved in designing for the crown of the Crown. In an interview in 2003 he recalled the stress of having to walk backwards out of the queen's dressing room when he went to do fittings at the palace, though he always remembered the advice given to him by Elizabeth's vendeuse: "be yourself. If you're nervous, she's equally as nervous; she doesn't like new people." When he came to design hats for Diana—which he did for about six years in the 1980s—the process was entirely different. Ahead of a trip to Japan, for example, Fox spread out sketches of his designs on the carpet at Kensington Palace while he and the princess sat on the floor reviewing each of them. Diana did, however, pose an unusual problem for milliners in that her head, said Fox, was like a huge rugby ball: It "came to a point in the front and very big at the back, and big, a really large head. . . . Very difficult head to fit."

The unwieldiness of her skull notwithstanding, Fox's verdict on Diana was that she was "really, really sweet," but "lost. Totally out of her depth." With his many years of dealing with royalty, he was at least able to give her the benefit of his experience when it came to clothing. But of the key designers Diana recruited to shape her constant reimagining, very few had significant experience of designing for the Windsors. The Emanuels, barely out of college, were astounded by how little direction they were given by the Palace when working on Diana's wedding dress—surely liberating in one sense, but daunting in another. Bruce Oldfield, a key influence in transforming Diana from frilly Sloane to glamourous knockout, came from a background even further away from royalty than the Emanuels, but their lack of experience certainly resulted in clothes that allowed Diana to inhabit and project aspects of her personality that might have been occluded in the hands of grander couturiers.

The Emanuels' wedding dress, conceived in concert with Diana's wishes, was almost cartoonish in its representation of a princess bride, and expressed more about Diana's voluminous if, at this stage, shapeless sense of mission and destiny than it did royal tradition. In their way, Oldfield's most notable designs for Diana were equally fantastical: a shimmering gown of green that she wore to the premiere of *Shirley Valentine* in 1989 made her reminiscent of a mermaid; in an extraordinary open-backed silver lamé dress, Diana moved like a gliding shard of moonlight on the night of the premiere of *A View to a Kill*, one of the many Bond premieres Diana attended. The two of them—Bond and Diana—were a good match. Both embodied a class-ridden, tradition-bound world of the Anglo-British past, but in a way that allowed them to be reimagined as contemporary and international. Hollywood helped Bond achieve that; in Diana's case it was designers such as Oldfield and Catherine Walker. Perhaps the central designer in Diana's life, Walker made a vast array of outfits for her between 1984 and 1996, at which point Walker began treatment for breast cancer, and Diana headed in new directions. Born and raised in France, Walker moved to England as an adult and, by her own telling, became a fashion designer practically by happenstance at the start of the 1980s. Without any roots in the country, and with no particular interest in popular culture, she claimed to be clueless about either royal dress or recent fashion movements when she made her first designs for Diana, a number of maternity garments for Diana's first pregnancy. But Walker was stirred by the challenge of designing for a royal, especially one with Diana's supermodel frame and cultural reach. As such, Walker's designs for Diana are the most interesting she ever wore, a conversation between the individual personality she wanted to project and the traditions she was tasked with upholding; Walker's fabric allowed its wearer to stray back and forth between Diana the global celebrity and the Anglo-British princess.

Perhaps more than any other designer, Walker consciously engaged with Englishness as a theme for the outfits she created for Diana's various foreign tours. She was inspired by the English photographer John French who, she said, "captured the femininity and elongation of the body" and by her own observations of the "quirkiness and freedom" with which Englishwomen dressed, as well as an aristocratic tendency for cool, pale colors and "an absence of fussiness." She dedicated herself to making Diana a vision of Englishness. For a 1988 trip to Australia, "indigo and pink were chosen for an English princess to wear for an Australian summer." The following spring, Diana travelled to the UAE, for which Walker provided "English country garden colouring," intended to provide a pleasing contrast to the arid desert, and to display Diana as an "Arthurian Princess," the soundboard of English and royal mythology dialed up to eleven. It was Walker who designed one of Diana's most famous garments, the so-called Elvis Dress, named as such because Prince William thought its high collar and glittering sequins looked like something The King would wear. In fact, Walker had styled this on a queen—Elizabeth I. Hampton Court Palace meets Caesar's Palace: Diana and her clothes were always laden with the mythologies of others.

* * *

DIANA'S APPARENT reinventions were a stellar incarnation of something that was going on in homes across the country, a recalibration of the British public's relationship with shopping, consumption, and personal presentation. In 1980, two magazines launched—*The Face* and *i-D*—both of which treated fashion and design in the way pop music had been treated for many years, as being utterly accessible, yet worthy of serious criticism, and pivotal to the development of a sophisticated, modern sense of self-identity. In 1986, the editor of *i-D*, Caryn Franklin, became the co-host of *The Clothes Show*, a new BBC TV series that brought the world of high fashion into the living rooms of millions of people every Sunday evening. Soon after, TV formats and print publications performed a similar feat with other areas of consumption and domestic life, including gardening, food, and home décor. It is worth noting the joy Diana found in splashing Windsor cash on not just clothes, but also working with the designer Dudley Poplak to decorate her homes at Kensington Palace and Highgrove in Wiltshire. As the beige of Britain in the seventies gave way to the technicolor eighties, Diana was a cheerleader for the transformation, a consumerist Britannia both replicable and irreplicable.

Being worn by Diana could transform the meaning of a garment. The so-called "black-sheep" sweater, which Diana was first photographed wearing in June 1981, is now quite probably the most famous item of knitwear in history. A vibrant red sweater dotted with rows of little white sheep and one black one, it has become woolen shorthand for Diana's strife with her birth family and her in-laws, and the impudence that her admirers cite as her superpower. When "Princess Diana: A Tribute Exhibition" opened in Las Vegas in September 2022, black-sheep sweaters were available to buy in the gift shop, as though they were official Diana merchandise.

The makers of the sweater—a tiny company named Warm and Wonderful—were deluged with requests after photos of Diana wearing the design were first published; the same happened with the Sloppy Joe sweatshirt Diana was pictured wearing to the gym a decade or so later. In the United States, JCPenney sold out of a particular scarf within hours of Diana buying one from a shop in Virginia. Not only individual fashion labels, but entire industries experienced the sugar rush of a Diana endorsement, no matter how casual or inadvertent. In the early eighties, she was credited with saving millinery in Britain and—so it was claimed by certain journalists and department stores—sent sales of thermal underwear through the roof when she was overheard saying that this was how she kept warm on cold days, though why the thought hadn't already independently occurred to hordes of shivering Brits is curious. Ahead of her wedding, the Labour MP George Foulkes suggested that Diana get hitched in a pair of jeans made in his constituency of South Ayrshire, Scotland. "A £5,000 dress might inflict damage on the taxpayer," he argued, whereas a "smart pair of tight jeans would do her and our export trade the world of good."

Diana—her body and her public position—was a precinct for designers to indulge their fantasies. In the spring of 1981, *Vogue* published ideas for her wedding dress by various different designers, including the Emanuels, who ultimately were rewarded with the commission. For *Woman's Own* magazine Karl Lagerfeld sketched his vision of Diana wearing one of his designs, a predictably skeletal depiction of the princess in brown silk. The very same month, October 1984, the designer for the TV series *Dynasty*, Nolan Miller, published his very different vision of how he would dress Diana—a Disney princess in off-the-shoulder apricot and ruffles. "If the Princess doesn't like it," he said, "I'll make it for Joan Collins."

Diana's patronage could transform a designer's career, but the removal of her imprimatur threatened serious damage. Bruce Oldfield said that when Diana decided to cut him off, it was a blow both personally and professionally, as a flock of customers in thrall to their black sheep also stayed away. And as slews of courtiers experienced over the years, she could be unfeeling when discarding those who had outlasted their purpose or done something to displease her. Anna Harvey claimed to have received several enquiries from designers puzzled as to why they had been suddenly frozen out. One of Diana's original image makers, her hairdresser Kevin Shanley, went through a similar ordeal. Shanley had been Diana's hairdresser for several years, starting before her relationship with Charles was publicly known, but he made himself persona non grata by advising against her stated desire to wear her hair up at the State Opening of Parliament in 1984. He felt the style was too old for such a young woman, and anyway, he told her, her hair wouldn't be long enough to pull it off properly. It was the kind of small but fatal misstep made by countless people in Diana's orbit, a trusted confidant who told her something—sometimes consequential, sometimes not—that she didn't want to hear and found themselves sent first to Coventry, then to Siberia. "There were long, uncomfortable silences," he recalled of their final appointments at Kensington Palace. "Some days she would barely speak to me." On 14 September 1984, he told Diana that he thought it best to end their association. "She seemed relieved."

Such was the interest in Diana's life and looks that Shanley's reminiscences as keeper of the royal locks were published in the *Sunday Mirror* in a five-part series a few months later, which told of his role in creating Diana's public image, helping to transform her "from a shy, unworldly teenager fresh out of finishing school to Delightful Di, with her 'cover girl' looks and world-wide acclaim." Like the Emanuels and Catherine Walker, Shanley was not versed in royal history nor very au fait with high-society fashions; Felicity Clark was among those who believed that his inexperience showed up on Diana's wedding day, her hair not styled properly to accommodate a tiara. Yet Shanley's work had a rare, if brief, cultural impact. As Diana's profile rocketed, her side-swept shaggy haircut became a phenomenon. The style itself wasn't wildly original. But once Diana started to appear in national newspapers on a daily basis, her hair was copied by droves of young women, and shops and mail-order companies did a brief but lucrative trade in Diana wigs, an echo of when The Beatles had surged from nowhere to occupy a similar grade of cultural presence, wigs of their mop-tops selling by the truckload. Newspapers and TV shows ran items on the craze, inviting famous and ordinary women to transform themselves into a princess by slipping on a replica of the Shanley cut. The glamorous West End actress Stephanie Lawrence wore one for the cameras, as did the less glamorous Wee Jimmy Krankie, the character of a ten-year-old boy played by the thirty-something comedian Janette Tough.

In her twenties, Diana was definitively not a fashion influence on the youngsters of the post-punk era who raided jumble sales, flea markets, and secondhand shops for their signature looks. Yet in a way, she was the ultimate vintage dresser of the 1980s. She married, of course, in the Spencer tiara, a family heirloom that dates from before the Second World War. On at least one other occasion, she paired the tiara with an emerald choker that was created for Queen Mary in 1911 to mark the Delhi Durbar and the start of her reign as Empress of India. At a function in Australia in 1985, Diana wore the choker as a headband, a jaunty, very 1980s flourish, that flattened—perhaps obliterated—the item's historical meaning in the way that modish secondhand dressing often does. It was perhaps aspirational working-class young women of Thatcher's Britain who most embraced Diana as an aesthetic north star. Of course, they'd be hard-pressed to ape jewels from the collection of the Spencer and Windsor families, but with the proliferation of high-quality color images of her, in print and on television, it was possible to copy her hairdo, track down her clothes and accessories, and imitate her makeup, especially as—in these early days of the fast-fashion revolution—British high-street shops were actively filling racks with Diana-led trends.

Elsewhere in the world, Diana was equally flattered by imitation. Teri Wilson is a self-confessed Diana fanatic who, as a teenager in 1980s Texas, followed and emulated her every fashion choice, using Diana as a portal to ways of being and identifying that would have otherwise seemed ludicrously distant. "I wore

Diana's high neck blouses, ruffles and ballerina flats," she says, before getting her own version of the Shanley cut and ultimately graduating to her first designer handbag when Diana was photographed carrying a Gucci bag in the very un-Texas-like surroundings of a polo match in England in the 1980s. When JCPenney stocked reissues of the black-sheep sweater in 2020, Wilson, now in her fifties, snapped one up. By one count, eleven Japanese women's magazines issued Diana-themed special editions in advance of her visit to the country in 1986, each including tips for readers on how to look more like the princess. In a market in Cairo in 1985, a British journalist came across a range of hosiery branded with Diana's name, face, and purported endorsement. Adopting Diana as an unofficial official brand ambassador is a trend that has never gone out of fashion. In 2010, a Chinese lingerie brand, Jealousy International, ran adverts with the slogan "Feel the romance of British royalty" for its "Diana" line that featured a Diana lookalike in nothing but underwear, high heels, tiara, and jewels, smiling at a small child as she plays the cello, a kitsch mélange of cultural associations as startling—and silly—as anything André Durand has ever managed.

AT THE height of her global fame, it seemed like Diana was self-regenerating with imperfect replicas of her popping up all over the place. The photographer Anwar Hussein followed Charles to New Zealand shortly after the engagement during which he snapped a clutch of Dianas who lined up to greet the prince as he arrived in Wellington. Ahead of Diana's first solo trip to New York in 1989, a Diana lookalike contest was held at Oliver's restaurant on East 57th Street, shop windows in the surrounding streets filled with pictures of the real thing. Diana lookalikes were a staple of British popular culture in the eighties and nineties, as guerilla marketing gimmicks, features in local newspapers when the princess came to town, and the evening's entertainment at holiday camps. Television producers seemed to look for any excuse to supplement their program with a woman who looked a bit like the Princess of Wales—and if she didn't, everyone would just pretend that she did. To give one example, on the show *Just Amazing* a cavalcade of thirty underwhelming Diana lookalikes was brought into the studio, whereupon the memory champion Harry Lorayne was set the task of remembering all their real names. Women from all kinds of backgrounds were noted, sometimes celebrated, for bearing even the vaguest physical similarity to Diana. "In a certain light, blonde, blue-eyed, stylish Fiona Shackleton could almost be mistaken for the Princess of Wales," suggested a journalist for Dublin's *Evening Herald*, one of several commentators to point out the faint, passing resemblance between Diana and Prince Charles's formidable divorce lawyer. Diana was herself fascinated, amused, and perplexed by the preponderance of all these dodgy doppelgangers. "People say you look like me," she said on meeting Selina Scott, a BBC journalist who had been one of the first hosts of *The Clothes Show* and who was frequently compared to Diana during the eighties and nineties. "Well, your Highness," Scott, older than Diana by ten years, replied, "I was here first."

Britain's leading theatrical newspaper, *The Stage*, carried frequent ads placed by numerous Diana lookalikes, some of whom made a good living from having the mark of Diana upon them. The most prominent impersonator of the twenty-something Diana was Julie Wooldridge, who appeared as the princess on magazine covers, in comedy sketch shows, advertising campaigns, and the cinematic classic, *National Lampoon's European Vacation*. But over time, Christina Hance probably became the best known of the impersonators. As Diana, Hance opened health clinics, became embroiled in a tabloid hoax, and—a little confusingly—voiced Diana for a premium-rate phone line. It was often very lucrative work, earning her thousands of pounds a day. Her profile grew to such an extent that in 1996 she appeared on the cover of the BBC's *Radio Times* magazine, her hand shielding most of her face, a sign of the inescapable fact that she didn't really look very much like Diana at all. Her success seemed mainly down to having similar eyes to "those eyes" that Diana possessed. "If you look at our features one by one there's little comparison," Hance admitted, "but there is something in my face that reminds people of her and they want to believe it."

The *Radio Times* cover was promoting a BBC documentary all about Hance's career, which had begun when her boyfriend entered her for one of those innumerable Diana lookalike contests, this one on the popular breakfast TV show *Good Morning Britain*. In her telling, Hance's journey to becoming "Diana" parallels that of the real Diana's. Winning the *Good Morning Britain* contest began a fairytale transformation from "a shy, unconfident girl who hid behind her fringe and never spoke" to a princess—or, at least, someone who looked a bit like a princess. But she tells the BBC crew she has allowed into her home, the attention from the public can be overwhelming. The constant staring—even though she deliberately encourages it—makes her extremely uncomfortable. "I've had Japanese people crying when I tell them I'm not Diana," she says, and has grown weary of men trying to pick her up because they feel it's the next best thing to pulling a princess. "I'm very cynical," she confesses, "I just don't trust anybody now." Racing to the depths of uncanny valley, in one scene an Elizabeth II lookalike dishes the dirt on the friction that existed between her and Hance when they first began working together. "Christina didn't behave," says Jeanette Charles, in full queen costume; "She thought she could giggle her way around [and] flirt a lot. . . . That is not the way to have people think it's a real thing." Hance explains it wasn't vainglory or attention seeking that caused her to behave this way, but nerves and naivety: "I didn't have a clue what to do at all."

A few months later, Hance was in the papers again, this time announcing that she was stepping back from her duties as a Diana lookalike, a weird parallel with the decision Diana made in 1993 to temporarily withdraw from public life. "Being Diana sent me mad and made me very ill," she was quoted as saying in one newspaper. "I ended up a zombie just like her. . . . The strain of public life has been too much for both of us." Yet nine months later, in December

Dianamania goes global. A parade of Diana lookalikes greets
Prince Charles in Wellington, New Zealand, March 1981.

The premier Diana lookalike of the 1990s, Christina Hance,
exhibits "those eyes," March 1997.

1997, Hance was the star of a further documentary—*Looking like Diana* on Channel 4—which followed her and other Diana looka-likes to see how they were coping now that Diana had passed away. Some time later, Hance posed for the press once more, this time revealing that she had swapped looking like Diana for acting like her, now working as a caregiver.

Hance also features as one of several Dianas in *Diana & Me*, the 1997 film starring Toni Collette and Dominic West that was rendered obsolete by Diana's death—and which is overflowing with Dianas. In addition to Hance's version, there is the Diana Spencer played by Collette, a male Diana impersonator, and the *real* Diana who appears in dreamlike archive footage. The film's depiction of London is as a kind of Diana-opolis; almost everyone is either in pursuit of her or warms themselves in her radiance. When West calls out "Diana" to Collette's character, the dozens of people crowded around him shout out "Diana!" in Pavlovian unison. In the universe of the film, she exists in a trinity: there are the plentiful facsimiles of her, the bit of her that is in every one of us, and the one true Diana whose untouchable magnificence can never be replicated.

The paradox of authentically reproducing Diana's uniqueness was—and still is—evident at the unveiling of each new artistic depiction of her. "No one plays the Princess of Wales nearly as well as the Princess of Wales," wrote *The New York Times* of a 1996 TV drama about Diana and the Windsors. "All the players seem smarter and better-looking than their real-life counterparts, except for Diana." The more we move from the moment, the more impressive is the first portrait of Diana, painted by Bryan Organ in 1981, which renders her in one of her phases of metamorphosis, Shy Di the Supersloane sitting alone inside the vastness of Buckingham Palace, on the cusp of becoming royalty, but still a private person. When the painting first hung in London's National Portrait Gallery in the days leading up to the wedding, it was slashed with a knife by Paul Salmon from Belfast who apparently claimed, "I did it for Ireland!" Salmon saw not a trace of Diana Spencer in Organ's brushstrokes, only a preening representative of monarchy and British imperialism. Diana might have agreed. She sat for a dozen portrait painters, and the only one that she felt came close to "getting me" was Nelson Shanks, a devoted practitioner of realist portraiture. However, even Shanks found his finished canvas lacking; stymied by the strictures of the commissioning process, he felt the person he could have captured—Diana in the midst of the very public breakdown of her marriage in the mid-1990s—was left unpainted. Other commissioned artists fell into the same trap. Emily Patrick wanted to capture Diana's "distress and neuroses" but the "stultified, quiet restraint" of Kensington Palace was a daily reminder of the impossibility of doing so. In a very different way, David Hankinson—who painted a portrait of Diana to hang, like a very chaste pinup, in the mess of *HMS Cornwall*—said his traditional sense of deference to authority led him to paint an idealized and romantic picture of Diana that he later conceded was "kitsch" and "overdone." Similar words were used to describe Anthony Snowdon's highly stylized photographs of Diana, including one taken in 1991 that looks like a scene of a family picnic as arranged by Thomas Gainsborough. Yet as an ex-husband of a princess, Snowdon had a conscious awareness of precedent and allusion in all depictions of royalty, and knew that Diana was more—or, perhaps, less—than an individual. Similarly, André Durand's paintings of Diana attempt to capture the invisible things we see whenever we look at her—though the agglomeration of stories and symbols he draws upon is so vast that one wonders whether any real person could ever be as protean as the Diana on his canvases.

While some have panned portraits of Diana for not accessing the woman beneath the tiara, others have raised the more fundamental objection that they don't look anything like her. Writing in 1992, the editor of *Harpers & Queen* lambasted Douglas Anderson's new portrait of the princess wearing an off-the-shoulder purple ballgown by trashing all paintings of her. "If you are beautiful enough and charismatic enough to be beloved across the world . . . what on earth goes wrong between you and the canvas?" Implicit in the criticism is that a portraitist's first and last objective is uncanny realism. It follows, therefore, that the iterations of Diana that should be most praised are the very ones that are most criticized: the press and paparazzi shots that caught her in the living of her life. Felicity Clark, who saw Diana's photographic potential when Diana was only fourteen, agreed that the paparazzi captured her best, as did Patrick Demarchelier, the photographer who shot several famous images of Diana in the 1990s. Demarchelier said the paparazzi photos of her are "all so fantastic" because they caught Diana off-guard. "I had to recreate that, to make her relaxed." In several of his photos, Diana's smiling head protrudes from darkness, her body either unlit or shrouded in dark, amorphous clothing. This is the *real* Diana, we're being told, "the woman behind the clothes." Whether this soft, accessible Diana is any more "authentic" than, say, the regal vision of Elizabeth II painted by Pietro Annigoni is debatable. One might say that Demarchelier swapped one language of iconography for another. The woman behind the clothes was still silent—and still a princess. Once applied, that layer could never be removed.

DIANA APPARENTLY considered it part of her solemn duty to appear as the Princess of Wales as often as possible; her public, she felt, expected nothing less. She was probably right, too. Chronicling Diana's holiday with Harry and William on the Caribbean island of Nevis in 1993, James Whitaker reported disappointment among the hotel staff that the woman who arrived in the dining room for dinner each evening was not dressed to the nines. "Why can't she wear some diamonds?" one employee asked.

Such acts of crossdressing—being seen in public in jeans and T-shirt—caused consternation among those who looked to Diana and her wardrobe to project what Catherine Walker's designs hinted at: a notion of magical Englishness. When Diana appeared in public in the early nineties wearing white jeans and chunky gold jewelery, she was ridiculed by *Tatler* magazine, while Anne de Courcy, in the *Daily Mail*, lamented the "Sharonisation of Diana," Sharon being a name that came to be associated with the aspiring working-class population of Essex in the 1990s. With a reference to the popular sitcom about the lives of two unhappily married sisters from Essex, another piece in the *Daily Mail* pleaded, "Will the real Diana please sit down, turn off *Birds of a Feather*, forget the Queen Vic [the pub in *EastEnders*] and dress like a princess." Essentially, this was Diana's favorite newspaper's more genteel way of instructing her to do what a paparazzo told her one day in the mid-nineties: "put your head up and start acting like a fucking princess." Even when Dillie Keane defended Diana in *The Mail on Sunday*, she did so out of irritation that "parvenus at *Tatler*" had insinuated Diana was some kind of "common woman pretending to be a Princess." In Keane's mind, Diana's stellar genetic inheritance could not be masked by a bit of sartorial slumming, "elephant belts or not."

If Diana's mid-nineties attire unsettled right-wing commentators with its supposed vulgarity, to some of those on the left her personal appearance evinced her vacuity; Nigel Fountain labelled her a "trash icon for our times" in *The Observer* newspaper five weeks before her death. Fountain's screed was triggered by a sugary article published by the *Daily Mirror* earlier that week about Diana consoling Elton John at the funeral of Gianni Versace, who had been murdered a few days prior. Fountain betrayed no interest in Diana's clothes, but her recent association with the high priest of Eurotrash was highly symbolic of her rancorous uncoupling from the House of Windsor. Versace's clothes for her—including a purple suit that Diana wore when giving an anti-landmine speech in Washington DC in 1997—were something close to a uniform for the post-divorce Diana. Reviewing the appearance of the suit in an episode of the fifth series of *The Crown*, the fashion journalist Rachel Tashjian noted the symbolism of not just that particular suit, but of Versace's presence in Diana's new wardrobe. His was "a talent unmatched by any other male designer," stated Tashjian, "to create gorgeous, sexy armor, clothes that made a woman look powerful and yet no less soft or feminine. You can see how the suit would be perfect for coming to Washington to ask for empathy for her cause but still be taken seriously." But the fact that the Versace association would be regarded as lowbrow and distasteful among certain of her compatriots surely added to his appeal for the Princess of the Black Sheep. As her namesake Diana Vreeland once said, "We all need a splash of bad taste."

A few weeks before Versace's murder, Diana held what *Vogue* called her "divestiture," an auction of seventy-nine dresses that had marked her time as an official, frontline royal. Diana said that after years of being appraised on her clothes, she was relieved to be entering a period of her life when clothes might not be quite so central to her profile. If she really did dream of a day when her public would ignore what she wore, the devoted younger following she has amassed since her death have denied her that wish. For millions of people under forty, Diana's clothes are a primary method of engaging with her reputation and her biography. Retailers and designers reissue famous garments, turning women around the world into historical reenactors, Civil War uniforms replaced by Virgin Atlantic sweatshirts. Pop stars, actors, and models restage memorable photographs of her, recreate her famous outfits, and buy her clothes and accessories; in 2023 Kim Kardashian paid $197,453 for an amethyst and diamond necklace Diana wore once in 1987. Later that same year, the original black-sheep sweater went for $1.14 million at auction.

The world has never been so full of Dianas, all the various iterations of her walking among us at once, the chronology of her life squashed and rearranged in the way that the Internet has done for all of our lives. Harvesting the giant trove of paparazzi photos that is now freely available online, Instagram accounts document, categorize, and celebrate Diana's innumerable looks: her gym looks and her glamour looks; her lesbian looks and her fairytale looks. Eloise Moran collated what she called Diana's "revenge looks" and published *The Lady Di Look Book*, pushing the notion of Diana's silent communication to new lengths. Moran sees all manner of things as Diana's conscious effort to speak to her public via her clothes. Perhaps, she suggests, Diana's choice to wear a pair of red heels was a "hint at a subtle rebellion," Diana telling us that she longed to tap her heels together and get back home, like Dorothy in *The Wizard of Oz*.

Moran even identifies something "a bit punk" about Diana's attitude to clothing, ironic given that Vivienne Westwood and Malcolm McLaren, whose boutique SEX had shaped London's punk look in the late seventies, viewed her as anathema. Yet Moran isn't alone among a younger generation of Diana's followers in identifying her as punk. In the 2021 documentary *Diana: Queen of Style*, the drag queen Bimini goes as far as to proclaim Diana "the biggest punk that's come out of England." Maybe such hyperbole is evidence that Diana has become an all-purpose cultural figure, Johnny Rotten to one crowd, Mother Teresa to another. Certainly, her capacious dress-up box has created confusion about who she really was. With her clones and impersonators crowding the streets from Kensington to Kyoto, at times over the last half century it has been difficult to tell where Diana stops and the rest of us begin.

4

Don't Do It, Di!

Diana holding her newborn son, Harry, outside
St. Mary's Hospital in London, September 1984.

A S WE LATER came to learn, Charles and Diana's marriage never truly had a honeymoon period. From their earliest wedded days together, discrepancies were screamingly apparent between their personalities, their senses of humor, and their interests. Diana, it turned out, wasn't the least bit interested in the country pursuits of huntin', shootin', and fishin' that the Windsors loved, and had no time for Charles's predilection for reading aloud from the philosophically inflected novels of Laurens van der Post, the conservationist to whom the prince was in thrall. Worse than that, Charles's heart never seemed remotely in it—or, at the very least, he had no intention of either abandoning his old friends and bachelor lifestyle or devoting himself to his young wife in the way she thought a dashing prince ought to.

Despite these early, glaring problems in her marriage, Diana became pregnant very soon after the wedding. It was thrilling news; she had longed to be a mother for as long as she could remember, though bouts of severe morning sickness made her first pregnancy very difficult. On 21 June 1982, Diana gave birth to her first child, William. The new mother's joy at her baby's arrival was accompanied by further difficulties. Over several months, Diana endured a dreadful, lonely experience of postpartum depression through which she felt unsupported by her in-laws, adding to her general feeling of being royal helpmeet, overlooked and underappreciated not just by Charles but by his parents too and the entire royal institution.

As wife to the future monarch, Diana's journey into motherhood was not considered a private rite of passage in the life of one very young woman, but a historical event, a moment of constitutional importance, national pride, and spiritual significance; as news spread that she was in labor, crowds of people gathered outside St. Mary's Hospital. One hundred and fifty miles away, at Eglwys Wen School in Cardiff, the children were convened in a special assembly to commemorate the arrival of an heir to the throne. Neil Welton, one of the school's former pupils, recalls that before singing the national anthem, the headmaster, as though conducting a religious ritual, instructed the children to "clear our minds of all our ideas and to just imagine we could see The Queen." Welton was eight years old at the time, and the assembly triggered in him a "magical feeling deep down inside. A profound feeling of duty, loyalty and protectiveness towards the baby Prince." This moment, he says, instilled in him a lifelong love of the monarchy and inspired in him the same feelings that those of an older generation experienced when celebrating Empire Day—a feeling of belonging to "something so special that even our forefathers were willing to fight and to die for it."

The day after William was born, the *Daily Mirror* published a review of the previous year of Diana's life, during which she had gone from Shy Di, the Cinderella of Sloane Square, to Princess of Wales and provider of the royal heir, the nation's ideal mother. The tone of this month-by-month recap, written by the gossip columnist Paul Callan, was that unmistakable mixture of lasciviousness and archaic deference that the tabloids favored when writing about Diana. Callan described Diana during pregnancy in chivalric terms: her skin "gleamed like newly burnished gold," and her eyes "scintillated with health and happiness," an angelic vision of expectant motherhood. Then came the obligatory nudge-nudge wink-wink: "There is one inescapable fact about pregnancy—a woman's bust becomes more generous." By April, her *"generous contours . . . were amply evident"*—the italics of Callan's original piece emphasized his meaning for the hard of understanding. Finally June arrived and "nature . . . repeated the same miracle it does a million times a day." After all, Diana was only flesh and blood; "Being Royal makes no difference." Except ordinariness is the very thing that Callan's piece was not celebrating; her delivery of a male heir was "a majestic moment," gloriously, royally atypical.

Other papers ran similar features. Many were less silly than Callan's, but collectively they displayed the same dichotomy: Diana, the everywoman; Diana, the superwoman. These were the poles between which much of her reputation was framed. It was discombobulating for her, engrossing, sometimes enraging, for her public, and illuminating of contemporary conversations about gender and the lives of women in a way that is still bitingly relevant.

JUST EIGHTEEN seconds in length, *The Execution of Mary Stuart* was a landmark in the history of cinema. Produced by the Edison Manufacturing Company in 1895, the film was the first to demonstrate the "stop-motion-substitution" special effect, making the beheading it depicted shockingly realistic for the time. It also set in train the telling and retelling of tales about sixteenth-century royal women that have proliferated in film and television in the English-speaking world for more than a century. Anne Boleyn—the mother of Elizabeth I and ill-fated wife of Henry VIII—holds a particular fascination for modern audiences, as an ambitious young woman who soared from the margins of the Tudor court, only to be felled by intrigue and misogyny. Couched in a discomfiting gothic glamour, her story has become the definitive archetype of the dark side of the princess reverie, a tale of female agency thwarted by male power and violence. Boleyn even pops up in the 2021 film *Spencer*, a highly fictionalized take on Diana's unhappiness within the royal family, as an unsubtle reminder to Diana of, to quote words that Diana once used about herself, what happens to "a strong woman" who "won't go quietly" in the patriarchal cage of royalty.

From the beginning, Diana's public reputation was swaddled in princess mythology, as though she were womanhood in its ideal, natural state, the very essence of femininity. She inherited aspects of this identity from royal women who had gone before her. Throughout the eighties, Diana was incessantly likened to a young incarnation of the Queen Mother, while some saw in her notes of Princess Margaret and the previous Princess of Wales, Mary of Teck, Charles's great-grandmother. There were also certain things about her that evoked Princess Alexandra, Elizabeth II's cousin, who was celebrated in the fifties and sixties for her "common touch," chatting easily and informally to members of the public. Years before the moniker was ever attached to Diana, Alexandra was sometimes referred to as "the People's Princess," a designation that certain newspapers were still using into the 1980s. The historian Colleen Denney suggests that Diana's image was decisively shaped by the long tradition of royal portraiture that reached its apotheosis in another Alexandra, a previous Princess of Wales, who later became queen alongside Edward VII. In both the official portraits of Diana as well as many of the press photographs taken of her, Denney identifies a reprise of Alexandra's image as the model of British femininity. Little of this was a deliberate attempt to revive memories of Alexandra, Denney says, either on the part of Diana or those who documented her existence. Rather, Alexandra's mythology remained in the ether as an unconscious cultural inheritance, "memories that became layered through a constant revisiting over time."

Of all the similarities between Diana and Alexandra that Denney points out, it is in their role of ideal mother that the parallels were most obvious. From the birth of her eldest son in 1864, Alexandra posed for dozens of photographs with her children, many of which were disseminated to the public, often in commercially published books that offered an insight into the princess's home life. Some of the photos included her husband, but for the most part she was captured alone with her children, at the center of the frame, her arms stretched across some of them, while others clasped her shoulder or leaned their head on her lap. This being the Victorian era, she and the children are all unsmiling, but in every other way, the images are strongly redolent of those taken of Diana and her sons. Diana buttressed her maternal portfolio with public pronouncements of her dedication to her role as wife of one future king and the mother of two potential others. In a much-publicized 1985 interview with ITV newscaster Alastair Burnet, Diana presented herself plainly as a devoted mother, who would have been at home in the Britain of a century earlier. "I feel my role is supporting my husband whenever I can, always being behind him, encouraging. And also—most important thing—being a mother and a wife." One might read into this a desire for Diana to redress what she saw as her mother's dereliction of duty, though it's also consistent with sentiments her father publicly expressed in 1987. "I am the boss in our marriage," Johnnie said of his relationship with his second wife, Raine. "It's important for the man to be in charge. . . . It's better for the man and for the woman." Perhaps not incidentally, he also claimed that "most women are bird-brained."

Though Diana's posed photographs with her children presented her in the traditional imagery of royal mothers, she famously took opportunities to frame herself as an exception to the past: teaching the children to swim in the sea, taking them to theme parks, sprinting barefoot in the mothers' race at the school sports day. It's debatable whether these photographs amounted to a rejection of the past or an emphatic reinforcement of it. It could be said that the projection of Diana as ideal mother was a celebration of motherhood at a moment when increasing numbers of women were confounding the idea that the progressive force of feminism and the traditions of femininity were necessarily in conflict. Equally, one might think of Diana's representation as essentially postfeminist: a woman who was both tethered to tradition and relentlessly modern, occupying the late-nineteenth-century imagery of femininity while simultaneously living the life of a late-twentieth-century female, having leapfrogged the complicating business of feminism altogether. While pregnant with her first child, she was praised for "glowing" in her maternity daywear like a Victorian lady and "stunning" in a bikini on the beach like a swimwear model. Before William was born, speculation about what type of mother Diana would prove to be was bathed in soft-focus Victoriana about her soft, nurturing character, while stories about her maternity care focused on the modernity of those—mainly men—who were looking after her, especially the gynecologist George Pinker, depicted in the tabloids as a heroic figure with no time for white coats or stuffy protocol. One article combined the two: a profile of Pinker, a modern man of science who vehemently opposed the queen's wish that Diana give birth at Buckingham Palace, was complemented by a panel of photographs of Diana in the company of other people's offspring and the caption "Natural love of children."

Acknowledging Diana as a magnificent mother was—and still is—common among even those who couldn't stand her. That's not to say that her mothering was considered beyond criticism. In fact, Diana's parenting was frequently dissected in the British media, especially after the Waleses' marital problems were made public. In the eyes of the Labour MP Frank Field, neither Diana nor Charles was fit to be a parent, given the scandals they were embroiled in during the early nineties. In 1994, he proposed that a "panel of parliamentary 'wise men'" be tasked with the responsibility of raising William and Harry, though he was prevented from posing the issue in the Commons by the speaker who said the children's upbringing was no business for politicians. In a similar vein, Claire Rayner, Britain's best-known advice columnist of the time, dismissed any notion that Diana's mothering should be the source of special praise. "She's the last person who ought to be an icon," she fulminated in 1996. "All her achievements rest on three penises: she married one and produced two more." In fairness, procreation within wedlock is the first and last responsibility of royalty, and one could just as easily make the argument that Charles owed his public standing to two women: the one who gave birth to him and the one who delivered him an heir and a spare.

Other criticisms were less scathing, but apparently no less serious. When Moreen Simpson of the *Aberdeen Evening Express* saw Prince William in an outfit that she thought unacceptably similar to clothes that his fusty father would wear, it was Diana she took to task. "Would any self-respecting mum actually dress her little boy in [this] appalling gear," she asked. "Why on earth does the Princess of Wales let it happen?" This might sound trivial, but it's highly instructive of Diana's significance as an ideal of motherhood. In the age of Victoria, the royal family had been projected as the ultimate British family, the gold standard of domesticity for which all decent, patriotic people should strive. In postwar, post-Suez, post-Beatles Britain, things were a little different; now, the tail sometimes wagged the corgi. Consequently, a lot of people seemed to perceive Diana not as an example of motherhood to be followed, as had typically been the case with Alexandra, but as a glamorous establishment validation of things that the middle classes already identified as common, normal, and good. But when Diana's mothering was seen to stray from those standards, she was rebuked.

Yet in occupying this status as representative mother, Diana performed another function, one that evinces how significant she was in the abstract, as an agglomeration of identities and perceptions through which millions of others could explore their own lives; for many women, Diana was not necessarily someone to extol or to criticize, but a trigger for debate and self-reflection. Eight months into her first pregnancy, the *Buckinghamshire Examiner* printed a discussion among readers instigated by the widespread coverage that had been given to Diana's maternity care. A nurse named Joyce Lister wrote in to argue that all women should be given those things Diana had access to, including scans, and if necessary, genetic counseling, and the option of an abortion. Up in Lincolnshire a couple of weeks following the birth of Prince Harry, Diana's experience was cited as the example of best practice in reports about potential reforms to midwifery in the area. Two years earlier, Angela Candlin in the *Liverpool Echo* had marked the impending arrival of Diana's first baby with a sardonic reminder of some of the things that motherhood meant for millions of women: "Nappy rash and teething problems interest relatives, not your vanished waistline and postnatal depression. Expect to stay invisible for at least ten years." For better or worse, that was not to be Diana's fate.

ANOTHER WAY in which Alexandra foreshadowed Diana's experience as Princess of Wales was as a wife who was expected to turn a blind eye to her husband's affairs. Edward VII—or Bertie as he was colloquially known while the Prince of Wales—was an unashamed philanderer in the manner of so many men of his social world over the centuries. "It was an aristocratic curse," explains Lady Anne Glenconner, one of Princess Margaret's closest friends who endured decades of her husband's infidelities, some of which he told her about over the breakfast table. Charles and Diana's situation was a long way from this, but Diana felt the sting of betrayal just as keenly.

As Diana recounted events, incriminating evidence that Charles was secretly still involved with his ex-girlfriend Camilla Parker Bowles was discovered even before they tied the knot. A few days before the wedding, as presents flooded into royal residences, she found a package on the desk of Michael Colborne, Charles's personal secretary. It was a gold bracelet that bore the initials G.F., or Girl Friday, Charles's nickname for Camilla. Diana realized this was not a present in celebration of the wedding of the century, but a forget-me-not from her fiancé to his old flame, who, to Diana's great discomfort, was still a valued confidante and in any number of ways closer to him than the unworldly, very young Diana could have hoped to be. Biographers differ as to whether this was the smoking gun of Diana's description, or evidence of Charles's sentimentality and blithe insensitivity. At the very least, it implanted in Diana's mind the unshakable thought that the man with whom she was meant to be sharing her life was emotionally, if not physically, committed to another woman. When Charles countered the idea that he had never really broken things off with Camilla—during an interview with Jonathan Dimbleby in 1994—he did so by claiming that their relationship had lain dormant until his marriage had "irretrievably broken down," in the mid to late eighties.

"Affairs were expected and wives just worked around it" was Anne Glenconner's description of how she dealt with her husband's infidelities. There were some—both in aristocratic circles and among the wider population—who felt that Diana should have adopted the same attitude. "She had everything and threw it away," said one man of Diana in his 1998 interview for the Millennium

Memory Bank, a BBC project that recorded the experiences and outlooks of an array of British people at the end of the twentieth century. In his opinion, "if she had any intelligence whatsoever and she had read history," Diana would have used Alexandra as her role model for the dutiful wife who looked the other way: "Edward VII had a whole string of mistresses, but Alexandra was the queen, she knew that; nobody else could become queen." Alas, Diana never signed up for any such antiquated scheme. Rather, as a devotee of the romance novels written by her step-grandmother Barbara Cartland, she hoped that marriage would undo the upset caused her by her parents' own unhappy union. By her own account, she married Charles assuming he would be a "father figure" to her, and the intense, dependent relationships she formed with older women such as Annabel Goldsmith, Lucia Flecha de Lima, and Elsa Bowker suggested she was looking for things she either could not get or would not take from her mother.

When Diana began to doubt Charles's commitment to her in the days before the wedding, the advice she got from those around her was to steer a course between blitheness and sufferance. Her sisters, perhaps only half joking, told her that it was too late to pull out as the commemorative tea towels had already been printed. In fact, royal wedding merchandise of every conceivable kind was being churned out; there was barely a British kitchen in the 1980s that didn't possess a mug or a plate, or some trinket of the big day. But in amongst the crockery, the dolls, and the collectors' editions of the *Daily Mail* were badges exhorting, "Don't Do It, Di!" produced by the magazine *Spare Rib*, the pioneering second-wave feminist publication that expressed itself aghast and deflated by the public enthusiasm for an event that seemed to glorify a Victorian view of gender relations, complete with alleged tests to determine the bride-to-be's virginity and reproductive capacity. The magazine sold the badges for twenty pence each, and they proved exceptionally popular. Fittingly, there was also a commemorative *Spare Rib* tea towel for sale, featuring text that read "You start by sinking into his arms and end up with your arms in his sink." One of these was sent to Charles and Diana as a wedding present; the Palace responded with a letter of "sincere thanks for the useful tea towel."

Spare Rib was far from the only voice of dissent regarding the wedding. The parish councillors of Clay Cross in Derbyshire declared the day of the nuptials Republican Day, while thousands of people in London attended Funk the Wedding, an anti-monarchist concert held in Clissold Park, four miles north of St. Paul's Cathedral. But the badges struck a resonant chord. *Spare Rib* staff were interviewed on TV networks in the US and Japan, written about in *The New York Times*, and given a prominent mention in *The Sunday Times*'s feature on the wedding merchandise bonanza. The badges also seemed to stir something among the public. "People who don't usually blink an eye if you sit opposite them in a bus wearing a lesbian, pro-abortion or women's liberation badge, frothed and foamed and questioned the sanity of even such a slight message," claimed a *Spare Rib* editorial looking back at July 1981. "We did wonder if they disliked the badge because it spoke too directly to women about marriage." Maybe Diana herself had been listening. Fifteen years later, her divorce in the bag, Diana was in the back of a car in Sydney when she spotted a wedding congregation on the steps of a nearby church. As the car drove past, she wound down her window and shouted at the bride, "Don't do it!"

Critics of *Spare Rib* included certain fellow travelers on the left who derided the magazine for deigning to give the wedding any attention at all. Vindication for the coverage came, in part, in the intriguing letters from readers who shared their conflicted feelings about the wedding and the person of Diana they had encountered through the media. One reader, Caroline Hearst, wrote to confess that she and many other feminists of her acquaintance were fascinated by Diana, or at least the mythological construction called Diana they encountered in the media. That she had guiltily feasted on the newspaper and magazine articles about Diana and found herself glued to the television on the day of the wedding caused this correspondent genuine consternation. But, she concluded, it was vital that women like her admit to their Diana fixation: "if we are unable to admit our feelings we will never be able to change them" and will wind up "rigid and sterile" like much of the male-dominated left. In retrospect, that sounds like a distinctly Dianaist sentiment. Of course, Diana was a long way from being a leftist; the *Daily Mail*'s Richard Kay is one of several of Diana's friends who finds her current popularity among young progressives more than a little peculiar considering she was an identifiably "small *c* conservative" her whole life. But Caroline Hearst's appeal to bear difficult emotional truths, and in so doing begin a process of self-change, would become a tenet of the Diana creed, especially when she spoke to other women about the difficulties of being a woman in a world governed by men, a conversation that began in earnest in the summer of 1992 with the publication of *Diana: Her True Story* by Andrew Morton.

Morton had been a member of the Rat Pack since the early 1980s and had written several books about Diana and the royals, all of them laudatory, uncontroversial, and steadfastly dull. In his 1984 history of the royal yacht *Britannia*—the Windsors' publicly funded floating palace, on which Charles and Diana spent much of their honeymoon—he attempted to portray Diana as both dazzlingly royal and dazzlingly ordinary, who was wont to do such radically free-spirited things as listen to a Walkman and "wander around barefoot, a bowl of Cornflakes in her hand."

Sensing that Morton was someone who could be relied upon to present her story in the way she wished, Diana approached him to write what was effectively an authorized biography. In addition to encouraging family and friends to cooperate in the form of private photographs and candid interviews, Diana contributed to the book by taping lengthy answers to questions from Morton, supplied to her via her friend James Colthurst, a strategy which would help to keep Morton's project a secret, as well as giving the princess the opportunity to accurately state that she had never spoken to Morton during his research. Just as Diana had turned to relatively unknown designers to help craft her visual image, so it was a publishing outsider, the tiny company Michael O'Mara Books, that was responsible for producing this extraordinary intervention in British public life. *"Only* a small, independent publisher could have done it," says Michael O'Mara, the man after whom the company is named. Originally from the United States, he found the process nerve shredding, exhilarating, and fascinating, giving him a "very good view of the deeply entrenched class system." While O'Mara copped some flak for being a foreigner, Morton received more for hailing from northern England and therefore not being the *right sort of chap* to write about such things. "It was fascinating for me as an immigrant, to see how the fact that Andrew was from Leeds apparently disqualified him from writing books about the royal family."

The moment the first extracts appeared in the papers in June 1992, the book was an international sensation. "The clippings from the time are incredible," says O'Mara of the many hostile pieces about the book, its author, and its publisher. "I laugh like crazy when I look at them now. You'd have thought we were under the Houses of Parliament with several barrels of gunpowder. It was treasonous, we should be banished—shot!" Alongside the delicately framed suggestion that Charles had been unfaithful, the book revealed Diana's struggles with bulimia, self-harm, and postnatal depression, and the deep wounds that her unhappy childhood had inflicted. Unprecedented though it was, *Diana: Her True Story* could be seen as part of the literary moment, belonging to the family of so-called misery memoirs that burst through in the 1990s and which can be read, particularly in the UK, as an early contribution to the way in which subjects such as mental health and emotional well-being are now publicly discussed. In the archives of the Great Diary Project, one woman's diaries from 1992 list the Morton book among many other accounts of unhappy female lives that she had read that year, including *Sins of the Father,* by Eileen Franklin, about the author's suppressed memories of the rape and murder that she witnessed her father commit and a memoir by Sheila Mottley titled *Tough Cookie: The Less Than Virtuous Tale of a Thalidomide Mum.* Morton's biography also arrived amidst a rash of huge bestsellers detailing the miserable state of modern marriage and the various ways in which men and women are apparently incapable of communicating. John Gray's *Men Are from Mars, Women Are from Venus* was published that same year, 1992, two years after *You Just Don't Understand,* by Deborah Tannen. Two years before that, Shere Hite published *Women and Love: The New Hite Report—A Cultural Revolution in Progress,* which detailed extreme dissatisfaction among thousands of married American women she had surveyed. Hite said the root of the problem was the fact that "democracy was praised in the outer world in which men were basically in charge. . . . At home we still had a kind of monarchical system." Something approximate might be said of Diana's peculiar situation as a woman whose existence was apparently modern and yet regressively ancient at the same time.

Diana: Her True Story was published five months after Rebecca Walker's seminal essay "Becoming the Third Wave" appeared in *Ms.* magazine. Walker's essay was written in response to hearings in the US Congress in which Anita Hill was cross-examined over her allegations of sexual harassment against Supreme Court justice nominee Clarence Thomas. The case was replete with complex dynamics of race, class, and party politics, but Walker homed in on the question of what happens to female testimony heard within a patriarchal institution: "Can a woman's voice, a woman's sense of self-worth and injustice, challenge a structure predicated upon the subjugation of our gender?" Infuriated by the treatment Hill received, Walker enjoined her audience to "let this dismissal of a woman's experience move you to anger." *Diana: Her True Story,* written by a man who had earned his stripes on the *Daily Star,* made no avowal of feminism, yet it tuned into a similar frequency as Walker's essay, albeit with the vexing irony that Diana always maintained a less-than-honest stance about her involvement with the book. Furthermore, the biography detailed the young Diana's habit of lying: "she had real difficulty telling the truth," her brother told Morton. Diana's rule of thumb seemed to be that a cluster of fibs, or an imaginative coloring of the facts, was perfectly alright if performed in service of what she considered to be a grander, more important truth. This is the feeling one gets when reading the lengthy excerpts of her interviews for the Morton book, which Michael O'Mara published soon after Diana's death. They are peppered with embellishments and exaggerations, but in a way as to underscore what she thought the key elements: her feelings of loneliness, neglect, and betrayal within an institution designed to swallow and smother.

The veracity of Morton's work was analyzed and debated exhaustively. Some laughed at what was described as melodramatic absurdity. Other commentators, disbelieving that Diana could have possibly been involved with the book, lambasted it as an insult to the dignity of the Crown. At different ends of the retail spectrum, Harrods and Tesco both declined to stock it. One columnist, perhaps with Diana the ideal mother in her mind, concluded that the book *must* have been a work of gossip and lies, as such heartrending stories as William pushing tissues under the bathroom door for his crying mother couldn't have come from honest, informed sources. "Most people," this writer stated, "feel that if Charles and Diana won't speak directly to the media themselves, it's because to do so would be to . . . get involved with scum." In fact, it became clear over the next five years that Charles and Diana were rather keen to "get involved with scum"—and the majority of the public believed the princess, even when her very sanity was questioned.

JOAN THWAITES from Yorkshire lived a full, varied life. Born in 1923, three years before Elizabeth II, she served her country in the Second World War by working in the Women's Land Army, after which she became a herdswoman. Later, she ran a farm owned by Lord Delamere for four years, before becoming a matron at a private school and a deputy matron at a nursing home for women. Her diaries from the 1940s to the 2010s—now part of the Great Diary Project—are punctuated by big royal events and her observations on the Windsor family and the monarchy, both of which she was clearly invested in, but had mixed feelings about. In February 1992 she watched a documentary marking forty years of Elizabeth II on the throne. "A bit drawn out," she thought. "It all seemed very artificial and traditional," a sentiment that was probably echoed in living rooms around the country, even among those who, like Thwaites, considered themselves politically moderate patriots. "The wind of change needs sweeping through their world." What prescience: by the year's end a hurricane of modernity had battered the walls of Buckingham Palace. It started a few weeks later when the Duke and Duchess of York announced their separation; "It's lasted about 6 years!" Thwaites recorded with obvious astonishment. "It can't do royalty any good." Then came the seismic event of the Andrew Morton book, which Thwaites read within a month of its publication. "The Princess of Wales has had a rough time with Charles," she wrote. "Very revealing."

Among the more shocking revelations included in Morton's biography was that Diana had suffered with bulimia for most of her adult life. The first whispers that Diana was affected by an eating disorder appeared in the early 1980s, when James Whitaker reported, inaccurately, that she was suffering from anorexia nervosa. It wasn't until 1993, a year after the Morton disclosures, that Diana made a speech pressing the need for better understanding and treatment of eating disorders, and only in 1995 did she directly acknowledge that she had lengthy, personal experience of the condition.

In Diana's telling, the onset of her bulimia was linked directly to her becoming a princess. A week after their engagement, Charles put his arm around her waist and said, "A bit chubby here, aren't we?" From that moment, Diana began to worry obsessively about her weight. It was the kind of story that was horribly familiar to Dr. Susie Orbach, a psychotherapist and founder of The Women's Therapy Centre, who Diana saw regularly in the early 1990s. In 1978, Orbach had published *Fat Is a Feminist Issue*, a book that explored the myriad factors that lead many women and girls into dysfunctional relationships with eating, food, and body image. The book is a classic now, its arguments and observations having entered the cultural mainstream, but at the time it was groundbreaking. A close analysis of the mass media discussion of Diana could serve as a compelling case study to reinforce so much of what Orbach wrote. Frequently Diana was held up as an ideal female body to emulate. A 1984 newspaper article about the Diana impersonator Julie Wooldridge (née Pocock) from Romford in Essex, explained how a "14-stone fatty known as Porky Pocock has transformed herself into a sylph-like Princess of Wales looka-like." Wooldridge is quoted as saying that her facial resemblance to Diana gave her a motivation to lose weight and realize the potential of her true self—one which looked very much like Diana, who was her "personal ideal in every way." But Diana's weight elicited some furious criticism from the general public, journalists, and certain supposed experts. When she fainted on a trip to Canada in 1986, the *Sandwell Evening Mail* invited readers to write in with their opinions on whether she was too "fastidious in her diet." Of the six letters they printed, none voiced any concern for Diana's health, but four of them criticized her for being too thin, and for recklessly setting a bad example to other young women. "Princess Di looks ridiculous," was one woman's scathing opinion, with another lambasting her for deliberately cultivating the "malnourished look." A third expressed anger that Diana was encouraging young women to become dangerously slight, which was especially troublesome as ordinary women lacked Diana's "unknown numbers of specialists," who would, so this person believed, instantly step in whenever the princess's vanity impinged on her health.

Such responses were common, even after Diana spoke publicly about her eating disorder for the first time in 1995. To some extent, one can put this down to cultural factors; as the success of *Fat Is a Feminist Issue* indicates, eating disorders were among the plethora of mental health conditions that were then, even more than now, smothered in stigma, taboo, and misconception, perhaps making it more difficult to gain empathy and understanding. More conspicuous is the criticism Diana received in 1996 from the prominent British psychiatrist Dr. Sidney Crown and Claire Rayner, the famous advice columnist who went from adoring the princess in the early 1980s to inveighing against her about all manner of things in the 1990s. Rayner and Crown both condemned Diana for glamorizing bulimia. "Oh, my dears," Rayner said in a sarcastic imitation of Diana, "don't be bulimic, don't be anorexic or, shock horror, you might finish up like me."

Crown and Rayner's views were published in a 1996 book by Chris Hutchins and Dominic Midgley titled *Diana on the Edge: Inside the Mind of the Princess of Wales*, which attempted to provide a psychological reading of Diana who had exhibited "conduct . . . sufficiently baffling to leave both the Queen and the Prime Minister at a loss." That conduct included recent incidents such as her decision to dispense with personal protection officers whenever possible, her aggravated run-ins with the paparazzi, and her apparent obsession with the art dealer Oliver Hoare that resulted in Hoare's wife making a complaint to the police about hundreds of nuisance phone calls that were tracked to Kensington Palace. And, of course, there were the distressing admissions and allegations that formed the spine of Andrew Morton's biography. The first extensive rebuttal of Morton—headlined "CHARLES: HIS TRUE STORY"—had been written by Penny Junor, who accused Diana of manifest dishonesty. Junor was also among the first authors to seriously question Diana's state of mind, suggesting that the princess's behavior was consistent with borderline personality disorder. Jonathan Dimbleby, in the early drafts of his 1994 authorized biography of Charles, had proffered a similar explanation for what he termed Diana's "temporarily aberrant behaviour." At Charles's request, Dimbleby excised that section of the book, but in 1995, reports appeared that senior figures within the Palace had commissioned a detailed study of the Princess of Wales's psychological state.

Plenty of those who were close to Diana around this time vehemently reject the notion that her behavior was indicative of mental imbalance. "Considering the life she lived," says Patrick Jephson, who served Diana as equerry and private secretary from

1988 to 1996, "considering the pressures she was under, she wasn't just sane, she had a kind of ability to restore sanity to crazy situations." Still, by the end of 1995, it was open season on Diana's mental health; "Shy Di" and "Dynasty Di" had a successor in "Dotty Di," as she was called in several publications. Infamously, Charles's good friend Nicholas Soames told the BBC that Diana exhibited all the signs of being in the "advanced stages of paranoia," in the immediate aftermath of her *Panorama* interview in which she alluded to an establishment conspiracy against her. Five months later Helen Mirren—who would subsequently win an Oscar for her depiction of Elizabeth II in a film set in the days after Diana's death—told *Us Weekly* magazine that while she considered Camilla to be a "powerful statement about how a woman can look and still be attractive," she found Diana "nauseating," "incredibly stupid," and "half crazy." Three weeks after that interview was published, Channel 4 was due to air the documentary *Psychoanalysing Diana*, in which the psychoanalyst Dylan Evans used Diana's words and behavior to put her on the couch, so to speak, with Nicky Lilley— one of the professional Diana lookalikes—playing Diana in dramatic reconstruction scenes. In the face of pointed criticism from various quarters, Channel 4 cancelled the transmission at the last minute, but according to the journalist and future government minister Michael Gove, who was one of the few people to have seen the program, Evans described Diana's romantic relationships with men as being an echo of her bulimia, all about "consumption and regurgitation," and that she married Prince Charles because he has the same name as her brother. Gove found the whole thing specious and distasteful, further evidence that Sigmund Freud is "second only to Karl Marx in his baleful influence on the intellectual life of this century."

Diana was not the first royal to have their mental state publicly scrutinized, and neither should she have been considered exempt from such scrutiny. She was, after all, a prominent public figure who—as she was at pains to emphasize—had an important responsibility in molding a future head of state. But running through the discussion of "Dotty Di" were two prominent themes: first, was the mixture of glee and disgust that many took in identifying her supposed mental health problems; second, was the suggestion that the exposure of these problems risked destroying her popularity. Tellingly, on page one of *Diana on the Edge*, Hutchins and Midgley underline that "despite a history of mental fragility—postnatal depression, self-mutilation, bulimia, and alleged suicide attempts—she had, until recently, the sympathy and support of the public and a tight-knit circle of friends." The word "despite" leaps out here, the apparent—perhaps unwitting—implication being that experiencing a condition such as postnatal depression would necessarily lead to a loss of sympathy or social standing. Diana herself interpreted the conjecture about her mental health as dreadfully tarnishing, an effort to have her locked away in a "loony bin," which she interpreted as a response to her being a woman who had stepped out of line. "I think every strong woman in history has had to walk down a similar path," she told Martin Bashir. "It's the strength that causes the confusion and the fear."

That Diana died at the Pitié-Salpêtrière hospital in Paris was bleakly fitting. It was here in the nineteenth century that Jean-Martin Charcot made his famous studies of patients suffering from hysteria, ninety percent of whom were female. The term "hysteria" derives from the Greek word for uterus, and it was Charcot's belief that the root of his female patients' maladies could be located in their ovaries. He photographed the women in his care extensively, including when they were under hypnosis or in the midst of a hysterical episode. A number of these women attained something like celebrity status and established an aesthetic for glamorous women in the thrall of supposed insanity that, rather like the princess iconography described by Colleen Denney, has filtered down the years to our own times, and was detectable in so many paparazzi photographs taken of Diana following her separation from Charles at the end of 1992, after which she frequently went out in public without bodyguards. *Dicing with Di*—the paparazzi chronicle of chasing Diana around the world—mocks Diana for being "confused, scared, vulnerable and alone ... sometimes obsessive, neurotic and dangerously out of touch with the real world," and proudly displays photos of her "loon attacks," those occasions when Diana lashed out either physically or verbally while being pursued by photographers. *Diana on the Edge* reproduces a picture of Diana leaving a gym in a trench coat and walking in an unusual way to avoid having her photo taken, which the authors cite as evidence of her unhinged state. There is a parallel between these images and more recent photographs of young female celebrities at times of tumult whose mental crises—whether real or perceived—have been feasted on by the mass media and their audience; think of Amy Winehouse walking barefoot and dishevelled in Camden, or Britney Spears shaving her head in public. "I'd been eyeballed so much growing up," wrote Spears about her decision to cut off her hair in front of seventy photographers, "had people telling me what they thought of my body, since I was a teenager. Shaving my head and acting out were my ways of pushing back." Worlds separated her from the Princess of Wales, but in that respect, Britney and Diana shared a common bond.

Diana first publicized her work with the charity Refuge in a segment on the late-night TV show *First Sex*, broadcast on Channel 4 on 11 June 1993. The show was frank, in some ways provocative, in its exploration of women's issues, not the sort of thing that elder royal women would have been involved with, but very much part of what was Diana's new strategy of publicly allying herself with, and likening herself to, marginalized women. A few months earlier she had visited a housing project in northeast London and remarked on how few men there were. A female resident told her that women always outnumbered men in their community, to which Diana replied, "There you are. It's the story of our lives," indicating that even as Princess of Wales her difficulties in life mirrored those of her working-class sisters.

By coincidence, the woman who had founded the precursor

to Refuge, Chiswick Women's Aid, was Erin Pizzey, the author of a novel—*In the Shadow of the Castle*—that was partly based on stories of the violence that allegedly marred Diana's parents' marriage. Pizzey was ousted from the organization she had founded in 1971 and subsequently became heavily involved in the men's rights movement. In her view, Diana's involvement with Refuge was, at least in part, a cynical attempt to insinuate that she had been a victim of domestic abuse in her marriage to Charles. This seems a step too far. Sandra Horley, the woman who led Refuge at the time, was unequivocal in her belief that Diana had a sincere interest in the cause. Furthermore, the charity's service users seemed to cherish Diana because she offered acceptance, a sense that they were being listened to and respected by a source of moral authority.

The same was true of the women Diana encountered at the Glasgow Women's Reproductive Health Service, established in 1991 by Dr. Mary Hepburn to provide specialist care for pregnant women living with HIV, drug dependencies, mental illnesses,

Diana competing in the mothers' race at a school sports day.
Wetherby Preparatory School, June 1991.

homelessness, or who had experienced some form of abuse. To the delight of the service users, Diana agreed to officially open the facility, though there was one moment that reminded everyone of the enormous social divide that separated the princess from the women she had come to visit, when Diana asked one of them whether she had a husband. "None of the women were married," says Hepburn, who describes "the look of horror that went across this poor girl's face . . . she said, 'I'd love to be married, if I could have a wedding day like yours.'" Diana brushed this off: "No, you wouldn't. It was ghastly. Ghastly. Ghastly." That tricky moment aside, her presence was valued. "She didn't need to say anything to them; her being there was what mattered . . . to say, 'there you are: you are important.'"

That Diana, the person and the public myth, made meaningful connections with women who had been placed on the margins of society is powerfully evident in an interview given by an English-woman known only as Tina to Dr. Wendy Rickard as part of the Oral History of Prostitution project. Across eleven hours, Tina relates the story of her life, one that had often been exceptionally testing. After a chaotic upbringing, she spent many years working as an escort and involved in a series of unhappy, abusive relationships with domineering and controlling men. Being only a year older than Diana, and a fellow Cancerian, Tina had felt some vague connection to her during the eighties, but it was after reading "her books"—which likely refers to those written by Morton—that she began to feel that she and the Princess of Wales led parallel lives. "She had the same sort of shite when she was a kid. You know, she didn't do particularly well at school, and even with the marriages. . . . I just feel so many similarities." Perhaps Diana would have discerned congruencies, too. In *Diana: Her New Life*, Andrew Morton's follow-up to *Diana: Her True Story*, she is quoted as referring to herself as "the biggest prostitute in the world."

Tina reckoned the similarities extended to their appearance, accentuated by the fact that she had her hair cut short like Diana's in the 1990s and wore a sapphire and diamond ring that looked a lot like the princess's. Around that time, Tina worked in Bahrain, where her clients were struck by the resemblance and took to calling her Lady Di. Similar to Diana's life story, marriage seemed to offer an escape from the unhappiness of her past—but in retrospect, it was doomed from the start. Throughout her difficulties, she always looked to Diana as a source of inspiration, a woman who, in Tina's eyes, refused to give in or to feel ashamed of who she was or the choices she had made: "She said 'up yours' to so much hierarchy. . . . It took guts, it took courage and determination, and she done it." Tina believed that she and Diana shared an antipathy for "the pompous English race," and although Diana died before she could realize her ambition of emigrating, Tina hopes to make the leap, disavowing her compatriots with "no feelings for anybody else in the world except themselves," those same sneering, judgmental English people who, Tina believes, tormented and demeaned Diana, labelling her as thick and mad and egomaniacal. Since childhood, Tina had a desire to care for others—"maybe," she says, "it's because I've never felt worthwhile as a human being myself"—and watching Diana's interactions with those in need and on the margins kept that ambition alive. At the end of 1997, a few months after Diana's death, she told Wendy Rickard that "all this has made me think, 'yeah, I can do my bit now.'"

Tina's arresting testimony evokes a loose comparison with the way that the artist Stella Vine approached Diana as a subject. Vine's profile soared in 2004 when the art collector Charles Saatchi bought her portrait of Diana *Hi Paul can you come over I'm really frightened*. The painting depicts Diana in "her princess gear," a tiara and what looks to be one of her early 1980s romantic ballgowns, but it could barely be further from the Victorian princess portrait tradition: her eyes are startled and brimming with tears, her face flushed red, and blood pours from her mouth. The title of the painting—which is written on the canvas next to Diana, as if scrawled in lipstick on a bathroom mirror—comes from a message that Diana apparently sent her butler Paul Burrell when she was fretting about "dark forces" that she sensed were aligning against her. This was one of dozens of portraits Vine had created of Diana, inspired by an intense interest in Diana conspiracy theories that incorporated all manner of things including "aliens . . . masons . . . satanism." Vine was drawn to Diana as both a personality and an artistic muse; "I like the way you could kind of see everything at once in her: the vulnerable woman who wants to be loved by everyone, and the more scheming kind of side of trying to get by and make the best of your situation." Before her career as an artist, Vine had worked as a stripper, an experience which she feels allowed her to see Diana in a particular way, a woman objectified and distrusted. "The picture is about two women," said Vine, referring to her feelings of identification with her subject. "One who lived in Kensington Palace. And the other who lives down the Whitecross Street," Vine's address in a much less salubrious part of London. The painting caused controversy—as did another of Vine's paintings: her take on a photograph of a young woman who had died of a heroin overdose—some of which the artist attributed to a widespread cultural conviction that there are some women who simply cannot be trusted, essentially the same notion that Rebecca Walker critiqued in "Becoming the Third Wave." "People think, first of all it's gratuitous, sensationalist, jumping on the bandwagon trying to make a buck," explains Vine; "then throw into that the stripper stuff as well . . . you're kind of considered a bit of a liar, I think, a bit of a thief and a fake and a cheat." Whether Diana was a conniving fraud or radically authentic are the distant poles between which her contested reputation still resides.

THROUGHOUT DIANA'S adult life, a recurring feature that appeared in British women's magazines was one that either imagined an alternate reality in which Diana had never become Princess of Wales, or in which she decided to pack it all in and turn herself into a "normal" woman. It was a rare reversal of celebrity media coverage, not fantasizing what it would be like to live in her world but dreaming of the wondrous ways in which she might inhabit ours.

In January 1987, *Woman* magazine speculated about a future world in which Diana lived among us as a nurse, a teacher, a model, a dancer, or a broadcaster, rationalizing that "if an actor can be President of the USA, why can't a Princess do a Wogan?," a reference to Terry Wogan, the genial talk show host who was a household name in Britain and Ireland at the time. Several years later, *Tatler* put a post-separation spin on the feature, sketching five hypothetical future lives that Diana might lead once Charles had been kicked to the curb, and encouraging readers to vote on which outcome they thought the most likely. Illustrations show Diana as a lifestyle guru; in opulent, remarried bliss in rural Ireland; jetting the globe as a "living saint"; and as a chain-smoking socialite in a British republic. The latter is marked as the nightmare scenario for Diana and the rest of us, while the best of all possible futures, says *Tatler*, is Diana as kingmaker; an illustration spread across the first two pages of the article shows Diana standing alone on the balcony of Buckingham Palace behind a newly crowned King William V, the power behind the throne, and a fulfilment of the princess myth as nurturer-in-chief of the future monarch. "Charles, you may note," runs the caption, "is nowhere in the picture."

Even for some of those who were solidly underwhelmed by Diana, imagining her future had an urgency. In her 1997 book *Different for Girls*—completed before Diana's death—the writer Joan Smith considered the mythology that tied together Diana, Marilyn Monroe, and Jackie Onassis, a celebrated triumvirate of "soft, vulnerable and *sad*" women, each of whom represented a "femininity which is both out-of-date and extremely seductive." The tendency to view Diana as part of this melancholy, glamorous trio was well established before her death. When Andrew Morton read of Diana's holiday romance with Dodi Fayed in the summer of 1997, he predicted it would not end well, and cast her as "lonely and unstable, combining elements of the two great tragic female icons of our century Jackie Onassis and Marilyn Monroe." Smith asked what it said about the world at the end of the twentieth century that "two of the women we most admire are dead and all three are linked with tragedy in its various guises: suicide, assassination, a desperately unhappy marriage?" She lamented that Diana was celebrated as a heroic wronged woman, like a real-life Anna Karenina with "I Will Survive" as her unofficial theme song, and derided certain figures in the media for "hailing the Princess, however improbably, as a heroine for the women's movement." In Smith's view, Diana was not someone who projected strength and independence, but lachrymose victimhood. Though her decision to "make a career out of her unhappiness" was popular with her followers, it would only lead to "more tears and loneliness. Her public likes her this way," continued Smith with awful prescience, "but is it a role she is prepared to die for?"

Among the parts in which Diana is cast today is that of inspiring role model to girls and young women, some of whom could be identified as belonging to the fourth wave of feminism. In 2009, the *Female Force* series of American comic books about "strong and influential women" published an edition dedicated to Diana, in which she is depicted as the fairytale princess who warmed the hearts of all those icy, uptight Brits and touched people around the world with her beguiling femininity. But there's something jarring about including a princess among the other women detailed in the series—a diverse bunch from Gloria Steinem to Cher to Condoleezza Rice—all of whom came to prominence through things they contributed or achieved rather than the entrenched, unearned privilege they were born with, then married into. Yet Diana's biography has been accepted by many as an emphatically feminist tale; "a feminist icon" is how the *Sydney Morning Herald* described her in 2022, "though during her lifetime, the idea was unimaginable." Perhaps not quite. One woman writing for Mass Observation in 1997 was explicit in identifying Diana as just that: "It is as a woman, and as a feminist that I most deeply admire what Diana achieved." Another female respondent thought such talk was absurd. "I thought perhaps a famous revolutionary had died," she said, having heard the news of Diana's death at a trade union rally. "It surprised me to find that trade union activists expressed genuine grief over the death of someone from the aristocracy. . . . It seems absurd to call a woman brought up in wealth and privilege the people's princess."

From a different perspective Kinsey Schofield, the American journalist behind ToDiForDaily.com, "a pop-culture take on the British Royal Family and a celebration of the life of Princess Diana," finds the feminist labelling of Diana just as wrongheaded; "I'm literally racking my brains trying to find examples of when she would have expressed any sort of feminism, and I can't," she said in March 2023. In her view, at least some of the popularity Diana enjoys among young progressives is because Diana has been distorted into a "martyr character . . . the ultimate victim" in a culture that says, "If you're a victim and you're willing to talk about your victimhood, for some reason we elevate that." She also thinks a simplistic calculation of my enemy's enemy is my friend is made on the part of those who can't stand the idea of royalty. That kind of sentiment comes through in a 2022 article by Róisín Lanigan which labelled the monarchy a "corrupt and archaic" vestige of "oppression, imperialism and colonialism" but hailed Diana as "the only bitch in this house (palace) we respected," at least until Meghan Markle "graced us with her disruptive anti-monarchical presence." If we're being honest, it's mightily difficult to identify the Duchess of Sussex, wife of Prince Harry, mother of Prince Archie and Princess Lilibet as an anti-monarchist—and impossible to identify her late mother-in-law as such. Diana's greatest ambition was not to tear down the monarchy but to future-proof it, which in her role as mother to the future king she had the capacity to do. It all goes to demonstrate that Diana is a crossbench emblem, proudly claimed by left and right, progressives and conservatives, who all see in her a reflection of themselves, and a means of accessing the critical issues.

When the BBC produced *Great Britons* in 2002—a TV series profiling celebrated figures from British history, culminating in a public vote—Rosie Boycott was invited to be Diana's advocate, attempting to persuade the audience that the Queen of Hearts deserved to be recognized as the ultimate representative of her nation. Boycott was an apt choice as Diana's champion. In 1971, she had co-founded *Spare Rib*, and in 1984 she published *A Nice Girl like Me*, a memoir that presaged Diana's confessions of a few years hence. She too felt that her father had been disappointed that she was a daughter and not a son; she too had contended with suicidal thoughts and struggled with the shame of disordered behavior, in her case alcoholism. In telling her story with such frankness, she made a deep connection with many women who recognized themselves in her story. Some of them wrote to thank her for sharing her experiences, alleviating a little of the stigma and making them feel not so alone. "Far from proving a liability, having told the truth turned into an invisible armour," Boycott writes. Diana had felt much the same in the final years of her life when shedding secrets became an ever-replenishing source of energy. In *Great Britons*, Boycott argued that a vote for Diana was a vote for love and compassion, a different form of greatness from those conveyed by the men who crowded the shortlist. A lot of viewers agreed. Diana finished third in the poll, behind Churchill and Isambard Kingdom Brunel, but above Newton and Shakespeare. The only other woman in the top ten was Elizabeth I, the daughter of Anne Boleyn, who once said she had "the body of a weak and feeble woman" and "the heart and stomach of a king": two very different models of royal womanhood, four hundred years apart, side by side in public estimation.

5

Follow the Fairytale West

An American Princess. Diana on her first visit to
the United States, Washington DC, November 1985.

JANE PAULEY WAS confused. The co-anchor of NBC's live coverage of Prince Andrew's wedding to Sarah Ferguson at Westminster Abbey on 23 July 1986 was trying to straighten out why the queen had announced, that very morning, that her son and his new wife would henceforth be known as the Duke and Duchess of York. "Won't Americans think that 'I'd rather be a prince, thank you very much, than a duke'?" Pauley mused aloud, as though Her Majesty had made an awful blunder by failing to consult US public opinion on the matter. The British pundits who sat beside her attempted to explain that Andrew and Sarah's new titles were, in fact, a considerable elevation. Neither Pauley nor her co-host Bryant Gumbel seemed satisfied with that answer, a little anxious, perhaps, that after all the hullaballoo of a live broadcast from outside Buckingham Palace and inside Westminster Abbey, the *Today* show was not giving its viewers what they had tuned in for: another girl next door magically transformed into a princess. Twenty minutes later, Gumbel raised the issue again. "Doesn't it seem a bit of a comedown?" Not at all, the natives assured him. But once the ceremony had concluded, he was back at it in one final effort to deliver viewers in Albany and Albuquerque the fairytale they had been promised: "Can she still be the Princess Andrew?" he asked, referring to an archaic royal style that requires some princesses to be addressed by their husband's name.

That last question—to which the answer was "no"—was fielded by Diana's twenty-two-year-old brother, Charles Spencer, who was one of a trio of royalists on hand to add insight to the proceedings, alongside the historian and biographer Robert Lacey and Tina Brown, whose coverage of Diana in Britain's *Tatler* had helped catapult her to editor in chief of *Vanity Fair* in New York. Spencer's association with Diana would soon help him break America, too. A few months later, on New Year's Day 1987, he would join the *Today* team, providing one interview or report every two weeks about a different facet of life in Britain. His lack of broadcasting or journalistic experience didn't matter; aristocratic suaveness and a deep connection to the Princess of Wales were qualification enough.

Diana had been a hit in the US from virtually the moment that she began appearing in the British newspapers, and her recent first visit to the country in 1985 had confirmed her as a star of the brightest order, in a category all her own. Arriving in Westminster Abbey on the day of the Yorks' wedding, she provided an abundance of the radiant princess glamour that NBC had come looking for. In the last five years, Diana had grown into Dynasty Di, no longer the uncultivated English rose, but a fashion-forward star who, to the delight of the US media, seemed distinctly American. Throughout the long history of the so-called Special Relationship between Britain and the United States, each had regarded the other as a locus of fantasies and resentments. By the mid-1980s, Diana was morphing into a unique figure, claimed by each side as evidence of their national genius. She herself felt the push and pull of both, a devoted royalist swathed in the Stars and Stripes.

INCONGRUOUS THOUGH it may be, a deep and enduring fascination with royalty permeated the pop culture of the American Century. Walt Disney's empire emanated from the Magic Kingdom and its enormous cast of royals, while queens of homecomings, proms, and drag shows can be found throughout the vast expanse of the union. At the time of writing, Queen Bey is holding court in Las Vegas, where Elvis "The King" Presley once reigned supreme. Many American enthusiasts for British royalty admire the power of the monarchy to unite broad swathes of the population. In a way, America's explorations of royalty serve a similar function: royal watching and royal role-playing cuts across the characteristic markers of social division; you're as likely to find Windsor wedding excitement in Martha's Vineyard as you are in Birmingham, Alabama. Age is no barrier either. In the year Diana died, the investigation into the appalling death of six-year-old JonBenét Ramsey introduced the rest of the planet to the only-in-America phenomenon of preschool beauty queens; that same year Disney's merchandise catalogues included an adult princess costume, with the tag line "You're never too old to dream of being a princess." Emulating royalty is vital to the pursuit of happiness: American self-help authors Kathy Kinney and Cindy Ratzlaff instruct women how to be *Queen of Your Own Life* while Robert Moore and Douglas Gillette show men how to access their *King Within*. Angelise M. Rouse's *The King Inside: Practical Advice for Young African-American Males* specifically urges readers to "unleash the King inside" as a way to "put an end to the negative statistics and media portrayals of your doomed future."

The allure of royalty even disturbs the pristine republican surface of American politics. When JFK scattered the fairy dust of youth, beauty, and celebrity over the executive branch of government he was said to have turned the White House into an all-American Camelot, the president as King Arthur alongside Jackie, his Guinevere. A few years before the Kennedy presidency, the film of Elizabeth II's coronation broke box-office records across the United States. In a survey of the film's impact, one young American woman told a researcher that she had been overwhelmed by what she saw: "oh, gosh, this is *wonderful*, this is like a fairytale, this is something America hasn't got." Perhaps that's the essence of this republican love affair with orbs and scepters: by definition, a monarchy is the only thing Uncle Sam cannot possibly own.

It is part of what Katharine McGee calls America's "castle envy." McGee, from Houston, Texas, is the author of *American Royals*, a series of young-adult novels about the twenty-first-century lives of Princess Samantha, Prince Jefferson, and their twenty-something sister Princess Beatrice, who is in line to become the USA's first queen regnant. There is a plump tradition of high-concept fiction about Americans colliding with royalty, stretching from Mark Twain's ingenious *A Connecticut Yankee at King Arthur's Court* to *The Princess Diaries,* a series of novels which was adapted into a film starring Anne Hathaway, via *Roman Holiday* and *Com-*

ing to America. But McGee goes a step further by creating a counterfactual world in which George Washington had been installed not as the first president of the United States but its first king, the founder of the greatest royal dynasty on earth. American readers find the premise "either massively entertaining or quite troubling," says McGee, although it's spun from historical fact: in the *American Royals* universe, George Washington accepted the crown at the end of the Battle of Yorktown upon the prompting of Colonel Lewis Nicola, who in real life had urged Washington to become king of the United States in 1782. McGee stops short of advocating an American monarchy, but she does recognize in herself and many of her compatriots "a sense of wistfulness . . . that we don't have anything like that as a society to pin our aspirations on, and to feel we've all been brought together." This captures a dominant strand of American interest in the Windsors, who McGee says are pretty much the sole royal reference point for both her and her readership: they embody a nagging sense of loss, a feeling that as good and as great as America might be, it mislaid something on its journey from the Declaration of Independence to global supremacy. At the same time, of course, American popular culture never tires of mocking royalty as old-world hokum; not America's innocence lost, but Europe's absurdity jettisoned. In *Hamilton,* the most traditional moment of musical theater is reserved for the effete caricature of George III; not for him the dynamism of modern rap, but a British pop throwback—and not the brilliance of a Kinks single, either, more like a bland B-side that Manfred Mann never got around to recording.

Thus, American popular culture affords the British monarchy space to be both antediluvian and prelapsarian—but in all cases, it remains a curious fantasy, a sandpit in which America can explore some aspect of its identity. When Diana came into view, she was a two-in-one gift: a contemporary and relatable figure of interest to those who looked askance at the backward institution she was joining—but also someone who pushed back on the American creed of the primacy of the individual, a reverse Rapunzel who was swapping her liberty for a life locked up in a gilded tower on behalf of her prince and the people, for whom she professed an equal, endless love.

These dual American visions of Diana come though strongly in two made-for-TV films which aired within three days of each other in September 1982: *Charles and Diana: A Royal Love Story* on ABC and *The Royal Romance of Charles and Diana* on CBS. These two films are part of a rather large canon of American-network-TV interpretations of the Diana dynasty—that is, Diana herself, her sons, and their wives—and both romanticized her beyond even the laudatory guff produced in the UK. CBS, in particular, showed Diana as a walking, talking length of tulle, all softness and light as she cuddles toddlers and delights everyone with her authenticity, hopping on and off buses; a humble London girl, devoid of sharp edges, exhaling rose-scented wholesomeness with every breath. Equally silly is the depiction of Charles as a royal Heathcliff, brooding and pained because of all the terrible things he has endured as the Prince of Wales: "The nature of my life," he confides to Diana, as though recounting his days fighting in 'Nam, "makes me aware of so many sorrows, so much human suffering, sometimes it makes me difficult." It is Diana, her sweet, soothing soul and her innate connection with the people, who brings him peace and fulfilment. At the film's conclusion, the Queen Mother urges them to display their new baby, William, on the balcony of Buckingham Palace—like Rafiki presenting Simba to the animals beneath Pride Rock—with what sounds like a Disney rewrite of a line from the Arthurian cycle: "Come, my children, come greet all Britain."*

By and large, Britons were unexposed to these hyper-romantic TV chronicles of Diana, though their existence was always of interest to the British press. In 1993, NBC aired an adaptation of Morton's *Diana: Her True Story,* which in the UK was available only to a relatively small number of satellite TV subscribers, though

---

* The American podcaster Aminatou Sow has described the custom of displaying new Windsor babies in public as "*The Lion King* for white people."

it garnered extensive coverage in the papers. Reviewers gleefully reported that a preview audience in London laughed at some inadvertently hilarious dialogue: Diana: "I just need you to hold me and touch me"; Charles: "Yes, but you're always being sick." They also relayed scathing comments made by Serena Scott Thomas, the British actress who played Diana in the series, about the "bum" script. "It was made for America," she was quoted as saying; "everything in America has to be spelled out."

British takes on American iterations of Diana were—and still are—a layered mixture of amusement that the daft Yanks had got everything wrong, offence at the liberties taken with the royal family, and pride that they should expend so much time, effort, and money in examining a facet of British public life. In his interviews with British people about the royal family, the academic Michael Billig found that many of his interviewees had an unshakable conviction that Americans were sick with envy that Britain had a special clan to bow down to, and they did not. "It puts us *above* America because they've got none," said one of Billig's interviewees. On the day of Diana's wedding, Mass Observation participants chimed in with remarks such as "The Americans must be green with envy, they will have their majorettes out tomorrow." In truth, most Americans with a fascination for the Crown can submit themselves to it secure in the knowledge that it will never be anything more than fantasy. As Katharine McGee puts it, "Americans hate having to pay for anything, and we don't have to pay a dime for the upkeep of the British royal family, so therefore we can enjoy it completely guilt free."

Michael Billig pointed to British certainty about American envy of the monarchy as a symptom of a deep national insecurity. "World power may have been conceded to the Americans," he said of this British logic, "but monarchy is a prized consolation." If this was true of British public feeling about the royal family in general, it was especially so of Diana and her immense popularity in the United States. In the final sentences of their book *Dicing with Di*, the paparazzi duo Glenn Harvey and Mark Saunders describe an experience of following Diana around Manhattan in 1995 when hundreds of New Yorkers began applauding and cheering as the princess stepped out of her car. After all their ridiculing and taunting of Diana, Harvey and Saunders suddenly heap praise upon her for being popular among Americans. "The woman being feted across the road wasn't the Loon," they state with characteristic anticharm, "this was a genuine princess, an international mega-star on an unprecedented scale. . . . Disarmed by her sheer and utter beauty, we both understood something about our country that we had not realised before: everybody else may have the gold . . . but by God, we've got the diamond." Within this same passage, they include a startling admission: "In that moment we both felt an emotion neither of us had ever experienced before. For the first time in our lives we felt proud: proud of Diana and proud of our country. We realised that though Britain may be struggling to be a major economic and military force, Diana is one of the reasons we are still the envy of the world."

For the first time in our lives we felt proud . . . we are still the envy of the world. And to think these men accused Diana of being a psychological mess. Yet bitter and self-deluded as they might seem, Harvey and Saunders were articulating the sentiments of many other Britons, for whom Diana was a source of national self-worth, a reassurance that no matter how much it existed in the shadow of its former colony, Britain's luster had not faded.

"CINDERELLA REDUX." That's how Diana's story was condensed for the readers of the *Washington Post* in the autumn of 1985, days before the Princess of Wales made her first visit to the United States. "She wasn't born royal, she's won no awards, she worked in a kindergarten," wrote the journalist Carla Hall in her "Diana Factbook," sticking to the fairytale narrative—though Hall added the important detail that Diana's appeal rested on "the distance between her and the rest of the world. You can see her, but you can't know her."

Tina Brown had aired something similar in her *Vanity Fair* profile of the princess a few weeks earlier, in which she noted that at official functions Diana had "perfected the art of detaching herself and being a presence." The nature of that presence, however, was undergoing a startling transformation. The Sloane Ranger who had once been a borderline parody of prim English femininity had ditched her demure princess persona for something unmistakably modern, starry, and American. Throughout her article "The Mouse That Roared," Brown uses American popular culture to explain the new identity that Diana was forming for herself in the mid-1980s, the separation she was underlining between herself and the other Windsors, and the role reversal taking place in her marriage, she becoming increasingly prominent while Charles withdrew into the background. In drifting from the royal family—whom Brown translates as the Ewings from *Dallas*—Diana has tossed out the "senior prom manner" of 1981 and "gone Hollywood," though it's "Jackie O" whom she most resembles in her conspicuous consumption and first-family glamour. It is not royalty that has put a spell—or a curse—on the princess, Brown suggests, but fame, American-style, and she wonders whether this ultimate A-lister has already entered her "Graceland" period, "when the real world melts away altogether."

In the final weeks of 1985, Diana brought this identity with her on an official visit with Charles to the US—her first ever trip to the country—and in doing so fully realized a new character type: the American princess, royalty untethered from the British crown. Of course, there had been other popular royals in the United States. As Prince of Wales, Edward VII's visit to New York in 1860 had astonished observers on both sides of the Atlantic with the enthusiasm that New Yorkers had shown for Queen Victoria's eldest son. Even Diana's husband commanded a sturdy American following. One aide sneeringly recalls that of the masses of cards Charles received on his fortieth birthday around one in every six was "from a Millicent of the USA, using HRH's birthday as an opportunity to push forward her claim as a future mistress or wife." Then, of course, there is Grace Kelly—though in transitioning from Hollywood superstar to European royal, her journey was the opposite of Diana's, who used her first visit to America to pay homage to a culture that the British establishment tended to consider hollow. In the famous moment when Diana danced with John Travolta at the White House, the fairytale was no longer about Diana Spencer becoming Princess Diana with a kiss from her prince, it was about a British princess being magically transformed into an American celebrity in the arms of a Hollywood heartthrob, with Ronald Reagan, the movie star turned president, looking on as the cameras flashed.

Diana had choreographed the moment, which a 2022 CNN article cited as one of the three iconic images of Diana's life.* Travolta's presence at the White House had been at Diana's personal request, and it was she who nudged Nancy Reagan into getting Travolta to request a dance. It is possible that she was living out the general flow of a daydream that had played in her mind for many years: the White House's checkered marble floor was similar to that in the Wootton Hall at Althorp House where Diana spent many hours as a teenager dancing by herself. And she had long looked upon America as a place of immense glamour and excitement. Her former nanny Mary Clarke tells a story of taking an eleven-year-old Diana to Harrods and Hamleys, London's famous toy store, in both of which they spotted numerous American tourists, "the men dressed in brilliant coloured checked trousers with striped shirts and sometimes wearing Stetsons," which apparently perturbed Diana, as did the "comely, well-covered women in polyester dresses" who "did not match up to Diana's idea of an American, mostly gleaned from pictures of Hollywood."

As an adult, Diana continued to regard the United States as a fabled place of promise. Admittedly, just about anywhere that wasn't the UK came to represent escape and revival once it was

---

* The others were of her approaching St. Paul's Cathedral on her wedding day and her wearing Christina Stambolian's so-called revenge dress in 1994.

clear that her marriage was mired in deep, insoluble difficulty. As Clive James observed of her pipe dreams about life after divorce, she held at the center of her imagination "some kind of enchanted place called Abroad, where she would be understood and where she could lead a more normal life." The middle-of-nowhere territory of Abroad encompassed many unlikely places, from Lahore to the South of France, an example of her capacity for magical thinking. When Joan Collins, soaking up the Mediterranean sun in the summer of 1997, learned that Diana was onboard a neighboring yacht, she and her companions were told to keep their distance by Dodi Fayed's bodyguards, who brusquely informed them that the princess was in search of nothing but peace, quiet, and complete privacy. "What," said a bemused Collins, "in St. Tropez in mid-August?"

Manhattan and Los Angeles were no more likely to have provided her with sanctuary and anonymity. Nevertheless, it was these American places she looked to as the epicenter of her post-royal life. "America is where my destiny lies. . . . It is a land where anyone can achieve," her butler Paul Burrell claims she told him, as though she might have imagined herself among the huddled masses sailing into Ellis Island. Naturally, part of Diana's ardor for the United States stemmed from the fact that she rarely encountered an American who wasn't besotted with her. To quote Patrick Jephson, "She liked foreigners and, of course, the only ones she met abroad were the ones who liked her. In fact it must have seemed to her that they adored her, unreservedly and unconditionally."

In reality, of course, there was no shortage of people outside the UK who, at best, regarded her with total indifference and, at worst, contempt. New York was the location of Diana's first official solo tour, in 1989, where she was met by screaming fans everywhere she went. But had she been able to see any of the local press beforehand, she would have gained a radically different impression of what the average New Yorker felt about her. "The most famous welfare mother in the world . . . [who] does no work [and] has no known talents" is how Pete Hamill of the *New York Post* described her ahead of her visit, which was accompanied by Irish-American protests at which a placard named her "DIM DI THE AVON LADY." Similar insults attended her visit to Chicago in 1996 and to Florida in 1985; "You Stuck Up Little Twit," is how the *Miami Herald* suggested Americans should address her. In the immediate aftermath of her death, the British-American writer Christopher Hitchens appeared on a number of network and cable TV programs, and at least a dozen radio shows, where he spoke pungently, not only against the royal family—"the House of Dracula" as he called them on MSNBC—but against the American media praise of a woman he thought "a spoilt kid . . . a borderline airhead, a gold-digger." He could barely believe his ears when he heard Kathie Lee Gifford tell her studio audience that Diana's demise was proof that the US Constitution needed to be altered to make sure that the right to a free press doesn't impinge on anybody's pursuit of happiness. "Where to begin?" he wrote in an account of that weirdest of weeks. "I could write a letter, pointing out that the 'pursuit' stuff isn't in the Constitution but in quite another document which declares American independence from the British monarchy. But . . . nah. This wouldn't be the week to bring *that* up." Though, in a way, he did bring it up on C-SPAN two days later, when he recalled Diana's first trip to America: "she could have met anyone she liked. They said, 'Who do you want to meet?' She said, 'John Travolta.' *That* was this princess." A viewer from Nashville called in, her voice shaking with anger. "You're in this country criticizing the royals," she said. "That's very easy to do. I would like to see you go back to England and criticize them over there." That, of course, in the traditional telling, had rather been the point of 1776 and all that—but evidently Diana had the capacity to make even some plain-speaking folks from Tennessee momentarily forget the essential point of the United States.

As it happened, a few months later Hitchens did return to England to make a documentary in which he criticized the princess, the royals, and the collective mourning that had taken place during "Diana Week," as some called it. He placed her iconography alongside other legends of the American Century—James Dean and JFK—whose premature exits made sure they were "mourned for what they never became, to say nothing of what they never were." Yet there might be a layer of Diana's significance in American culture that Hitchens did not address. More emphatically than any royal figure since Independence, Diana fulfilled a distinctly

"Media Overkill!" A mural in honor of the late Diana, Princess of Wales, by the street artist Andre Charles, on a wall in the East Village, New York City, September 1997.

American expectation of royalty, one that runs through Disney depictions of good monarchs—that they radiate love, treating the people in the manner of an adoring grandparent, infinitely affectionate and forgiving. It was exactly this that the rhetoric of the revolution charged King George III of failing to do. By refusing to interfere in Parliament's governance of the American colonies, he was accused of betraying the people he was meant to love and protect. Though charged with being too much of a king for freedom-loving Americans, for some who rebelled against British rule he was perhaps not king enough. If Diana is regarded—accurately or not—by many Americans as the anti-Windsor because of her capacity to touch the hearts of ordinary folk, it would follow that she is also the anti–George III, the king who is identified by many historians as being the prototype for the Windsor monarchs. For monarchy-curious Americans of the late twentieth century, Diana delivered what two centuries' worth of British royals could not.

WHEN DIANA visited the Henry Street Settlement on the Lower East Side of Manhattan in February 1989, it evoked memories of the time the Duke of Windsor—formerly King Edward VIII—toured the same part of town forty-eight years earlier. In 1941, *The New York Times* reported that the duke was straying so far from the beaten track of a royal visit that he had by his side a Yiddish translator to help him communicate with the people he met in one of New York's poorest tenements. As he travelled from one location to the next, crowds of local people followed, most of them astonished that royalty should be among them. A photograph was taken of the duke at the Vladveck Houses public housing development, a female resident smiling as she meets her celebrated guest. In 1989, newspapers printed similar photographs of Diana sitting with women who ran the Henry Street Settlement shelter, one of whom couldn't contain her excitement at being in the presence of a real princess. "I'm trying to compose myself," said Shirley Reese on what had been going through her mind when the photo was taken, "and I just burst out, 'Listen, I just got to say it, I don't know if I should say it or not, but oh my God, your skin is so pretty!'"

If Diana and Edward were able to charm working-class Americans, it was nothing compared to the effect they had on the filthy rich. Hyman Roberts, a resident of Palm Beach, Florida, who experienced visits by both Diana and Edward, stated that in the years of his exile from Britain, Edward and his wife Wallis Simpson were "lionized by Palm Beach's international set as their reigning monarchs." But it was the visit of Charles and Diana in 1985 that Roberts claimed to be "the social event of the Century." The showpiece occasion of the visit was a ball, tickets priced at five thousand dollars each. In advance of the big night, the local press urged Floridians to be on their best behavior, and master royal etiquette. "Curve the elbow gently unless holding a glass" was the advice of the *Palm Beach Post*, and "Smile just enough to turn up the corners of the mouth. Don't grin." Try as they might, the locals could never get it *quite* right. According to Hyman Roberts, when the photographer Mort Kaye did what he thought was the correct thing and bowed to Charles and Diana after taking their picture at the ball, Charles asked him, "Why did you do that? You're not Japanese." The prince had another withering Windsor moment at the ball when he saw the hotel valets dressed up in Beefeater costumes and pointed out that their sleeves didn't fit properly.

Diana, on the other hand, seemed a different sort of royal magnificence; she would never make you feel like a heehawing colonial. At least part of that is because, from the start, she could be identified as an eighties material girl, existing on the same plane of American consumerism on which so much of the planet grazed. Her ability to deploy this lingua franca reinforced her popular reputation even in her homeland. In Britain, one of the stories that became part of the lore of her wedding day was that as Diana readied herself in the morning, she started to sing "Just one Cornetto," a song written to the tune of "O Sole Mio" that was part of a very famous advertising campaign in Britain and Ireland for a brand of ice cream. The incongruity of Lady Diana singing about a consumer product that was available in every supermarket in the country while in the midst of her magical transformation into the fairytale princess clearly captured the imagination of journalists and biographers. Diana and her Cornetto represented a British, or maybe European, redraft of what Andy Warhol said about Coca-Cola:

> What's great about this country is that America started the tradition where the richest consumers buy essentially the same things as the poorest. You can be watching TV and see Coca-Cola, and you know the President drinks Coke, Liz Taylor drinks Coke, and just think, you can drink Coke, too. . . . When Queen Elizabeth came here and President Eisenhower bought her a hot dog, I'm sure he felt confident that she couldn't have had delivered to Buckingham Palace a better hot dog than that one he bought for maybe twenty cents at the ballpark.

How much of what Warhol said is actually true is debatable. But it seems pretty certain that this reflects how great swathes of twentieth-century Americans felt about their culture. And in Diana, Americans perceived the first stellar royal who embraced the same philosophy of consumption that made America great—to the extent that when she was in the United States, Diana shopped at JCPenney.

To millions of Americans, Diana offered a commercially obtainable version of royalty. It is noticeable how many collectors of Diana ephemera live in the United States, where the market for objects connected to her continues to be astonishingly buoyant. One of the key dealers in this market in recent decades is Alicia Carroll, a former actress who in the 1970s appeared on *General Hospital*, the show—coincidentally—on which Meghan Markle's parents worked and first met. In 1981, Carroll was swept up in the glamour and romance that surrounded the royal wedding, and spotted a business opportunity in the frenzy for the princess among Americans just like her. She set up shop as a dealer of royal memorabilia, and over the years has sold millions of dollars' worth of Diana-related artifacts and has been offered everything from Diana's nail clippings to a trove of letters Diana wrote to her lover James Hewitt.

Likewise, Darren Julien has sold dozens of items owned by Diana over the years through his auction house, Julien's Auctions, that is dedicated to the world of entertainment and pop culture. At Julien's in 2020, Bob Goldsand of El Dorado Hills, California, bought a Paul McCartney gold disc to add to his impressive collection of Beatles and other pop culture memorabilia. At the same auction he also bought a bracelet formerly worn by Diana as a present for his wife, Pat, to thank her for the love and support she gave him following his mother's death during the COVID pandemic. Pat has her own collection of Diana memorabilia, including a Diana doll in a replica of a Catherine Walker dress, in mint condition and stored in its original packaging. "Even though she was royalty, I felt I could go up to her and talk to her," says Pat on her love for Diana, which she and Bob say was instrumental in work they do for various children's charities; they own one of the original Batmobiles from the 1960s *Batman* TV series and arrange for seriously ill children to take rides in it. "You look at what she did," says Bob of Diana's example, "it was all about giving back and kids."

If Americans have been able to use American pop culture and consumerism to draw Diana closer to them, then something similar might be said of Diana's engagement with the USA. One of the reasons Diana is perceived to have launched a sartorial rebellion against the House of Windsor is her wardrobe of clothing that marked her out as an Americanophile: cowboy boots, NFL sweatshirts, baseball caps, T-shirts and jackets with the stars and stripes emblazoned upon them—the kind of clothing that Borat might suppose are the marker of an authentic Yankee Doodle. She had the clothes and, so it seemed, the dissatisfaction with the Old World, so why not cross the Atlantic for good? "Move to New York!" shouted an audience member at a ceremony in Manhattan at which she received an award for Humanitarian of the Year in 1995. She was considering it, apparently, though it's impossible to know how it would have panned out. Legendary columnist Aileen Mehle, an authority on New York high society, predicted that "after a year with the novelty gone she'll be just another blonde divorcee." Perhaps California was a more likely destination; she was reputedly considering whether to purchase Julie Andrews's house in the Hollywood Hills in the final months of her life. The Golden State, of course, was to be the place where her younger son and his wife would flee "in fear for our sanity and physical safety" and where he would exploit his royal title to build a personal entertainment brand, which rests in part on disparaging the very idea of royalty. In an ad for a profile in the *Los Angeles Times* ("Harry & Meghan: Their American Life"), readers were entreated to "FOLLOW THE FAIRYTALE WEST"—an almighty pileup of contradictory, transatlantic allusions of exactly the kind that Diana elicited, but which can be disaggregated in the figures of Harry and Meghan. From the outside, it seems Harry might be struggling to wrap his head around some of the fundamental American ideals: when giving his thoughts on the US media in 2021, he described the First Amendment as "bonkers. . . . You can capitalize or exploit what's not said rather than uphold what is said." The Duchess of Sussex had similar difficulties understanding the basic point of the monarchy when she and Harry began their relationship. She was, she says, surprised to learn that she would be expected to curtsy to the queen on their first meeting, assuming the bowing and scraping was only for show, just "part of the fanfare . . . I said, 'but it's your grandmother.'" It was moments such as these that made her realize the difference between the idea of royalty that she had acquired from American film and TV and the reality as lived in a place where it's been a constitutional lynchpin for more than a millennium. "I grew up in L.A., I see celebrities all the time. It's not the same. This is a completely different ball game." Perhaps only in the figure of Diana have the two identities of Beverly Hills celebrity and royal icon ever been successfully reconciled.

*   *   *

IF THE entreaties to move to New York and California were not enough to indicate Diana's popularity in America, then the commercial offers that came her way removed all doubt. She was approached to star alongside Kevin Costner in a sequel to *The Bodyguard*, and Disney was keen to have her associated with its theme parks. News reports in the summer of 1996 claimed that Diana had been offered millions of dollars by the corporation to attend Walt Disney World's twenty-fifth anniversary celebrations later that year, though Diana's spokesperson told the press that the princess had "no intention of attending, and the correspondence with Disney will make clear those intentions."

There is no record of any official contact between them, but a surprising association had also developed between Diana and McDonald's, to the extent where one might consider her a de facto brand ambassador. Among the British, food and drink has often been used to stress the gap between royalty and the populace. Interviewing families about their opinions on the royal family in the 1980s, Michael Billig discovered that fish-and-chips had a totemic quality for the British, as though it were the definitive marker of British identity, British freedom, and the living of an authentically British life. Several of his interviewees earnestly cited the fact that the royal family couldn't queue up at their local chippie for a bag of chips as a reason why they didn't envy the royals their exalted status. Of course, the royals do eat comfort food like the rest of the population; Prince Charles was an occasional customer of the fish-and-chip shop nearest to his and Diana's Gloucestershire home, Highgrove. Back in the forties and fifties, the supposedly maverick, modernizing tendencies of Prince Philip were said to be revealed in his unfussy, proletarian culinary preferences. Early in his career, Winston Churchill's valet John Gibson served as a royal footman, and was astonished to learn that Philip's favorite meals were bangers and mash and fish-and-chips. But when it came to Diana, it was her consumption of American fast food, especially

McDonald's hamburgers, that was repeatedly highlighted as a sign of her connection with ordinary people.

American-style fast-food restaurants were a relatively new addition to British life when Diana leapt into the spotlight in 1980. In May 1981, BBC News ran a report that detailed the huge sums of money that McDonald's and their competitors were investing in an attempt to transform British eating habits, putting the future of fish-and-chips in peril. "It's a multi-million-pound gamble," said John Craven on his *Newsround* show, "and whether it works or not depends very much on you," meaning the children and adolescents that constituted his audience. It appears that the teenage Diana did her bit. In his memoir of serving the princess, her butler Paul Burrell tells the story of how he and a colleague raised Diana's spirits during one of her lonely first nights at Buckingham Palace by getting her a Big Mac from the McDonald's on Victoria Street. As the years passed, Diana developed a reputation for being a lady who lunches under the golden arches—even though she far more often frequented the forbiddingly expensive restaurants of Mayfair. It gained her kudos in the United States, where it was often pointed to as incontrovertible proof of her accomplishment as a mother. A very large proportion of the books written about Diana by American authors include at least one reference to her taking William and Harry to McDonald's, and they always do so by way of praising her parenting skills. Diana fans in the general American population seem to agree that her trips to McDonald's were an important part of her contribution to the world. "Diana was a different breed to the other royals," said one woman in Chicago, speaking to a local news crew as she lined up to sign a book of condolence in September 1997; "She fed her children McDonald's." "I saw how much she loved her children," wrote an American reviewer of a book about Diana on Amazon in 2022. "I saw her taking those children to normal places like McDonald's." Specific instances of Diana in McDonald's are very rarely cited, but the fact that she went there and educated her sons in its ways has taken on a folkloric aspect, a little like the legend about King Alfred burning one of his subject's wheat cakes while masquerading as a peasant, a tale designed to keep alive the memory of an epochal leader with a common touch. It's also never really stated why being treated to junk food necessarily helped William and Harry become better people, physically or morally. Princess Margaret practically lived on gin and cigarettes, but nobody ever claims it made her at one with the multitudes. Moreover, it is well known that as children Margaret and Elizabeth took trips on London public transport, queued up and paid for tea and bread and butter at the YWCA, and joined the Girl Guides—known in America as the Girl Scouts—alongside working-class war evacuees. But quite rightly, in the United States none of this qualifies the late queen as a person of unique distinction—perhaps because, unlike Diana's patronization of McDonald's and Disney, it doesn't remind everyday Americans of their own lives, conforming to and endorsing their own experiences and expectations.

The myth of the People's McPrincess is enshrined in the popular imagination, albeit with an occasional variation on the theme: *Spencer* ends with Diana rescuing her sons—whom she has dressed in the freedom threads of blue jeans and baseball caps—from what the film implies is a barbaric English custom of killing birds one-by-one with gunshot. She then takes them to KFC, an altogether more enlightened American environment, apparently, where the birds on the menu have been industrially slaughtered by the truck-load. The American novelist Peter Lefcourt ran with the Diana-McDonald's association in his satirical novel *Di and I*, published in 1994, in which Diana ditches the royal life to work at a McDonald's franchise in the Freedom Mall in Rancho Cucamonga, California. Diana takes her sons with her, too, giving them "crew cuts and Bart Simpson pj's," transforming them into "average American kids." Lefcourt wrote this with tongue firmly in cheek, but beneath his novel's layers of irony rests a feeling common among Diana's American admirers that only in the USA could Diana's true self be realized, because she was, at her core, an American princess raising American princes. "A piece of her was definitely American," claimed the front page of *The Kansas City Star* the very day after her death, one of a number of American obituaries to make such an assertion.

Nearly thirty years later, Diana's perceived Americanness is undimmed. "There's something very trailblazing about Diana that feels very American to us," says Roberta Fiorito, co-host of the US-based *Royally Obsessed* podcast. "You know, not having the stiff upper lip but showing emotion, forging her own path—it *feels* so American to us." Pat Goldsand, the collector of Diana memorabilia, describes Diana as "a little bit of both" British and American; her husband, Bob, believes Diana's story is inspirational as it tells people that "no matter who you are, you can eventually become members of the royal family," which is an unmistakably American spin on the Diana Spencer story. Hyman Roberts, who documented Diana's 1985 visit to Palm Beach, reaches further, stating explicitly that Diana "personified 'the American Dream' by emerging from relative obscurity, overcoming adversity, and becoming a superstar."[*]

Diana had some American ancestry through Frances Work, one of her maternal great-grandmothers. But for her—the ultimate fairytale princess from a land far, far away—to be considered an American at heart seems an especially bold claim. Perhaps this is evidence that Alexis de Tocqueville's feeling that "the American is the Englishman left to himself" is a presumption that still holds in the American mind. Or, from a less Anglocentric perspective, the belief in Diana's fundamental Americanness maybe reveals an assumption that "the American way" is simply humanity's default setting; like everyone else, Diana was an American stuck inside a foreigner's body.

If some Americans felt that Lady Di was stripping off the British cladding to access her inner Lady Liberty, a good number of Britons were troubled by what they saw as the increasing layers of American identity that Diana wrapped around herself in the last

---

[*] In his praise for Diana as a mother, he cites her "attempts to orient William and Harry firsthand to the real world" by "paying for hamburgers at McDonald's."

years of her life. In their book of 1996, which aimed to unpick Diana's psychological state, Chris Hutchins and Dominic Midgley quote at length the American PR expert—and self-described Anglophile—Mary Spillane, who confirms that Diana is losing touch with her sturdy English roots. "I'm an individual, I can stand on my own two feet, I don't need a man," says Spillane of Diana's mindset, "in-your-face-stuff, which is American. Therefore, the American flag sweatshirt, with the cycling shorts and the rest of it, is all part of this. . . . It's a very self-centred existence." Later in the book, the Venerable George Austin, Archdeacon of York, voices his dismay at a similar American influence on Diana—and the rest of his compatriots—which he deems morally corrosive. It's her interest in spiritualism and psychotherapy that really sticks in his craw. "The American disease," he calls it, "everyone has to be counselled. There's no acceptance of personal responsibility." Julie Burchill, who rejoiced in Diana's thoroughbred Englishness, conceded that one of Diana's least attractive traits was her use of "damp, self-dramatizing American therapy-speak," against which her "dry, self-mocking, very English wit was to provide a welcome balance."

For more than a century, the threat of being possessed by American culture has haunted the British just as the promise of being transformed by it has thrilled them. More than Charlie Chaplin, Cary Grant, John Lennon, or any other single cultural figure, post-1985 Diana embodied both the dreaded Americanization of the UK and the degree to which the United States offered the British a means of reinvention and escape. For it wasn't just she who was looked upon as an American convert; her devoted British followers, too, seemed to many traditionalists like a mob of crass, sentimental colonials. The mass mourning for Diana was regarded in some quarters as the ultimate proof that Britain was, culturally speaking, a fifty-first state, displaying synthetic "McDonaldized emotions," as one British academic termed it, to honor its McDonald's princess.

Much of the world outside the US and the UK also saw Diana

as more American than British. "The explanation for her cross-cultural appeal would seem to be that she appeared so American," says Joke Hermes, the Dutch writer and critic. Though the Netherlands has a strong tradition of lamenting the pervasive impact of an American popular culture that is critiqued as glib, vulgar, and hyperbolic, it is still the case, Hermes reminds us, that the United States "saved us from totalitarian Nazi rule" and helped to forge the postwar Dutch nation "by introducing us to the joys of consumer capitalism." And Diana seemed to be a shining example of that audacious spirit of reinvention. America is "the land without frontiers . . . where a paperboy can become a millionaire and a kindergarten teacher can become a princess."

On the surface, that might sound odd: it was, of course, very much in Britain that Diana became a princess. Yet Hermes is essentially correct. In Britain, the young woman who became a princess was Lady Diana Spencer, the "well-bred" aristocrat who volunteered to carry out a constitutional function. It was in America that Diana's backstory as a kindergarten assistant and house cleaner had a supercharged power, filtered through the myth of the American Dream and Hollywood fantasy. Arguably, it is this Diana that has held the attention of millions around the world for nearly half a century; only in America did Diana fully become *Diana*.

6

Upstairs, Downstairs

Duty and service. Diana at a function on the
Isle of Wight, December 1988.

S PENCER HOUSE IS an astonishing place. With beautiful architectural features, antique furniture, and sumptuous art, it is a rare and sparkling relic of the eighteenth-century days when aristocrats rather than oligarchs lived the most opulent London lives imaginable. Though this gargantuan mansion, which is less than half a mile from Buckingham Palace, hasn't served as the family's pied-à-terre for a century, it is still in Spencer hands and still in splendid condition thanks to a renovation that began in 1987. Soon after that restorative work had begun, however, it became apparent that the building's treasures were just too enticing for some to resist. In August that year, a caretaker—disgruntled with his pay and working hours—was sentenced to nine months in prison for stealing thirty-five thousand pounds' worth of paintings from the Spencer House collection. It seems to have been a bumpy year for Spencer property staff: in the spring, newspapers reported that police had investigated peculiar goings on at Althorp, including alleged sex parties thrown by domestic servants.

Such behavior from the staff must have left Diana's father aghast. Johnnie prided himself on having a firm grasp of service; the obligations involved in serving and being served were central to his idea of what it meant to be a Spencer. In various ways and with varying effects, he bequeathed this to his children. And at this very moment Diana was making strides in refining her own idea of service within the royal family. Initially, her main role as Princess of Wales had been exceptionally well-defined: breed an heir. Beyond that, however, there was a void; she felt both lacking in direction as to what she should do to fill her days and unsure about how to conduct herself while doing so, insecurities that were exacerbated by low self-esteem, the slow but inexorable collapse of her marriage, and a feeling that her judgmental Windsor in-laws failed to give her the support she desperately needed.

By her telling, there had been a time during her second pregnancy when she and Charles were close, and it seemed that a happy future as man and wife really was possible. But those hopes were soon dashed. Diana said that when Harry was born, in September 1984, Charles stood by her bedside and complained about the baby's sex, and even his hair color. The old problems resurfaced, most damaging of which was perhaps their mutual neediness and essential incompatibility; the marriage lurched ever closer to the cliff edge. According to Charles, it was only at this point, sometime in 1986 that he took up with his old flame, Camilla. A minority of royal watchers think this is the case; most believe Diana was correct in thinking that Charles and Camilla had been involved for much of the preceding five years. In any event, it was around the same time that Diana began an affair with James Hewitt, a captain in the Life Guards regiment of the British Army. What Diana craved—a flood of loving enthusiasm and praiseful validation—were things the Windsors could never provide. In a sense, she compensated for that by carving out a public existence that focused on service to the suffering.

From the late 1980s, she embraced causes which were considered by many to be distinctly inappropriate concerns for a future queen, but which she felt passionately about—and which semaphored to the rest of us how she felt about herself: abandoned, rejected, and misunderstood. Her idea of service collided with that held by "the Grey Men," as Sarah Ferguson called the courtiers and bureaucrats—"essentially well-marinated Sloane Rangers"— whose role in life was to serve the Palace and, as Diana saw it, to silence, thwart, and disempower her. Often caught up in the uncivil war were those whose duty it was to keep her buoyant—people who adored her and were infuriated by her, who resented her and found their life's meaning in her, and who sometimes questioned the wisdom of a life of service when it meant serving the royal family, reputedly the ultimate servants of the British people.

JOHNNIE SPENCER wasn't the only lord of the manor who struggled to get the staff. In the mid to late decades of the last century, light-fingered servants seemed to afflict grand homes throughout the land. Take the case of Anthony Collingwood, a butler who in 1973 was found to have stolen from his employers at Borde Hill, in Sussex, more than a quarter of a million pounds' worth of silverware, paintings, and objets d'art. As Adrian Tinniswood reveals in his book *Noble Ambitions: The Fall and Rise of the Post-War Country House*, the thefts were especially remarkable considering Collingwood had twenty-two convictions for theft prior to being taken on at Borde Hill. That this rogue had been deemed the best available candidate for such an important household position says much about the decline of domestic service across the twentieth century, especially after the Second World War. In an era of vast societal change, serving in a stately home was no longer attractive to most working people, and reduced aristocratic incomes meant many landowners simply couldn't afford the army of knowledgeable and skilled servants that were needed to keep their ancient homes running as before.

The young Diana had a mixed record with the Spencer family servants. At Park House, she and her brother were watched over by a succession of nannies, whom Diana resented, feeling they were there to replace her mother or steal her father. When she decided they deserved punishment she delivered it, placing pins in their chair, locking them in the bathroom, or throwing their clothes out of windows. "It was mostly due, it seemed, to Diana's high spirits and pranks that my predecessors left," says Mary Clarke, one nanny whom Diana did not torment. Clarke encountered difficulties with the other domestics and "the back-stabbing which could go on among members of staff in this type of household," but she believed that the Spencer children—though often ill-disciplined—were raised to be mindful of their position in life. "I always got on very well with everybody," Diana told Andrew Morton via James Colthurst. "Whether it be the gardener or the local police. . . . My father always said: 'Treat everybody as an individual and never throw your weight around.'"

This was, in essence, the Spencers' *noblesse oblige*, an ancient aristocratic sense of duty to the less privileged who orbited around them, something Johnnie professed to take deadly seriously—though perhaps he didn't always live up to the ideal. The biographer Angela Levin records that when Johnnie inherited his earldom in 1975 and moved the family to Althorp, he reneged on a promise that he would take with him Elsie and Bertie Ellis, the married couple who had served at Park House for many years. The Ellises, who were two years away from retirement, found themselves in need of a new home and employment at very short notice. According to Bertie's diary, Earl Spencer had the hot water to their cottage switched off while they were still packing up his lordship's antiques and fine wine, leaving Bertie feeling "very bitter" that he had given his "whole life to private service," only to be treated so shoddily by a man who, Bertie said, was not the honorable chap he claimed to be. Years later, the chauffeur who had famously helped Johnnie navigate the steps at St. Paul's Cathedral on Diana's wedding day was informed that his services were no longer required by a note sent to him on the back of a postcard.

In the leaner, more democratic times that followed the end of the Second World War, new thinking about Britain's stately homes and their owners had come into play. Reflected in cultural works such as Evelyn Waugh's celebrated novel *Brideshead Revisited*, an idea took hold that the mammoth seats of titled families constituted Britain's greatest artistic achievement, for which the nation should be immensely grateful. Writing in *The Telegraph* in 1995, Charles Spencer's friend from Eton and Oxford, Boris Johnson, summed up the thinking in crude but efficient terms, arguing that "societies need rich people, even sickeningly rich people. . . . If British history had not allowed outrageous financial rewards for a few top people, there would be no Chatsworth, no Longleat"—and no Althorp. Instead of being the "sickeningly rich" beneficiaries of great privilege and political power, in the second half of the twentieth century Britain's aristocrats were frequently cast as conservators of the nation's heritage who shouldered the burden of living in their ancestral homes for the sake of Queen and Country. Lord

Montagu of Beaulieu invited photographers to capture the preparations ahead of welcoming the paying public into his residence, Beaulieu Palace House, in 1952. The pictures, published around the world, showed him on his hands and knees scrubbing the floors, and sleeves rolled up as he polished the family silver, the perfect image of the aristocrat-servant, a tradition that Diana would briefly join during her stint as cleaner and nanny in her late teens.

Diana's grandfather Jack, the 7th Earl, was known as "the curator earl," because of his passionate interest in, and encyclopedic knowledge of, the Spencer properties and their contents. He was the first to allow members of the public to visit Althorp, though there are stories of him checking visitors' shoes for mud and following them around with a duster. "He detested them so much," said Johnnie about his father's feelings toward the great unwashed, "he used to stand at the front door with a shotgun." When Johnnie took possession of the estate, he and his second wife, Raine, embarked on a project of modernization: visiting hours were increased, a café and gift shop were opened, and both of them made an effort to engage with the public. Raine, in particular, was seen as a force of change, much to the outrage of the Spencer children, whose feelings of animosity toward their stepmother were entangled with her alterations to their family home. Both Diana and her brother were appalled that Raine had carpets fitted on top of Althorp's oak floorboards, and that, at Raine's instigation, some of the most prized items from Althorp's vast art collection were sold to pay the bills. The resentment towards Raine burned deep in Diana and her brother and resulted in some shocking behavior. In 1989, the Spencer family gathered at Althorp for Charles's wedding to his first wife, Victoria Lockwood. Ostensibly aggrieved by the lack of attention being paid to her mother, Diana pushed Raine down the stairs during an argument, an incident she seemed rather proud of when she described it to her speech coach, Peter Settelen. According to Angela Levin, the scene was reprised two and a half years later, in the days after Johnnie died, when Diana and Charles, now the 9th Earl Spencer, swiftly banished Raine from

Althorp, stuffing her clothes into trashcan liners and kicking them down the stairs. No longer in possession of a place in the House of Lords—he and his heirs were excluded by reforms introduced in 1999—today, most of Earl Spencer's dynastic responsibility is the upkeep of Althorp, safeguarding it for his children and the nation. He acknowledges his great good fortune, though there are days when he thinks, "I could do without this." The struggle is felt by many of his caste. In August 2023, *The Telegraph* ran a piece by Emma, Duchess of Rutland, describing the "hellish reality" of living at Belvoir Castle.

Alongside their role as self-sacrificing defenders of Britain's cultural gems, the other pillar of the Spencers' twentieth-century reputation as public servants is their fealty to the monarch. Sir Arthur Bryant explicitly linked the two things in recalling a wartime visit to Diana's grandparents, Jack and Cynthia, "who were living at the time in great simplicity; their stately home and all its historic and artistic treasures were under dust-sheets," a scene that could have come straight out of the *Brideshead Revisited* TV adaptation that would air later that year. Suppers consisted of "Spam or some other austere wartime dish," eaten in a room filled with "tantalizing pictures of 18th century fat cattle." To Bryant, Cynthia represented "the perfect ideal of an English lady" and "a lifelong servant of the Crown," a reference to the thirty-five years she spent as Lady of the Bedchamber to Queen Elizabeth, who later became known as the Queen Mother. In the middle of that period, Diana's father also served as equerry to George VI and Elizabeth II. In 1954, Johnnie held numerous screenings of a ninety-minute silent film he had shot while accompanying the young queen and the Duke of Edinburgh on their recent tour of the Commonwealth. It doesn't sound like an hour and a half that would have flown by: the highlight was reportedly a sequence in which Prince Philip drove a tractor around a farm in New Zealand. But it publicly underlined the access that the Spencers enjoyed to the royal family, as well as their desire to be seen as humble servants of the sovereign. That mythology was sort of true, but also not: for much of the eighteenth and nineteenth centuries, the Spencers reveled in their status as leading Whigs, the political faction that stressed the rights of Parliament against those of the Crown.

These notions of service were a prominent part of Diana's familial identity which, as we've already seen, was exceptionally important to her. Her favorite hymn, played at her wedding at her request, was "I Vow to Thee, My Country," the words to which equate service to Britain with service to God.* At each milestone of her career in public life, she reiterated her commitment to serving— whether that was to her husband, her monarch, her country, or her people. Yet there was always a tension between these vows of self-abnegating service and other things that propelled her: her individualism, her urgent ambition, and her conviction that she had been born for a special purpose, something that had been with her for as long as she could remember. On the surface, this does not jibe with other things she claimed about her childhood, namely that she was unwanted since birth and always struggled with feelings of worthlessness. But she repeatedly told those close to her that while growing up she had felt, not only different from those around her, but in some way exceptional, and chosen. "I knew very early on in my life that I was born to do something special," she told her sometime friend and astrologer Penny Thornton. "I knew I was destined to marry a great man. Somewhere along the way I began to know that man was Charles."

To point this out is not to suggest that Diana was insincere about hoping to find happiness in her marriage or that her interest in good works was faked. Rather, in the context of her family circumstances, her education, and her social environment, the ambition that pulsed within her was funneled into making as spectacular a marriage as she could and living out a Spencerian life of "service" on the grandest scale imaginable. Vaulting ambition was not encouraged in a young woman of her background: it was con-

---

* The hymn was also sung at the funerals of Diana, Winston Churchill, and Margaret Thatcher.

sidered alien to her sex and beneath her nobility. But Diana clearly had it in spades, and she didn't know what to do with it, other than subsume it into this aristocratic ethos of service. Sometimes it made her sound disingenuous, if not a little bit ridiculous. When reflecting on the acclaim she received on the balcony of Buckingham Palace on her wedding day, she described it as "humble-making, all these thousands and thousands of people happy." As with the Hollywood stars who profess to be humbled by receiving an Oscar, this doesn't make much sense: in what world could such acclaim and adoration possibly cause a flush of humility?

Destined to serve; destined for greatness. It was a tension in her life that is perhaps best encapsulated in the memoir written by one of the few people who can claim to have been Diana's boss. In the People's Princess mythology, much is made of her supposed Cinderella period, the time between her moving to London and getting engaged, when she worked part-time jobs cleaning her sisters' flats, assisting at a nursery school, and taking care of the infant son of Mary Robertson, an American banker who published a book about her relationship with the nanny who became a princess. When Robertson returned from work one evening to discover that Diana had furtively eaten all the chunks of meat in the casserole intended for the family's dinner, she requested that in future Diana let her know if she had used up anything in the house so that it could be replaced. Diana promised she would, and apologized—"so sorry to have inconvenienced you." Shortly after this odd incident, Robertson found a bank deposit slip under the skirt of her sofa in the name of Lady Diana Spencer. Robertson, who had no idea about Diana's background, looked her up in *Burke's Peerage* and was astonished to learn that her child's caretaker was "blue-blooded and titled." Tina Brown shrewdly suggests that the bank slip had been misplaced accidentally on purpose: "That was Diana declaring to her boss she wasn't, after all, just the 'help.'" As Diana's former private secretary Patrick Jephson puts it, "people forget that Diana was not the girl next door; she was not Kate Middleton: she was Lady Diana Spencer." *People* might forget that; Diana never did.

*   *   *

THE TWENTIETH-CENTURY evolution of "service" among aristocrats paralleled developments within the royal family. In his 1954 memoir of cooking for Victoria and Edward VII, the chef Gabriel Tschumi lamented how few young people were now attracted to serving the great families, including the Windsors. Yet at this very moment the young Elizabeth II was pressing ahead with her own life of service, pursuing the example set by her grandfather George V whose reign from 1910 to 1936 marked the template of what might be termed the "service monarchy," reframing the most fawned-over, privileged, and waited-upon family in the land as servants of the people.

One of the problems with the service monarchy is that there is no clear definition of how members of the royal family are expected to serve nor how many of them are needed; each generation has to make it up as they go along. "There is no actual laid-down job or role," to quote Prince Charles, speaking in 1985; "it would be quite easy to do nothing." Consequently, every thirty years or so, there is some new member of the family who gains a reputation for radically overhauling centuries of tradition, as though nothing similar has ever happened before. Prince Philip once occupied that role and aggravated Palace staff with his newfangled ways. When it came to Diana, she too clashed with the Grey Men. Sometimes these were specific people, including various trusted aides to her mother-in-law and her husband, such as Robert Fellowes, private secretary to the queen and—in the way of the miniscule world of aristocracy— husband of Diana's sister Jane. Another of the grey suits was Richard Aylard, who served as Charles's private secretary between 1991 and 1996 and was identified by Diana's side as a field marshal in the War of the Waleses that raged during those years. Often, though, the term "Grey Men"—or "shadowy forces" as Diana sometimes referred to them—was a personification given to an oppressive sense of censoriousness and disapproval that Diana felt bearing down upon her from the upper echelons of the courtier class.

Diana's act of shaking things up came largely in the form of her charitable interests, which were increasingly personalized from the late 1980s onward. However, arguably of greater social significance than her embrace of any specific cause—homelessness, domestic abuse, addiction, mental illness, AIDS—was the emotional tenor in which she approached them. The architect Edward Cullinan designed the Lambeth Community Care Centre, and he tells an illustrative story of the day Diana formally opened the facility in 1985. As is seemingly the case with almost everyone who encountered Diana at such events, he was bedazzled by her, the combination of her royalty, her celebrity, and her personal charm producing a mesmerizing effect. But he was most struck by a brief episode involving his daughter, Emma, who, like Diana, was in her early twenties, and was among the many people who had turned up hoping for a chance to see or meet the princess. As Diana walked through the building as per the official itinerary, Emma found herself on the other side of a window from the princess, and so "pushed her nose against the glass and made her mouth into a kiss shape, and Diana just broke out of the procession and did the same," mirroring the kiss. Nobody could quite believe what they were seeing. "That was that woman," recalled Cullinan with breathless admiration, "she was just astonishing."

Inevitably, the princess's behavior wasn't entirely without precedent. An oft-told story about Queen Alexandra, for example, has her showing off her injured leg as a way of connecting with a hospital patient who had recently suffered a bad accident. The other Alexandra—Elizabeth II's cousin—supposedly marked her first official royal engagement by chirping "Wotcha!" to a little boy who had excitedly greeted her in the same colloquial way. But Diana's public bearing seemed reflective of a fundamental change in British manners, stemming from a fraying of traditional deference that in turn caused a widespread social confusion about etiquette and appropriateness. Tessa Baring—chair of the board of the children's charity Barnardo's between 1987 and 1993, when Diana was its president—captures this in recalling her visits to various Barnardo's projects. "Either people were going to practically curtsey to me when I arrived or else they'd say 'Hi, Tess!' and you never knew which it was going to be. It was an interesting transition that was going on at the time." Diana, it is fair to say, was at the vanguard of that transition, perhaps its unofficial figurehead. Baring marveled at Diana's ability to charm dignitaries with her best princess routine one minute, and in the next, plonk herself on the floor to play with small children or have heart-to-hearts with disaffected teenagers.

"She's one of us," thought Paul Burrell, later to be Diana's butler, when he first encountered her as a footman shortly before the wedding, "and perhaps that had something to do with the fact that the Spencers knew the life of service as well as that of nobility." It's surprising that Burrell—the son of working-class parents from a coal-mining community in Derbyshire—should imagine his experience of service to be comparable to that of the Spencers'. But a recurring theme of his memoirs of serving Diana is the suggestion that they enjoyed parallel experiences of the world; what Diana lived as a female aristocrat marrying into the Windsors, he went through as a working-class man in service to them. "If the princess was pinching herself over the magnificently surreal world in which she found herself, then so was a certain footman," he said of the early 1980s when he and Diana both found their lives rooted in Buckingham Palace.

Burrell, who entered royal service as a teenager in 1978 and acted as Diana's butler for the last four years of her life, is one of many who have published an account of their experiences serving the princess. In pre-Diana days, such books were rare, though not unheard of. The most infamous was *The Little Princesses*, Marion Crawford's tale of her time as governess to Elizabeth and Margaret, published in 1950. To the modern reader, the book is innocuous, presenting both girls as pleasant children who had a genuine interest in the world beyond their bubble. The royal family, however, was aghast that one of their staff would have ever cashed in on their service to the Crown in such a way. "Crawfie" was coldly shunned forever more; Margaret and Elizabeth even declined to acknowledge her death in 1988. After *The Little Princesses*, a couple of other servants' tales were published that mirrored the new, more voyeuristic approach to royal reporting that was taking hold on Fleet Street, but the sixties and seventies witnessed very little in the way of what the butlers saw behind the palace gates. Then along came Diana, and the service memoirs poured forth. Over the last thirty years astrologers and psychics, butlers and bodyguards, press officers and private secretaries—even her florist—have all given the inside scoop on working for Diana. No other figure in royal history has been so thoroughly discussed by those paid to serve them and clean up after them, in all manner of ways. One inevitable consequence is a recurring depiction of Diana as thoroughly childlike—lovable, dependent, and prone to tantrums. Burrell gives us an image of her skipping down the corridor at Kensington Palace at bedtime while he walks behind her switching off the lights; Rene Delorm, Dodi Fayed's butler, describes the moment when Diana and Dodi—thirty-six and forty-two—fell in love during a romantic dinner that turned into a messy food fight, a nursery habit Diana enjoyed. In fact, playing with one's food appears weirdly popular among royalty more generally: one of the Queen Mother's staff, for instance, told the writer Valentine Low that even in her eighties the boss took pleasure in hurling peas into the dining room chandelier. Perhaps knowing that there'll always be a servant to clean up the mess makes it more fun than it might otherwise appear.

Of these service memoirs, Burrell's book, *A Royal Duty*, is the most illuminating in what it says about the strange ambiguity that Diana brought to the notion of serving royalty. What he perceives as Diana's contempt for old-fashioned hierarchy is mirrored by his own disregard of old-fashioned humility. He places himself in a lineage of steadfast servants: "I was as dependable to her," he proudly states, "as John Brown was to Queen Victoria." Such boasting echoes David John Payne, the footman who published *My Life with Princess Margaret*, or "my princess" as he proprietorially referrcd to her. However, Burrell outstrips Payne, making himself the central character in *his* princess's life, describing their complete interdependence; he writes that even when on a short family holiday, he frequently had to sneak off and call Kensington Palace, so intense was their need for contact. Burrell tells us of Diana's secret trysts, her moments of despair, and flashes of joy. At all turns she is "one of us" to the extent that his children became firm friends with hers—weirdly, she apparently nicknamed his youngest son her "little sexpot." And, of course, she was at her most magically royal in those moments when she tossed aside the whole business of being a princess, such as when she would jump into a swimming pool fully clothed. "Splashing about in the pool in her clothes, she was on the same level as her staff. She loved seeing the look on people's shocked faces as she leaped in in her jeans or shorts, sweatshirt or T-shirt." Burrell wants us to see Diana as a force of social change just in her being, flipping the world upside down, dissolving the barriers between master and servant, princess and people, one watery jape at a time.

Some have questioned his account of his relationship with Diana. Until the queen swept in deus ex machina to shoo the whole thing away, Burrell stood accused of stealing 310 items of Diana's property, that he asserted were in his possession for safekeeping.* William and Harry have labelled *A Royal Duty* "a cold and overt betrayal." Perhaps so. But with her proclivity for oversharing and speaking her truth at all costs, it's also the kind of thing Diana might have done herself. It might even be that Paul Burrell is the Platonic ideal of a Dianaist, an inevitable consequence of Diana's recasting of royal interaction with the world. According to Burrell, the working-class butler and his aristocratic princess were indivisible, two devoted servants who formed a single entity

---

* In November 2002, the case against Burrell was dropped eleven days into his trial after Elizabeth suddenly recalled that many years earlier Burrell had—as he had always claimed to the police—told her that he was looking after some of Diana's belongings.

with shared goals; not only was she "one of us," but he was one of her: "I know what we had," he insists, "I know the depth of what we shared. I know the future we were heading to." If that sounds fantastical, perhaps that's because the world that Diana built—or, perhaps, the one that we all built around her—had outlandish fictions at its core.

Recognizing no formal separation between "upstairs" and "downstairs," as children at Park House and Althorp, Diana and her siblings would merrily walk into the kitchen to chat with staff as though they were old friends. Not everyone appreciated this: Mary Clarke recalls that one cook at Park House left soon after being recruited in part because she "could never get used to the children having total freedom of the house." Almost immediately on becoming part of the Windsor setup, Diana repeated this practice at the royal residences, including Buckingham Palace and aboard the *Britannia* on her honeymoon, where she shared cans of beer with the crew and struck everyone on board "by the way she related to them all—from the Admiral to the stokers," as Andrew Morton has written. Some staff, including Burrell, were delighted by her attitude. Others, adhering to the traditions of domestic service, were very uncomfortable with having a Princess of Wales sitting on the counter sharing gossip or talking about last night's telly. Those older staff were surely alive to the problems that could arise from pretending that there were no divisions between royal employees and royal employers—and they would be vindicated on numerous occasions when the essential, irreducible imbalance between Diana and those paid to do her bidding was revealed.

Burrell himself provides examples of this. When he became Diana's butler at Kensington Palace after the Waleses formally separated at the end of 1992, Burrell claims to have become his boss's confidant, a shoulder to cry on, and a go-between she called on to help resolve personal crises. So informal was their relationship, he says, that Diana would frequently let herself into the home Burrell shared with his wife, Maria, who for a time was also on Diana's staff, then made herself coffee, and "poured out her heart to Maria time and again, talking about life with her husband and how unhappy she was." By the end of 1994, Maria found the demands of working for the princess were eating too much into her personal time, so she decided to quit her job, a decision that apparently enraged Diana. "After all I've done for you? . . . I've bent over backwards to accommodate you and be flexible, and this is how you repay me." According to Burrell, his wife said, "She wiped the floor with me. She had me in tears." This act of throwing one's weight around—breaking what was supposedly the Spencers' cardinal rule—was not an isolated example. In her biography of Diana, the seasoned royal watcher Judy Wade relates the astonishing story of when Diana discovered that her driver, Steve Davis, was romantically involved with her dresser, Helen Walsh. Such relationships were discouraged by the Palace, and Diana was furious that two of her staff were conducting a relationship in secret. By the terms of their employment, however, they were doing nothing wrong—unless Walsh allowed Davis to stay in her quarters at Kensington Palace past midnight. So on one evening when Diana was certain that the two were together, she waited until the stroke of midnight at which point she began banging on Walsh's front door, shouting, "I know you're in there!" Hardly the behavior of "one of us."

Rumors of run-ins with staff came early in her married life. An indiscreet Princess Michael of Kent told Roy Strong in May 1984 that "being rude to servants is the lowest thing you can do and she does it," in a conversation about the ways in which Diana was ruffling feathers at the palace. This was apparently a revelation to Strong, but the papers had been full of Diana's alleged conflicts with members of staff, domestic and administrative, for quite some time. The first was Stephen Barry, formerly Prince Charles's valet, who resigned his position in October 1981, amid stories that he and Diana were in a kind of turf war over Prince Charles. A slew of others followed Barry out the door during the course of Charles and Diana's marriage, including those who felt aggrieved at having their service abruptly terminated once the Waleses' split was confirmed. Several former staff members have voiced their experiences, detailing the unpleasantness of being caught up in a royal match gone hideously wrong, and alleging instances of startlingly bad behavior from the prince and princess. Some of these accounts have never appeared in the UK. There are those who argue that this is just as it should be: no employees blessed with the rare privilege of glimpsing the Windsors' private lives should ever open their mouths about it. But perhaps by the end of their marriage Charles and Diana had invaded their own privacy to such an extent that it was unreasonable to expect discretion from anyone else. In speaking out via Andrew Morton, Richard Kay, Jonathan Dimbleby, and others, Diana and Charles loosened the lips of those who would share all kinds of intimate details about life behind the palace gates that take us light years away from the deference and discretion of Marion Crawford's book. In 2002, Diana's personal protection officer, Ken Wharfe, spilled numerous secrets in his (first) memoir, including that Diana owned a vibrator that she called *"le gaget."* Four years later, a disgruntled former member of Prince Charles's staff, Sarah Goodall, published a memoir of her twelve years of service in which she reminisces about urinating in the gardens at Highgrove, and a separate occasion when colleagues simulated sex acts in the kitchen of St. James's Palace. She also ponders whether Diana was "a fruitcake" or merely "a spoilt bitch."

Goodall admits that a large part of her motivation for writing the book was financial; royal staff are often not well paid, and her dismissal from Charles's team had reduced Goodall to selling ice cream in a theatre to pay the bills. In the spring of 1997, it was disclosed that Diana's housemaid of nine years, Sylvia McDermott, was paid only nine thousand pounds a year at the point at which the Princess of Wales had dismissed her the previous November. A few months later, in the weeks following Diana's death, Alicia Carroll, the American dealer in royal memorabilia, says she was approached by numerous anonymous people, whom she suspects were royal staff, offering her various of Diana's possessions, evidence either of unconscionable greed or resentment against parsimonious employers—perhaps some combination of the two. Patrick Jephson (at first Diana's equerry, then her private secretary) claims there was "nothing more guaranteed to stir up royal displeasure than the thought that those travelling on their coat-tails were enjoying the ride." Diana herself, according to Jephson, was of the belief that she was forever being exploited by staff: "She paid lip service to the need for staff 'R and R', but seldom missed a chance to make you feel just a little bit guilty for taking it."

The memoirs of Jephson and Wharfe detail rather a lot of unpleasant and capricious behavior from their boss, but both provide detailed and thoughtful context about the large and unusual pressures Diana faced and the insecurities that beset her. They also stress the exceptional qualities she possessed, those things that made working with her enjoyable and rewarding. Wharfe concedes that if Diana suspected any disloyalty from her staff, she was "capable of exacting ruthless punishment," but he rightly reminds us that "it must have been terribly embarrassing, if not humiliating" for her to work among staff who all knew about her marital problems. At the same time, some of Wharfe's stories detail a woman who was not beyond exploiting her privilege to get her own way, such as when she decided the laws of the road didn't apply to her and expected Wharfe and other police officers to turn a blind eye to it. As Wharfe puts it, "Being the Princess of Wales had its advantages." Jephson recalls the strange tensions involved in working in a close-knit team for a boss who was keen "to find reasons for feeling resentful or exploited" by her own staff, and who could "switch from warm intimacy to frozen exclusion in an instant." Yet how seductive were those moments of warm intimacy with Diana—an after-hours glass of wine and a gossip with the princess on her sofa. Such instances taught Jephson a vital lesson in working for royalty: "Deference protected the small people too, from royal favour too lightly granted and too quickly withdrawn." This was something that the staff of other royals were far less likely to lose sight of. When Sarah Goodall was removed from certain duties for appearing to become too familiar around His Royal Highness, she claims to have felt that the "chill of Royal disfavour hangs on me like an old, wet coat. . . . It is like being dumped by someone you love"—though she was never given any reason to believe that the feeling was reciprocated.

Desperation for royal attention could cause ructions among the staff. Burrell makes barbs against the snobbery and jockeying for position that is rife inside royal palaces—not among the royal family, but those who work for them, a traditional complaint among the downstairs staff of grand British residences where one's place in the pecking order is hard-earned and jealously guarded. Jephson is less bothered by such things; if anything, he sometimes seems to think that a tad more snobbery wouldn't have gone amiss at Kensington Palace. He despaired of the occasions when Diana let her hair down and indulged in the sort of vulgarity that Burrell found charming. "Consonants were an optional extra, so words often emerged in a lazy drawl," says Jephson—Diana's accent, again, being scrutinized for evidence of her true identity. "This suited the subject matter, which in private was not always very elevated. The cruder the humour, the more her verbal discipline deserted her, as if it shared our wish suddenly to be far away, preferably with someone not expected to ascend the throne."

Jephson bemoans the influence of slick, devious PR operators whose advice to the Windsors exacerbated the family's problems. This was an evocation of the figure of the evil counsellor who throughout the long history of English, and British, kingship has been blamed for corrupting monarchs from King John to Charles I to George III—and Elizabeth II. *The Crown*, the Netflix series on which Jephson was a consultant, stresses the importance of the senior courtiers in causing Elizabeth to make her sister Margaret's life a miserable slog by refusing her the marriage she sought to a divorced man. Prince Harry apparently was totally unaware of "Aunt Margo's" difficulties until he found himself in a vaguely comparable situation, but he too feels his family are the playthings of these overmighty servants. His memoir *Spare* is written, essentially, as the tale of a good prince thwarted in his attempt to serve his nation by a cast of guttersnipe journalists and unctuous, dissembling servants, to whom he gives animalistic nicknames: The Bee, The Wasp, The Fly. Even Granny was prone to the poison they poured in her ear. When Oprah Winfrey suggested to him that it must have been the queen who cancelled an appointment to meet him, Harry deliberated before saying, "No. When you are head of The Firm, there is [sic] people around you who give you advice." Less service monarchy, more servants' monarchy.

At worst, Jephson found his boss temperamental, immature, and manipulative. Diverting so much of himself into supporting her also put a strain on his own marriage. Yet he remains of the opinion that working for Diana was a rare privilege and an important duty. "Once it became obvious that my service for Diana went way beyond what was expected of a service equerry—which started pretty soon—then I knew that there was a cause. . . . *She* became a cause, because she represented in my eyes many of the good things that I believe that the monarchy was intended—is intended—to embody in a way that her in-laws, beginning with her husband, did not." By this he means a commitment to reducing the gap between royalty and populace—not in social or economic terms, but morally and emotionally. If pressed, he will boil those virtues down to one word: "decency."

This sense of Diana as a cause, beyond even the cause of royalty, is a common theme among many of those who worked for her, and those who didn't. It is a big part of the reason why people—whether they were on the payroll or not—would forgive her when she treated them badly. "She was capricious; she was cruel, actually," says Patrick Jephson. Yet she also had what he calls "the quality of forgivability," a compelling mixture of personal charm greatly magnified by her royalty, and multiplied by the feeling that she was doing something special with her status and influence, something of which no other public figure was capable. Ultimately he felt his position as her personal secretary was rendered untenable when he discovered, after the fact, that Diana had secretly admitted Martin

Bashir and the *Panorama* team into Kensington Palace to record that seismic interview. But he never lost the faith. "It was an honor to work for her, and it's an honor to still be encouraging people to remember her now."

IN THE days after Prince Philip's death in 2021, Britons were incessantly reminded of his decades of self-sacrifice. One MP described him as "the embodiment of duty and service"; another celebrated his "profound sense of duty"; a third hailed him as "an extraordinary public servant." Even Joe Biden joined in, saluting the duke's "devoted public service." The president, not known for his admiration of the British monarchy, made no mention of Philip's well-documented abrasive and dismissive attitude to those beneath him in the pecking order. There are numerous accounts of the verbal bashings he delivered to Palace staff, while the author Kitty Kelley makes the startling claim that another public servant—a US secret service operative—was struck over the head by the duke for the crime of not driving His Royal Highness to dinner fast enough during a royal visit to San Francisco.

The conviction that being a member of the royal family is a thankless grind of obligation is coupled with the commonplace wisdom that the Windsors' lives are intolerable, and that no ordinary person in their right mind would envy them. If anything, so the thinking goes, it is the royals who are jealous of the hoi polloi and their freedoms. This seemed to be especially the case with the Princess of Wales. When Diana was pregnant with William, a young woman named Barbara Nicholson wrote an open letter to a newspaper about having recently been cared for by Diana's gynecologist, George Pinker.* That Nicholson's experience of childbirth overlapped with Diana's in this way was remarkable considering that until the last four weeks of her pregnancy she had been living

---

* Pinker saw Nicholson as part of his National Health Service duties at St. Mary's Hospital in London.

at a homeless hostel. Yet despite the hardships she faced as a new mother in straitened circumstances, Nicholson said she wouldn't swap places with the Princess of Wales. "I wouldn't like to be in your shoes," she wrote, speaking to Diana directly; "you will never be able to go up to the market like I can and buy daft hats or frilly dresses for the baby." More than once, Diana appeared to have triggered such responses among members of the public in her interactions with them. During an official visit to St. Albans in 1988, Diana opened up to a pet shop owner about the difficulties of being royalty, a life that is "not all it's made out to be." Doris Bird, an employee at a nearby supermarket, asked Diana if she'd like to have a go at pushing a shopping cart down the aisle, imagining that this was something she would have never experienced. Diana explained that going to a supermarket was actually a chore she relished; Bird supposed it must provide brief but blessed relief from the "monotony of being a Princess."

It is important not to be too cynical; there is no question that postwar British royalty have been handed duties, expectations, and scrutiny that previous eras couldn't have imagined and wouldn't have tolerated. As far as the public is concerned, it is an important part of the deal. In 1993, the satirist Ian Hislop was asked why he thought Sarah Ferguson, Duchess of York, had seemingly fallen in the public's estimation while Diana's popularity remained undimmed, bolstered even by her very public clashes with other Windsors. "She was having too much fun," he said of the duchess. "People in Britain want the Royal Family to go and be cold in Scotland and get wet in Balmoral and traipse about in ill-fitting, uncomfortable clothes and have a generally miserable time and then we don't mind that they're the Royal Family." Diana didn't do a great deal of traipsing, especially not in ill-fitting clothes. But her glamour was offset by her evident unhappiness and her public statements of dissatisfaction. Perhaps, then, part of Diana's enduring popularity is that while embodying the fantasy of royalty, she also had the common decency to suffer for it, reassuring her public that being royal really was about duty and service, and nowhere near as desirable as being paid minimum wage or living in a homeless hostel while eight months pregnant.

The writer John Higgs argues that the monarchy is "intrinsically cruel" and likens the monarch to a pet parakeet: loved, pampered, and diligently taken care of—but still locked in a cage simply for the benefit of the people who own it. Picturing what Prince William's eldest child, Prince George, has in store for him, Higgs argues that "the cruellest aspect of his situation is that it will not give him the opportunity to earn status through hard work and personal achievement"—though, to be fair, through their military service and charitable endeavors George's father and uncle have worked harder and achieved more than many other offspring of the fabulously wealthy one can think of.

Diana's difficulties with the Windsor world of service underlines the essential archaism at the heart of the monarchy, in which twenty-somethings with no experience, qualifications, or training can be placed into a prominent public position and left to design their own job description. In the 1990s, there was much anguished questioning about whether the Windsors had it in them to learn the lessons Diana gave them and adapt sufficiently to save the institution. Similar questions were asked after Elizabeth II's death in 2022. Charles and Camilla are keen to slim down the monarchy, we are told, to make it more in tune with modern sensibilities. Antique titles such as Lady of the Bedchamber (which Diana's grandmother once held) are now being replaced, but the queen's "companions," as they are now called, are still drawn from the same tiny pool of the social elite that staffed them in the days of Anne Boleyn, and are not required to demonstrate any particular skills or knowledge to fulfil these influential roles, other than being a good egg.

Joan Thwaites—the Great Diary Project contributor who noted royal events between the 1940s and 2010s—recorded at the back of her diary of 1992, the *annus horribilis*, three bullet-point observations about the problems that beset the Palace that year: "Sex discrimination . . . Race discrimination . . . Queen doesn't pay taxes." More than thirty years of scandal, upheaval, and pledges to reform later, those are all still issues of controversy and criticism. *After Elizabeth: Can the Monarchy Save Itself?* asks the title of the book by Ed Owens that argues the institution is doomed if it doesn't radically modernize itself. The mystery is why the British, a majority of whom apparently still approve of The Firm, don't take matters into their own hands and modernize it for them. If the royals really are nought but servants of the people, perhaps it's time for their masters, the Joan Thwaiteses of the world, to lay down the law. Patrick Jephson has argued that the system in which the royals choose who serves them is ripe for abuse and manipulation, and inevitably leads to factionalism and favoritism—the very things that happened on Diana's watch. Others say that professionalizing the system by making the royal staff British civil servants in the conventional sense would be nonsensical as the monarch reigns in fourteen countries outside the UK—though for how much longer remains to be seen.

Diana's sons are waging a contest to see who's the humblest servant of them all. When the Sussexes retreated from the frontline of royal life, Elizabeth II announced that Harry believed he was unable "to continue with the responsibilities and duties that come with a life of public service." The duke and duchess responded, "We can all live a life of service. Service is universal." True—though the dukedom of Sussex is definitively local, and in the gift of the monarch. Reconciling privilege and individuality with institutional duty seems even more unwieldy for Harry than it was for Diana. Prince William, meanwhile, is persisting with a Diana-Windsor hybrid that includes a five-year plan to end homelessness in the UK, though whether complex social problems should be handed over to unelected figures subject to no official system of accountability is highly questionable. He recalls that it was his mother who introduced him to the scourge of homelessness which, he says, has no place "in a modern and progressive society," one retort to which might be that neither does the service monarchy—whatever "service" means.

7

The Royal Touch

Diana in Hong Kong, November 1989.

STEPHEN TWIGG BELIEVES that Diana's life changed the day she met him. It was 14 December 1988, and Twigg, a masseur and holistic health practitioner, arrived at Kensington Palace to treat his new client, who told him that her sore muscles made her feel "so down and I hate to disappoint people by not being on top of my game." Twigg quickly deduced that there was much more going on with the princess than a few troublesome knots in the neck.

At first glance, he was struck by Diana's "hunched shoulders," "heavy tread," and a "lack of coordination. She certainly did not have the smooth and graceful movements and posture of a person fully at ease with themselves." Worse was to come when the massage began: a sense of "turmoil and confusion" apparently emanated from Diana's stomach, pulsing its way into his palms. Working further up her body, "I suddenly felt an overwhelming wave of sadness sweep over me," Twigg says, "as if the release of her facial muscles had allowed a tidal-wave of emotion to surge out from the top of her skull." He took a mental note of the things he claims Diana's body was emitting into the center of his being:

> *Fleeting sensations of fear —*
> *Flashes of intense anger, bordering on rage —*
> *Excruciating self-judgement —*
> *Extreme sadness and abject loneliness*

When she told him "I make myself sick," the statement lingered, ambiguously, without explanation, but Twigg says he intuitively understood the double meaning. It was his certain belief that Diana's muscular aches were the result of a welter of emotional issues, which were in turn a symptom of post-traumatic stress disorder—though it's unclear what qualified him to make that diagnosis. According to Twigg, things could barely have been bleaker for the princess: her body was "what the body of a human being feels like when they are close to giving up on life." Yet in Twigg's telling, this alarming encounter also marked the beginning of Diana's renaissance. For the next seven years, Twigg not only treated Diana with his holistic "hands-on bodywork," but helped introduce her to a range of New Age philosophies, alternative therapies, and esoteric interests that, as a promotional blurb for the book states, propelled Diana's "transformation from unhappy young woman, suffering from depression, bulimia and thoughts of suicide, to powerful figure on the world stage who was able to challenge governments and cause a royal dynasty to bow to the wishes of a nation." In helping Diana to heal herself, Twigg believes, he had set her on the path to healing we, her people.

Even if his judgment on who Diana became and the things she effected is overblown, Stephen Twigg was an influential figure in the last decade of her life. Mind you, he was pushing on an open door. Diana's interest in the ineffable world of spirits and energies was deep-rooted, as was her belief that she possessed powers that strayed beyond the bounds of the material universe. Twigg is in no doubt that Diana transformed herself for the better by treating her mental and physical health as though it were one and the same thing, eagerly taking responsibility for her own well-being. Yet some of those who knew her worried about the intensity she invested in whatever latest fad came her away: colonic irrigation, crystals, homeopathy, aromatherapy, hypnotherapy, astrology, mediumship. Her search for spiritual healing knotted itself to her mission to heal others, the core of her understanding of the purpose of monarchy. Consequently, the world of the 2020s contains a posthumous Diana who speaks words of wisdom to true believers from beyond the grave. This is not the "thick as a plank" princess—as she once described herself to a member of the public—but a force of nature with access to knowledge that perplexes and terrifies the establishment among whom she lived her earthly life. To some Dianaists, even now she possesses powers mightier than any sovereign.

*   *   *

IN FAIRYTALE terms, Stephen Twigg had roused Diana from her spellbound slumber. It was several years into her awakening, in 1993, when she came upon Simone Simmons, a self-described "energy healer" who worked at the Hale Clinic on Harley Street in London. Like so many others, Simmons claims to have felt a powerful connection to Diana years before she had any contact with her; once they got to know one another, says Simmons, she and Diana agreed that "in some past life we might have been cousins, sisters, perhaps even mother and daughter."

A lifelong Londoner, Simmons was raised in a Jewish family of East European heritage with an ethic of self-improvement through education, hard work, and commitment to the community. In conversation, she proudly describes a great-grandmother who took in washing for a penny a load, and every Friday fried thirty pieces of fish: fifteen for her family and fifteen for the local poor. This great-grandmother was also known as a wise woman who was thought to have possessed psychic powers, powers that Simmons believes she inherited, and was aware of even as a child. With a schoolfriend, she set up an occultist society at the age of fourteen; at seventeen, she joined the Spiritualist Association of Great Britain. On the day of Diana's wedding, Simmons watched the TV coverage from a hospital bed, recuperating from an operation. Two or three weeks later she was back in the hospital, this time to visit her sister Rachel, who was in a coma following a car accident. It was then that she discovered her supposed gift for healing. Having seen "a rainbow aura emanating" from Rachel's body, Simmons insists that not only was she able to communicate with her sister, but that by placing her hands near, but not on, her "whilst quietly speaking loving, encouraging words, the needle on the machine monitoring her heart would flicker and then jump," which she apparently took to be a sign of something positive. It's not easy to grasp precisely what Simmons believes her powers are—something to do with altering electromagnetic fields—but she says that she saw Rachel's "aura and spirit . . . floating above her physical body" and realized that she could help "to pull the two forces together."

It's something of this order that she reckons she did for Diana, ridding her of various aches and pains. It wasn't only Diana's body that Simmons treated, but her home, too, directing her powers into casting out negative energies from each room of her Kensington Palace apartment, parallel to the way Diana had the place swept for bugging devices when she suspected some wing of the establishment of surveying her. Simmons claims to have performed healing on Prince Harry, too: "Sitting on Diana's lap, with his head snuggled into her shoulder. . . . Diana explained to him that it wouldn't hurt, that he would soon feel better, but he wasn't worried. I sat with my palms turned towards him and let the energy flow forth." Simmons also states that she taught Diana how to perform energy healing herself; she claims that the healing techniques Diana learned brought "comfort to the many hundreds of thousands of seriously ill people she met" in the last three or so years of her life.

That is a breathless exaggeration requiring us to believe Diana capable of biblical miracles—though Simmons is at least correct in stating that Diana was convinced of her power to heal. Many people in Diana's orbit agreed that Diana felt she had healing powers, and some were convinced that she did. Her friend Elizabeth Tilberis attributed her body's positive response to a bout of chemotherapy to Diana's intercession. "I believe the princess was single-handedly responsible for getting me home to family," she wrote in her memoirs; "no one will ever convince me otherwise." Diana's sister Sarah McCorquodale was struck by the apparent pattern in which severely ill people were able to cling to life long enough to experience a visit from Diana, only to die very shortly afterwards. "Because they knew she was coming, for some reason . . . they hung on," she explained. "It was very strange."

In the latter stages of her life, her mercy dashes to the bedsides of the dying were ridiculed in the press. But it was the British papers that first seeded the notion of Diana the heavenly, healing princess years before she clogged her diary with therapists, fortune tellers, and seers. A clear example comes from August 1985, when Diana and Charles visited Wythenshawe Hospital to meet survivors of a recent fire at Manchester Airport which had killed fifty-four people. Thirteen-year-old Lindsay Elliott lost her mother, aunt, and uncle in the disaster and had kept her eyes shut and her tongue silent ever since. But according to press accounts, the presence of Diana at her bedside had caused her to open her eyes and speak for the first time since the accident: "She was beautiful," is what she reportedly told her nurses. "Just the medicine," read the caption beneath a photograph of Diana sitting on the girl's bed that appeared in the *Liverpool Echo*: "a solemn Princess Diana unlocks the words Lindsay has found too painful to speak."

Charles was not ascribed a role in this act of healing and has rarely, if ever, been cast by the popular press as a healer in the way Diana was, this despite his very public championing of complementary medicine, alternative therapies, and spiritual questioning. In fact, in 1988 he opened the Hale Clinic at which Diana and Simone Simmons would eventually meet. During the Waleses' visit to India in February 1992—a little more than two years after Diana had her first session with Stephen Twigg—British newspapers reported that Charles had been rapt by a demonstration of the Unani practitioner Dr. Hakeem Abdul Hameed as he treated patients with "touch and intuition." According to one report, Charles had been tempted to offer his own wrist for healing, but was dissuaded by an aide who pointed out the watching eyes of every newspaper on Fleet Street. Michael Dixon, a prominent British physician who was formerly a senior figure within The Prince's Foundation for Integrated Health, has described Charles as "the Healing Prince" who "suffers with his people," precisely the kind of language routinely used to couch the myth of Diana.

Floating around these descriptions is, of course, the mythology of the so-called royal touch, the belief that royal personages had a God-given ability to rid the afflicted of scrofula with a touch of their hand, in imitation of Christ. In his 2015 study of the phenomenon, Stephen Brogan asserts that Diana's ancestor Charles II held twice-weekly ceremonies in which he touched sufferers of scrofula. The king began these ceremonies immediately after he took the throne in 1660; detailed contemporaneous records indicate that by the end of his reign in 1685, he had touched ninety-six thousand people in search of a cure. The royal touch ceremony came to an end with the accession of George I and the Hanoverian dynasty in 1714. Nevertheless, even as the notion of the "divine right" of kings diminished, it never entirely disappeared. According to research conducted in 1964, 30 percent of British people believed Elizabeth II had been divinely chosen. And though the ceremony of the royal touch now seems outmoded, the underlying impulses linger on in revised forms. The concept of the "royal walkabout," in which members of the Windsor family come face-to-face with the public, allows the populace the opportunity for physical contact with royalty, typically with a handshake. Diana is exulted for being the first royal woman to perform these handshakes without gloves, giving skin-on-skin contact that appears to have enhanced the feeling of intimate contact between princess and people—just think of those photographs of her among the crowds on her visit to Australia in 1983, a scene that lands somewhere between Christ among the multitudes and Beatlemania.

In other contexts, up-close contact with royalty has persisted and is frequently imbued with a spiritual quality that most of us would think of as "charisma," a word whose original form referred to a remarkable gift endowed by the Holy Spirit. When Elizabeth II died, memories of encounters with her poured forth from the British public. Over and over, Elizabeth's charismatic gifts were extolled. "She would have this incredible aura when she entered the room," said the photographer Chris Jackson, seemingly convinced that the queen had a capacity to alter her surroundings through the specialness of her being: "I certainly felt the change in the room when she arrived." The lord-lieutenant of Bristol attempted to be more precise about Elizabeth's charisma, recalling "the way she stared right at you when you talked to her." It's tempting to ascribe such behavior to basic good manners, but the lord-lieutenant flagged it as proof of the tremendous presence she had: "She focused on you, she listened to you, and when it was time to move on, turned her heel and went and spoke to someone else and created the same amazing atmosphere." The musician Nick Cave stated quite plainly that the queen was "almost extraterrestrial . . . the most charismatic woman I have ever met . . . she actually glowed." Some didn't even need to feel her hand or share a stretch of carpet with her in order to experience her powers. Amongst a crowd in Yeovil, one woman witnessed the queen waving in her general direction, a moment that burned into her memory. "She had this amazing ability to make you feel she had directly seen you and was waving to you alone," she told the BBC. Virtually identical claims have been made of Diana. "She had a gift," avers Chris de Burgh, one of Diana's favorite pop singers—though for him her magic is the spiritual watermark of the ultra-famous rather than the royal: "They carry an aura about them." Of course, the tributes paid to Diana predate those paid to Elizabeth; it's hard to make an empirical case for it, but perhaps this is evidence of one way in which the mourning for Diana altered the way that the British public responds to the Windsors. Just as Diana's death nudged the queen into the uncharted territory of speaking to the public "as a grandmother . . . from my heart" so the tidal wave of tributes to Diana's ethereal charisma set a precedent for the voluminous— and rather unlikely—praise of Elizabeth's personal charm, her warmth, her social skills, the bewitching aura she carried with her in one-on-one encounters.

If the premodern purpose of the royal touch was to connect people with the divine, its Dianaist refashioning isn't about communing with something beyond the self—whether that be God, nation, or empire—but with a sublime version of the self, expressed in the repeated claims that when a person stood face-to-face with Diana, she made them feel that they were "the only person in the room" or that "nobody mattered but you." In *God Save the Queen: The Spiritual Dimension of Monarchy*, Ian Bradley quotes the Reverend Dr. Alan Billings in identifying Diana as the world's leading figure in a late-twentieth-century religious movement that is "about people not God, about 'heart' not head, tailored by each individual." It's the search for the "best and true self"—to quote Meghan Markle—that is the commonplace aspiration of many post–World War II westerners. This certainly sounds like an accurate summation of the path Diana trod.

Some have interpreted Diana's spiritual roaming as evidence that she was in freefall, grasping for any branch to cling to. Perhaps, though, never settling on anything in particular was the

His Holiness and Her Royal Highness. Diana at the Vatican with Pope John Paul II, April 1985.

entire point. She flirted with numerous religious traditions—Islam, Catholicism, Kabbalah—but dogma and institutions not only bored and frustrated her, they seemed rather to antagonize her, a tricky state of affairs for someone whose husband and son were both in line to become a head of the Church of England. In a secretly recorded conversation she had with her confidant James Gilbey, her suspicion of church prelates and their orthodoxies is as clear as can be. "He looked horrified," she said of Peter Nott, the Bishop of Norwich, after she'd told him that she was protected in life by the spirits of deceased loved ones. "I thought: 'If he's the bishop, *he* should say that sort of thing.'" Warming to her theme, she challenged his credentials as a spiritual leader, and aggrandized her own: "I understand people's pain, people's suffering, more than you will ever know." Understandably startled, Bishop Nott steered the conversation in a less contentious direction. Diana was delighted: "I thought, 'Ah! Defeated you!'"

Despite—or, perhaps, because of—her pick-and-mix approach to understanding the mysteries of life, death, and the next world, plenty of people have espied a particular religious identity in Diana. Julie Burchill suspects that Diana likely had some distant Jewish heritage, passed down to her in what Burchill asserts are classic traits of Jewish women: "profoundly maternal, disliking horses, strong-nosed, comely, needing too much and giving too much." Hyman Roberts, the chronicler of Diana's adventures in Palm Beach, also believed that a recognizably Jewish ethic ran through Diana's later life, thanks to the charity work she did, the sense of suffering she communicated, and, most tenuously of all, because her friend Lana Marks was Jewish. Here she is again, Diana in her most potent form: Princess of the True Inner Self. Dig deep enough and you'll find a part of Diana that was Jewish, or American, or a republican—or anything else that she wasn't but you are.

A COMMON thread running through many of Diana's unconventional healers is the pride they take in "telling it like it is," perhaps as a means of counteracting accusations of charlatanism. Simone Simmons presents herself to the world as a straight shooter, and there's a relish in her anecdotes about how she treated Diana just like any other client. "I say what I mean, and I mean what I say," she claims to have told Diana. "I've never met anyone like you before" is apparently how Diana responded. "That's because you don't know many real people," Simmons countered. There were occasions when she kept things a little too real for the princess's liking. According to Simmons's recollection, when she warned Diana that "her relationship with a man she was keen on was not going to end in marriage and that everything wasn't going to be hunky-dory," a call from Kensington Palace came through the next day cancelling all their future scheduled appointments.

On the whole, however, Diana seems to have appreciated the bluntness of her healer-friend, and the things that made her one of the "real people." Throughout their friendship, Simmons lived in a flat above a Tesco supermarket in Hendon, northwest London. Simmons says that Diana "wanted to know what was going on in the world 'down on the ground in Tesco's'" and was "fascinated by my life out on the streets"—although that might be adding a little too much color: Simmons was, after all, a practitioner at a Harley Street clinic, not a crack dealer holding down a corner. Even so, the disparities between them perhaps helped their friendship work. "It was sometimes easier for Diana to explain things to me," Simmons reasons, "simply because our other lives were so different." At the peak of their association in the mid-nineties, these two women from vastly different worlds spoke to each other for hours a day, either in person or on the phone, Diana in her palatial surroundings, Simmons in the front room of her flat, the clank of shopping carts and the roar of passing cars playing in the background. In the stories that Simmons tells, Diana unburdened herself and sought advice on just about every topic: health, sex, family, handling the media, and working with the Red Cross. If Diana was fascinated by Simmons's ordinary life, Simmons was astounded by what she describes as Diana's ignorance of the everyday. Supposedly, the princess was in her thirties before she learned how one would go about making a bowl of pasta and tried paying for Simmons's services with a CD player rather than cash. In 1994, Diana told the *Daily Mail* that she didn't know how to use either a parking meter or a payphone. If Simmons's memories are accurate, Diana might have been telling the truth.

Both Diana's birth family and her in-laws have expressed discomfort with Diana's coterie of healers and spiritual advisors. "My sister was aware that I didn't agree with her seeing that much of soothsayers," said Sarah McCorquodale. It was one of the reasons why Diana kept her various circles of friends separate from one another. The accounts that people such as Simmons and Stephen Twigg give of their involvement with Diana are simultaneously detailed and detached: Diana allowed them extensive, intimate access, yet at the same time she held them at arm's length, an impressive feat she managed with all kinds of people. It could be that Diana's reliance on "soothsayers" is one area in which the impression of her as being more royal than the royals is accurate. Monarchy has always been closely tied to not only religion, but mysticism and magic. Simmons's claims of having practiced healing on a young Prince Harry (for what, Simmons doesn't say) evoke Rasputin's purported healing of Prince Alexei, the eldest son of Tsar Nicholas II, a cousin of Elizabeth II's grandfather. Nicholas and Elizabeth's common ancestor Queen Victoria attended seances, and it is thought that a batch of her correspondence that confirmed her interest in speaking to the dead was destroyed lest it embarrass the rest of the family. In her testimony to the coroner's inquiry into Diana's death, Sarah McCorquodale confirmed that she had also destroyed "publications from the aforementioned soothsayers with accompanying letters" to save William and Harry from "anything sensitive or that would be distressing." Even Prince Charles used his ITV interview with Alastair Burnet in 1985 to confirm his interest in parapsychology, but denied reports that he had used a Ouija board to contact his great-uncle Lord Mountbatten, who had died in 1979.

By her own admission, Diana believed she was watched over by her deceased relatives (her paternal grandmother, especially), that she had lived past lives, and that she had certain powers of foresight, though she frequently outsourced the reading of her future to numerous psychics and astrologers. The extent to which she believed what her seers told her is difficult to discern. When Diana's father died in 1992, Betty Palko, who for a while was Diana's favored supernatural intermediary, insisted that she had been visited by the late earl's spirit, carrying a "message of love and understanding" for his youngest daughter, declaring that Diana was destined to radically transform the monarchy and would certainly be queen one day. These purported messages from Johnnie Spencer contradict things that Diana believed her own intuition told her; she stated repeatedly that she never felt she would become queen. As she did with friends and associates who claimed no psychic powers, Diana sought constant guidance from esoteric sources, only to dismiss the vast majority of it if it failed to confirm her own hunches. Patrick Jephson learned to treat the boss's spiritualist interests as a benign indulgence. "My intention, with all these things, was to maintain a pretty jocular atmosphere between us," he says, "because I didn't think she really believed it and I certainly didn't."

That is not the impression Diana gave her crew of occultists. In the summer of 1997, she and Dodi Fayed made headlines when they arrived by helicopter in a Derbyshire village for an impromptu visit to the home of one of her favorite psychics, Rita Rogers, a woman who was described by her local newspaper in the 1990s as having "a big, black bouffant hairdo worthy of an 80's American soap." The previous week, Diana had called Rogers from aboard a yacht in the Mediterranean to consult her on the idea of using Fayed money to open an international chain of hospices in her name. The scene conjures an extraordinary image that exceeds the one of the marathon chats with Simone Simmons: the Princess of Wales on a superyacht with her billionaire playboy boyfriend, seeking guidance about the global advancement of her personal brand from a widow in a Derbyshire mining village. The purpose of the in-person visit of the following week was to allow Dodi to receive a reading, though what Diana said as she went back to the helicopter is Rogers's strongest memory of the day. "I always remember the journey . . . a fox run straight across her feet, and she said, 'Oh dear, Rita, is that bad luck?', you know. She was very afraid of the helicopter journey back." Diana's sensitivity to that possible bad omen was perhaps triggered by a warning that Rogers had given her a couple of years earlier, that "somebody had tampered with the brakes on her car," a seemingly baseless assertion, but one that Rogers said had come through to her from the spirit world and which Diana took to heart.

The astrologers and the psychics, the energy healing and weekly colonics, the cupping therapy, and dowsing—Diana deployed all of it, and lots more besides, on the unending project of healing herself. And relatively little of it was secret. From the late 1980s, publications as diverse as the *National Enquirer* and *The New Yorker* in the US, and *The Sun* and *The Guardian* in the UK published articles about Diana's embrace of the supernatural. "None discreeter than psychic Rita" wrote Chris Hutchins in the *Sunday Mirror*, one of several publications to write about Rita Rogers, referring to her disinclination to talk about her royal client. The astrologer Penny Thornton was more forthcoming. She was trumpeted by her publishers and her employers at *Today* newspaper as astrologer to the Princess of Wales and developed a media reputation as an authority on Charles and Diana. Thornton had first attempted to publish an article that outlined her belief, based on her astrological studies, that Charles would never be king, and that the Waleses' marriage would end in divorce, as early as 1987. She says that she sent the piece to Diana for pre-approval—which was given—but had been unable to find an editor willing to publish it. "Too astrological," she has said, which might be better expressed as "too specious," considering the nature of her predictions, though Thornton states that prominent astrologers had been predicting that Charles wouldn't make the top job since his birth in 1948. Eventually, in November

1988, the *Daily Mail* ran the article, which in Thornton's words, "caused a hurricane of outrage from the serious astrological faction": the Faculty of Astrological Studies was incensed and accused her of sullying the good name of astrology. Soon after, Thornton appeared on the long-running BBC radio program *Loose Ends* to defend her piece, and in subsequent years appeared in other places where her background as Diana's astrological consultant was cited as her qualification to discuss some aspect of the Waleses' affairs. That included an appearance on the ITV series *The Time, The Place* in December 1993, in which she was involved in a debate about Charles's future. By this time, she had fallen foul of Diana, as most of her soothsayers did at some time or another—but the important fact is that the reputation of the future queen was publicly entwined with spiritualism, superstition, and pseudoscience, and it became commonplace to discuss and evaluate her through those same lenses. As the years of Diana's life stretch further away from us, this fact seems increasingly important in allowing us to understand the ways in which she established herself as a unique figure in our culture at a time when royalty retained a patina of magic, but public respect for grand institutions—including spiritual authorities such as the Church of England—and demonstrable truth was waning.

In 1995 Thornton published an account of her association with the princess—a book that Thornton says Diana knew about while they were still on good terms. In *With Love from Diana*, Thornton devotes space to several vivid dreams she had about Diana, all of which she claims were rich with portent. Of two "big dreams" she had in 1989, Thornton describes one which featured Diana, a man named Peter, and a setting by the sea. Based on this, she mused upon some possible biblical significance, an echo of the life of Christ. "Oh, yes," Diana told her, "I was a martyr." The phenomenon of royalty invading their subjects' dreams is as old as royalty itself. The writer Brian Masters believes that Victorian Britons were forever meeting their sovereign in their sleep: "one only has to dip into the vast underground literature of the period to see what importance the old queen had assumed in the fantasy-life of her subjects," he wrote in his 1972 book *Dreams About H.M. the Queen and Other Members of the Royal Family*, which was primarily concerned with the monarch of his era, Elizabeth II. In research for that book, Masters reckons he canvassed a thousand people, roughly a third of whom recalled having dreamt about a member of the House of Windsor. In a great many cases, the dreamlike strangeness came from seeing the queen in very mundane settings: having tea with Elizabeth was a common scenario, and one person dreamt that the whole Windsor clan dropped in for a cuppa on their way to opening a fish-and-chip shop, hitting the mother lode of symbolic everyday Britishness. "Dreams make the distant royals more human," Masters asserts—yet rarely do the dreams in his book present the Windsors as entirely non-royal; the piquancy of the dreams is a kind of magic realist juxtaposition of royal magnificence and quotidian blandness. In one dream, Her Majesty is working as a truck driver but wears her crown while doing so.

It might follow, therefore, that when Diana arrived in the public consciousness nine years later, she was literally a dream version of royalty made flesh. One woman dreamt of the queen playing on a sleigh with the young Prince Edward; "How wonderful," the dreamer told Masters, "the Queen likes playing with her kids, the same as any working-class mum." This is precisely the type of praise that has been lavished on Diana since 1982 and brings to mind the famous image of Diana on the amusement park water rides with Harry and William. Another woman dreamt about the queen throwing snowballs; a third dreamt that Elizabeth barely made her way through a speech, so hampered was she by a fit of the giggles—both things that multiple people, including James Whitaker, recall Diana doing. A decade after Masters's book was published, the Mass Observation project made a specific request of its respondents to tell them about any dreams they had about Diana, so struck were they by the number of people who had mentioned them in their recent submissions. Those dreams often featured the queen, too, and—of course—Her Majesty popping round for tea, but respondent T545f had a typically Dianaist dream about walking down her local high street arm-in-arm with the new princess.

Diana herself placed great import on dreams, and in the last year of her life consulted Joan Hanger, a self-described "straight-talking" and "internationally-respected dream analyst." However, many of the dreams Diana apparently related to Hanger probably don't require a great deal of analysis. During Diana's engagement, according to Hanger, the princess had a frequent nightmare of being stuck on train tracks while Charles and his father tried to pull her free; in another she was abandoned by her mother in the midst of a natural disaster. She also told one in which Charles's crown kept slipping off his head; though to her friend Roberto Devorik, Diana claimed to have had a vivid recurring dream shortly after Harry's birth, in which she was the one whose crown kept falling off during her and Charles's coronation. In fact, Diana told so many people about so many different suggestive or symbolic

The royal touch. Diana among her people,
November 1982.

dreams one wonders how she remembered them all and whether they were all strictly true. Maybe she kept dream diaries, or maybe she embellished or invented some of them as a means of hinting her thoughts and feelings to a particular person, inviting them to interpret the dream for her and tell her what she hoped to hear—either as an exercise in self-assurance or as a test of loyalty.

Among this cornucopia of dreams Diana had a couple which, in retrospect, Hanger believes were probably premonitions of her death. Simone Simmons attests she experienced the same thing. In fact, for an event that seemingly shocked the world, Diana's demise in Paris was apparently foreseen by an awful lot of people. So convinced was the psychic Edward Williams of the princess's impending death that he took his concerns to a police station in Wales on 27 August, four days before the accident.

But more than premonitions, it is the tales of disturbed sleep that have bedded in as the lore of the British public's experience of Diana's death. Rita Rogers says she awoke unexpectedly at one in the morning and flicked on the TV to learn of the car crash. Simone Simmons claims much the same thing. Scattered across the evidentiary record are statements from people who never met Diana but insist they too were disturbed in the early hours, as though some spiritual force had been roused by her misfortune. Just down the road from Althorp in Northamptonshire, a woman named Joyce White woke up at three in the morning, feeling "absolutely freezing cold," or so she claimed in 1999 when asked about her feelings on Diana as part of an oral history project. "So did thousands of others," White said, "people like me who just pick up on *things*." White had never met Diana, but she sounds like a true Dianaist: a witch in a previous life, she believed, she had felt abandoned and unloved as a child, and treated horrifically by her husband, who had once deliberately cut the brakes on her car. She had no time for organized religion, looked within for her strength, and the years of her own strife only confirmed her conviction that she had been put on earth to absorb others' hurt and emit love. "People have been talking to me all my life. They come in and they home in on you, and they'll sort of, 'can you help me?', and they'll unburden themselves to you. . . . Is it a gift? Sometimes it's not! You want to get home and you're tired and somebody stops and you feel you've got to give them a couple of hours of time. . . . You can't turn people away." It could be Diana herself speaking.

IN THE minds of several of those involved in the project of Diana's supposed transformation outlined by Stephen Twigg, not only did her death send a spiritual shockwave across the world, it effected fundamental, irrevocable change. Debbie Frank—another astrologer, whom Diana consulted for the final eight years of her life— certainly believes so, as does Stewart Pearce, who acted as Diana's "voice and presence coach" from late 1995, and whose "spiritual guidance," according to Frank, "was a great catalyst in [Diana's] life, as she emerged into her full glory." Pearce—who lists Eddie Redmayne, Vanessa Redgrave, and Margaret Thatcher among his previous clients—appears sincere in his belief that on the day of Diana's funeral a "gargantuan wave of emotion arose from the heart of the world, moving the planet's magnetic field." Furthermore, "a vast archetypal flow of force arose from our collective mourning," he says, which then "poured into our bodies, literally startling our cells" and moving people across the planet toward a new "empathic wholeness."

Strong stuff, indeed—and it would be easy to dismiss, were it not for the way that such views often seep into mainstream coverage of Diana, and rarely face much scrutiny. To give one example, when Pearce published a book about his relationship with Diana in 2020, it was publicized in various prominent and mainstream places, including in an article on the Katie Couric Media website, in which Pearce outlined certain practical changes he had encouraged Diana to make to her speaking voice, posture, and presentation. The article carries photographs of Pearce, links to the book's Amazon page, an image of the front cover, and claims that Stewart "got to know the princess in a way few did." But it doesn't touch on any of the book's extraordinary assertions, such as that Diana triggered "a seismic shift in global consciousness," that she was "the major voice for change during the nineties," and someone who had been "chosen by divine decree, consecrated not by oil but by providence alone, and esteemed in the people's hearts. These facts cannot be denied." The article also presents a peculiar inconsistency in its account of the time Pearce spent with Diana. To the interviewer—and others—he states that he first met Diana shortly after her conversation with Martin Bashir had broadcast. Yet the article suggests that it was he who coined "queen of everybody's hearts," during a lunch with the princess—despite Diana having already used almost exactly that same form of words to Bashir.

More broadly, there appears to be a high cultural tolerance for overblown statements about Diana's capacities for changing the world with the touch of her hand or the power of her presence. Judging from the sense that Diana had of being born for greatness, having healing powers, being able to see into the past and the future, and to connect with the dead, it is tempting to think that she might have been convinced of it herself. Stewart Pearce appears to agree: in his book he claims that "Diana believed that she was an expression of Divine perfection." The mantle of the wounded healer has been picked up by Diana's youngest son—and he also believes that he and the royal family have it within their gift to transform the spiritual or emotional lives of people around the planet. An overlooked moment from his spate of interviews in 2023 was when Tom Bradby of ITV asked the duke whether he thought the fractured relationships between him and his wife and his birth family could ever be healed. "One hundred percent," he replied: "I genuinely believe, and I hope, that reconciliation between my family and us will have a ripple effect across the entire world. Maybe that's lofty, maybe that's naïve." "Grandiose" or "delusional" might be closer to the mark.

Shortly after that interview, Harry's memoirs were published in which he disclosed that he has sought to connect with Diana through a medium. It appears he believes that he really has made meaningful contact with her, and William, too, is of the opinion that Diana has been actively present in his life; "guiding me," he allegedly told Harry, "setting things up for me." Over the last quarter of a century, there have been any number of people who claim to have been in lengthy, frequent, and profound communication with Diana. Six years after her death, a television channel in the UK screened a séance with the purported intention of speaking with Diana from beyond the grave. *The Spirit of Diana* was broadcast in 2003, the era when conventional TV was still, just about, king. Roughly two years later, YouTube began, an outlet on which the peculiar and the marginal can thrive, and which today hosts a forest of self-proclaimed mediums who profess to be channeling Diana from the other side. There are also dozens of published accounts from those who claim to convey the authentic, authoritative voice of Diana. Some are clearly the works of grifters and pranksters. The short-lived Church of Diana was purportedly based on the word of Diana, as communicated to the church's leader, Richard Yao—Chairman Yao, he called himself—and written down in its foundational text, *Diana Speaks*. Around the turn of the millennium, Yao's church supposedly had seven thousand followers—but the whole thing was almost certainly a satirical hoax, mocking the apparent sanctification of Diana and the dangers of religious fervor.

Plenty of others seem sincere in their belief that the People's Princess had chosen them to spread her voice to the world. In some of these "conversations," Diana talked about personal issues; at other times, she wanted to chat about politics and religion. One consistent theme was the issue of her intelligence and education. In life, she was often ridiculed for a perceived lack of learning, something she was enthusiastically rectifying in the afterlife. "I am spending much time in the wonderful halls of education and knowledge that we have here," she supposedly told one medium; "I wasn't that academically capable in my physical body and I often felt shy and embarrassed with people who were obviously far more intellectual than I was." On the other side, however, she was free from the snobs who mocked her on earth and has become an expert on just about everything. "One has to ask oneself," implored the editor of one medium's account of her discussions with Diana on issues such as religious fundamentalism, global banking, and consciousness, "is this Diana whom critics call under-educated?"

Diana, Autodidact of the Heavens, was also preaching the gospel of self-improvement, self-reliance, and self-discovery— mirroring the projects of so many of the mediums, lots of whom appear to see something of themselves in Diana, that definitive Dianaist trait. Jack Stewart believed he interviewed Diana at length when she manifested herself in his wife, Anne, who stated she had been held back in life, "stifled by snobbery and discrimination." For his part, Jack noted he feels an affinity with Diana because of a dislocated childhood. At one point in the transcript of his conversation with Anne/Diana, he was overwhelmed. "You will forgive me for being slightly emotional . . . I have expected this all my life," he said of connecting with forces beyond this world that would help him make sense of existence; "I have known for decades, but not known how it would manifest." In almost every iteration, the Diana who supposedly speaks to the mediums urges each of us to turn our gaze inwards in our search for fulfilment and enlightenment. As she told one medium in 1999, deploying a very nineties cultural reference, "The truth is not 'out there.' To find the truth you just need to look within."

Again, this esotericism dovetails with an entirely mainstream post-1997 cultural trend of depicting Diana as ethereal and preternatural, someone who always had at least one foot in the world of ghosts and spirits. It's evident in the film *Spencer*, in which Diana seems to be trapped in a haunted house (Sandringham), then rummages through her derelict childhood home (Park House) as though she herself is a ghost. In *The Crown*, her first appearance is a fictional scene in which she is dressed as a tree, her costume for a school production of *A Midsummer Night's Dream*, a play about magic, enchantment, and nobody appearing to be who they really are; her final appearance is as a ghostly vision who appears to Charles just after her death. Showrunner Peter Morgan said this was a "unique way of representing her," though in Mike Bartlett's acclaimed play *King Charles III*, she is like the ghostly Banquo from *Macbeth*, haunting her ex-husband as he attempts to begin his reign. Diana living on after death is a main theme of the novelistic treatments of her, too. In Monica Ali's *Untold Story*, she fakes her own death and surreptitiously reinvents herself on the other side of the globe as an ordinary person; in *Diana: The Ghost Biography* by Emma Tennant and Hilary Bailey, Diana comes back to earth in the form of Sister Julia, a nurse who cares for Harry at Balmoral where he goes to convalesce after a bungee-jumping accident in Bali. Even in the ocean of documentaries that have been made about her—so many dissecting the controversies surrounding her death, or the strangeness of the week that followed—she frequently appears as someone whose life has always, and will always, be defined by her death. *The Princess*, a documentary film of 2022, stitches together her story entirely from archive footage of her life and times; no talking heads, no dramatic reconstruction, no narrator to pull us away from a Diana who we know from the start is dead and gone. It's as though we are being led through her story—the usual folkloric one of the fairytale turned nightmare—by a Dickensian ghost of princesses past.

In the four years of their association, Diana and Simone Simmons fell out repeatedly. The last time was in June 1997, when Simmons had been "excommunicated"—as Sarah McCorquodale describes her sister's habit of banishing the faithful from her retinue—over a perceived indiscretion. In such circumstances, Diana would sometimes even go to the lengths of changing her phone numbers, stranding the undesirable on the wrong side of the moat. Simmons claims she was allowed back in shortly before Diana died, though on the understanding that she wouldn't tell anyone. Simmons didn't ask why, so she claims. "I never questioned Diana."

In the investigations into the princess's death, Simmons stated that Diana had given her for safekeeping a dossier, six inches thick, of explosive information about British involvement in the international arms trade, which she intended to use at some point, naming and shaming those of her compatriots who profited from landmines. Simmons swears she never read it—and neither has anyone else. By Simmons's account, soon after Diana died, she doused it in olive oil and set it alight in her flat, singeing her floor in the process. "If they could bump Diana off, they could bump anybody off," she says by way of explanation. She told the world about the dossier in her 2005 book *Diana: The Last Word,* a follow-up to the more discreet *Diana: The Secret Years* in 1998, both of which Simmons wrote on the pretext that the princess had asked her to tell the world "the truth," should she ever meet a grisly end at the hand of the dark forces arraigned against her. For all the peculiar, unlikely sounding stories that Simmons tells about her friend, her rendering of Diana's personality and character seems sharp and accurate: to be in Diana's presence was life-affirming; she was funny, energetic, and loving; "refreshingly open and interested in everyone around her in an unaffected and outgoing way." Among her flaws, "she could be capricious, found it impossible to keep a secret, and had a tendency to fall out with people over the most trivial of matters. She was also inclined to tell little lies." Diana might have said much the same in return. To Tina Brown, Chris Boffey, news editor of the *Sunday Mirror,* claimed to have paid Simmons thousands of pounds in return for information about Diana's private life. It seems Diana's suspicion about tales she thought Simmons was telling led to their falling out in 1997; not really "the most trivial of matters."

Simmons was not invited to the funeral. When the day came, she walked the short distance from her flat to Hendon Way, to take up a spot among the locals who lined the pavement, waiting for the funeral procession to pass on its way to Althorp. It was a sad, bizarre, and beautiful way to say goodbye to someone she had come to know so well and loved very much.

Ever since, Simmons has said that she is still in regular contact with Diana, whose spirit visits her flat and sometimes conveys opinions about the state of the world, her family, and the monarchy. She occasionally hears her voice in more conventional ways, too: the messages that Diana left on her answering machine cassettes back in the 1990s that she replays from time to time. Her health has suffered in recent years, and she wonders whether her situation might be different had Diana still been alive; whether Diana, with her exceptional generosity and formidable force of will, might have been able to help her in some way; whether with her around, she might not have gotten ill in the first place. Idiosyncratic as she appears, Simmons can tell a tale known to so many in Dianaworld, the strangeness of having a dreamlike princess sweep into the everyday story of one's life, then vanish—though she feels as present as she ever did.

8

Dianaji

Diana in Pakistan, September 1991.

A FTER BEGINNING HER physical and spiritual revitaliza-
tion in the late eighties, Diana grew ever bolder in creating
a royal identity distinct from that of her in-laws—and in
using the levers of the media to antagonize them. In July 1991,
she turned thirty. Earlier that summer, Andrew Morton had published an article in *The Sunday Times* that suggested Diana would
be forced to spend her big day moldering lonely and alone inside
Kensington Palace as her husband was not intending to celebrate
it. The *Daily Mail* retorted with a piece by Nigel Dempster, explaining that Charles had offered to throw his wife a birthday party,
but she'd told him to get lost. As it turned out, Diana's thirtieth
was spent at the Savoy Hotel where she attended a fundraiser for a
children's hospice; a young child with cystic fibrosis was given the
honor of helping the princess blow out the candles on her specially
presented cake. Now fully aware of the power of her public profile
and the media's inexhaustible interest in her, she was laying down
rakes everywhere for Charles to step on while she sauntered ahead,
presenting herself as dutiful, demotic, and endlessly caring.

Beyond the petty point scoring, Diana made substantive
efforts to spread her roots in foreign soil by taking her reimagined royal touch on the road, especially in places that had once
been colonies of the British Empire—from New York to New
Delhi and in Pakistan, which in the autumn of 1991 was the
location of her first official solo tour. "I am a humanitarian"
is what Ken Wharfe remembers her saying in advance of the
trip. "I want to touch the people and I want them to touch me,"
she told him, a classic Dianaism, so lacking in ironic gloss that
it sounds close to parody. The Pakistan tour "was her chance
to establish the caring Diana brand," says Wharfe, though he
insists that his use of the word "brand" should not lead anyone
to doubt her sincerity. "This wasn't a cynical move," he avows,
"it came from the heart," as though there were always a clear

distinction between the two. In the royal family, public duty and private feeling are, virtually by definition, mixed in messy, complex ways. That was even more so with Diana, in whom the consciously self-serving and the instinctively selfless seemed so often to operate in fluid tandem.

Whatever her motivations, Diana's tactile style of international diplomacy proved hugely popular in Pakistan. "Lahore was a cauldron," Ken Wharfe recalls. "The crowds were huge, six or seven persons deep on both sides of the road." Of course, it was a tightly planned trip, minimizing the chances of her encountering anything other than beaming adoration—still, Diana proved immensely popular, and was feted everywhere she went. Newspapers back home published reams about the apparently mesmerizing impact she was having on her hosts. One story quoted the Pakistani government official Mahbub Ahmad hailing Diana as "the ideal, model mother for the Pakistan family planning programme." Ahmad, whose duties involved attempting to slow his nation's birth rate, which was among the highest in the world, said there were plans to produce posters reminding women that Princess Diana had only two children. One might imagine myriad reasons why Diana's example wouldn't be all that instructive to women in Karachi or Islamabad. Yet Ahmad's utterance demonstrates Diana's vast cultural reach.

For the remaining six years of her life, Diana's association with Pakistan would intensify privately and publicly. For many Pakistanis—and other South Asian people, too—the connection would likewise take deep root. It's not that she was universally adored or glorified; rather, her story—its mythic qualities magnified by her royalty, the power of the mass media, and the mercurial nature of her personal qualities—found resonances among populations everywhere. Thus, Diana, the pale English rose celebrated for strengthening the Windsor monarchy with the DNA of her indigenous British ancestors, coexisted with Diana, the postimperial princess whose image transcended all kinds of social barriers, real and imagined.

*   *   *

NEVER WAS the domestic adulation of Diana so complete as when she was on the other side of the world. Organs of the British media documented her popularity abroad with an embarrassing neediness. It was as if the very things that Diana sought from the crowds—the affection she was unable to get from her family; the esteem she found lacking in herself—were being passed on to the nation she represented, confirmation that Britain was still loved and admired around the world.

In May 1986, BBC One aired *Most Honoured Guests*, a documentary about the Waleses' six-day trip to Japan, a hub of Dianamania. The program, and the surrounding coverage in tabloid and broadsheet newspapers told the British public just how hard the Japanese had fallen for the Princess of Wales, detailing the recently released TV shows and books about her, as well as the "Diana robot doll" that was on sale in Japanese department stores, alongside Diana-inspired clothing lines, ceramic Diana figures, Diana-themed phone cards, a Diana comic strip that was being published in a Japanese newspaper, and a Tokyo pinball parlor that had changed its name to The Diana. The impact of the trip to Japan led to some talk in the papers that Diana had launched a new fashion craze for kimonos in the UK. The *Birmingham Evening Mail* claimed to have found one young woman who said that she would swap her usual tracksuits for traditional Japanese dress thanks to Diana's example: "it makes you FEEL like a Princess," she said after trying on a kimono for the first time.

Thirty years earlier, Diana's father had accompanied Elizabeth II as she toured the Commonwealth of Nations (the entity that emerged from the husk of the British Empire) to project not just her identity as a new monarch for a new era, but the personification of a nation with a new role on the world stage. Instead of embodying imperial rule, the young queen was envisioned as its antithesis. While in New Zealand, Elizabeth declared that "the Commonwealth bears no resemblance to empires of the past. It is an entirely new conception built on the highest qualities of the spirit of man: friendship, loyalty, and the desire for freedom and peace." On her foreign trips, Diana said little that was broadcast or reported, but her presence was routinely interpreted by the British news media as an extension of those things the twenty-something Elizabeth had transmitted to a previous generation. When Diana visited Oman at the end of 1986, the *Sunday Express* weirdly hailed her impact on the region as "a healthy smack in the yashmak," so gloriously did she represent the enlightened values of modern, postimperial Britain.

Powerful though that representation could be, Diana's mythology proved remarkably protean. Around the world, Diana and the narratives that formed around her were recast, poured into molds that had deep significance to the indigenous culture. The United States offers the best known example, with Diana's experiences being viewed through the legends of Marilyn Monroe and Jacqueline Kennedy. Such is America's cultural sway that the "Candle in the Wind" vision of Diana would quickly assume substantial prominence, though not ubiquity. In parts of the Vietnamese media, for instance, Diana's life and death was explored through Kieu, the female character at the center of a classic work of Vietnamese epic poetry who sacrifices herself for the good of her family by marrying a much older man who mistreats her horrifically and forces her into prostitution. This tendency to see Diana not as an update of a previous Princess of Wales or as a reincarnation of one of her famous Spencer forbears, but as a parallel to someone from a cultural background far removed from her own came as a surprise to some as the crowds of mourners, in London and elsewhere, began to amass on 31 August 1997 once the news of her death was announced. Reporting from the British Embassy in Washington DC, Mary Dejevsky for *The Independent* noted the heterogeneity of the people who turned up to sign the book of condolence: straight and gay, young and old, and "most extraordinarily of all, in this very white part of Washington, is the proportion of blacks and Hispanics for whom upper Massachusetts Avenue is alien territory." The same was true, she felt, of the scene outside the hospital in which Diana had died, where "there were more black people than you would see in most Paris crowds."

"Most people with a Black mum or auntie know that the love for Princess Di is almost unquestioned," says the writer Banseka Kayembe of the affinity for Diana felt among Black British women. Distant though she was in so many ways, Kayembe believes that Diana lived a high-status, establishment version of what many Black women in the UK experience, "a feeling of 'otherness,' being in an environment that is often unwelcoming if not downright hostile." This was especially true for older women "who suffered unimaginable hurdles. Diana's situation, though different, felt oddly relatable." Speaking on the BBC radio program *Woman's Hour* around the twentieth anniversary of Diana's death, the writer and editor Charlie Brinkhurst-Cuff voiced a note of skepticism, arguing that "princess culture" and the beauty myths associated with it have often excluded rather than embraced Black women. Participating in that same broadcast was the curator Chaédria LaBouvier, who spoke about Diana's popularity among Black American women, at least part of which LaBouvier attributed to Diana's sense of style. "She wasn't just well-dressed, she was bad, you know, she had a walk, she had a style, she had a look," which LaBouvier said set Diana apart in the minds of Black women as someone they could identify with and perhaps aspire to emulate. "I never grew up wanting to be Jennifer Aniston. . . . Diana was one of the few white women that black American women felt was truly a peer." The writer Ashley C. Ford expresses a similar sentiment when describing the adoration that her Black American grandmother had for Diana and the period of mourning she entered following the princess's death: "My entire life she had loved reading about Diana and discussing the woman's life with her friends. . . . Before her, British royalty seemed weird and outdated. She modernized it. And who do you know that thinks of themselves as modern princesses and queens more than Black women that age?"

As part of his TV show in 1998, Chris Rock riffed on the notion that Diana, Princess of Wales, was a heroine to African American people. To mark the first anniversary of her death, Rock said, "We wanted to know how the public is actually coping with the loss of the People's Princess. So we asked the people: the people of Harlem." Out on 125th Street, Rock teased those he spoke to by telling them that plans were afoot to rename a boulevard in Diana's honor—nobody thought that was a good idea—and then went into a wig shop for a Diana makeover. In an art gallery, the owner pulled out the one portrait of Diana he had, an exact copy of a photo taken by Lord Snowdon of the princess in the Queen Mary tiara and a very eighties pink ballgown, except this painting—the owner made sure to point out—showed Diana with dark brown skin. The studio audience reacted with a mixture of laughter and applause. Mocking as Rock was, it was all in good fun; the message was summed up by the young man who brought the segment to a close: "We support you, you get much love out of Harlem. . . . Big up, baby!"

DIANA'S LIFE took place during a time of a transformation of the UK's engagement with the rest of the world and a large increase in the nation's ethnic minority population. Yet the royal family continued to be regarded—proudly so, in some quarters—as a vestige of a glorious imperial past, and definitively white. Among those British families that Michael Billig and Marie Kennedy interviewed in the 1980s, there was unanimous agreement that having non-white people within the Windsor family was unthinkable; there was no way that Charles could have gotten engaged to a teenage girl who was Black, Chinese, or even Greek, said one young man, perhaps unaware of Prince Philip's origins.* Not that the interviewees themselves had a problem with ethnic diversity, they insisted. It was just that they didn't think the royals would stand for it, nor the population at large. One woman dismissed the very notion with

---

* Other than one family Billig refers to as West Indian, all the people interviewed appear to have been white.

brutal clarity: "they'll marry different nationalities, but coloured no. . . . I think they'd scrub them to get them clean, bleach them."

The social world from which Diana emerged was not one of great racial or ethnic diversity. A flurry of newspaper stories was generated in the mid-1980s (and again in 2012, when the story was rediscovered by various news outlets) by the revelation that one of Diana's great-great-great-great-grandmothers was Eliza Kewark, an ethnic-Armenian woman from Mumbai. In her 1992 biography of Diana, Lady Colin Campbell wrote that Kewark's story, combined with the fact that one of Prince William's godparents—the pale-skinned, blue-eyed Tally Westminster—was descended from the African great-grandfather of the nineteenth-century poet Alexander Pushkin, "should be reassuring for the ethnic minorities to know that their blood also flows in the veins of some of the grandest families in the land," though why they should be reassured, and about what, she doesn't say. "Foreigners are funny," declared *The Sloane Ranger Handbook*, that tongue-in-cheek anthropological study of the London set of the 1980s to which Diana belonged. "Nothing is funnier than a funny voice, particularly an Indian voice." Diana herself was known to have been amused by accents unlike her own and—without malice—enjoyed imitating them. Prince Harry seemingly followed her lead. According to Ken Wharfe, on one of Diana's attempts to introduce her sons to the "normal" world, Harry sat on a London bus waggling his head and loudly saying, "Bud bud ding ding," a common playground taunt of the day, in mockery of the Pakistani driver. Harry was only seven years old at the time, and Wharfe says Diana took the children off the bus after a few stops, apologizing to the driver as they went. Some years later, Harry was filmed using an explicitly racist insult against a Pakistani fellow cadet at Sandhurst. Clearly contrite about the incident, he wrote in his memoir that until the footage was made public in 2009, he was unaware that the word in question was a slur, assuming that it was "like Aussie. Harmless." It's difficult to imagine someone of his generation being that ignorant—but perhaps it simply reveals the bubble that was his upbringing.

The incident with Harry and the Pakistani bus driver took place in the spring of 1992, by which time Diana had cultivated an interest in the spiritual traditions of Asia and the Middle East, part of her search for emotional and physical healing. A seminal moment in the connection that Diana was to form with South Asia came when she met with Professor Akbar Ahmed, an expert on Islam's relationship with the West. At Diana's request Professor Ahmed gave a lecture on Islam at the Royal Anthropological Institute in London in September 1990, and gave her a further briefing at Kensington Palace ahead of her five-day trip to Pakistan in 1991. Ahmed gave Diana a copy of his book *Living with Islam* (which was adapted into a six-part BBC TV series in 1993) and was thrilled to see photographs of her holding it in several British newspapers the following day.

In his memoirs, Ahmed talks of the princess in explicitly spiritual terms: "a bridge builder between faiths. . . . Diana exuded a translucent glow that was touched by an undefined spirituality and it embraced and uplifted me." In conversation he is even more effusive: "Superwoman, like these Marvel characters," is how he describes her at one point; "like a Sufi, like a mystic" at another; "an almost saintly figure . . . an extraordinary human figure who was growing by leaps and bounds and whose presence was deeply spiritual." If this sounds like a romantic exaggeration, Ahmed politely suggests that her compatriots have always struggled to grasp Diana's true significance as a temporal leader with a spiritual calling. "I felt 'this is a soul in search of a road' . . . [but] the British public being what the British public is, and British journalists being what the British journalist is, they did not see this at all, so they were reducing it all the time to bulimia and vomiting and all the sordid aspects of the human flesh." Looking back on the nineties, those years between the collapse of the Soviet Union and the shock of 9/11, Ahmed believes that the "pendulum was moving steadily and visibly toward closing the gap between Islam and the West," and the Waleses were playing an important role in that process. In Ahmed's view, Charles belonged to the lofty tradition of Frederick

II, Holy Roman Emperor, and Alfonso X of Castile because of his commitment to learning and spiritual enrichment. He describes a speech the then Prince of Wales made in Oxford, October 1993, on the subject of Islam and the West as being "an event of great historic significance," making a case for putting Islamic tradition at the center of Western civilization. The prince and princess were two sides of the same coin, says Ahmed. Where Diana "saw God through nature and through love and through the ordinary person," Charles sees it "as an intellectual, as a scholar, through the head." In this sense, perhaps the Waleses were a match made in heaven after all; whether either of them quite measured up to Professor Ahmed's estimation is another matter.

The response to Diana's five days in Pakistan was feverish; huge crowds of the excited and the curious came out to catch sight of her as she moved around the country. Her escort on the trip, the Pakistani cabinet minister Seyeda Abida Hussain, told Diana's biographer Kate Snell how beguiled she was by the princess—though she worried that Diana was cultivating a romantic idealization of what Diana thought of as Muslim masculinity, "great macho men" as Hussain put it, "the strong Muslim patriarchal type" who are "protective towards women." Diana pointed out how attractive she found Pakistani men who, to her, appeared to be unusually tall, elegant, and handsome. She said the same to friends back in London. "Aren't they a good-looking race?" she remarked to Natalie Symons when watching Pakistani films at Kensington Palace.

If there was some exotification going on here, it didn't appear that way to many British Muslims and British Asians who were buoyed by the connection she forged with Pakistan. Now a practicing GP working in East London, in the 1990s Attiya Khan was a teenager (from an Indian Muslim family) and recalls a feeling that Muslims in Britain at the time were thought of in polarizing terms, either disruptive and intrusive or silent and invisible. That echoes criticisms that were made at the time of broadcast about a controversial 1993 *Panorama* investigation called "Underclass in Purdah," which reported on what was claimed to be a crisis among the (mainly Muslim) Pakistani and Bangladeshi populations in the cities of Birmingham and Bradford, afflicted by poverty, low academic attainment, and religious extremism. Diana never engaged in debates about anything as contentious as that. However, when she was photographed wearing shalwar kameez, or reading about Islam, and—perhaps most significantly—was known to have close relationships with Muslim men, in Khan's view she made a welcome contribution to filling the void that existed between the two poles of invisible and vilified, even if all she did was share a little of her own her hypervisibility. The writer Yasmin Choudhury is emphatic about what Diana represented: "In a country where immigrant women were solely visible when subjected to bigotry, Diana made them feel truly seen."

Yasmin and Jaffer Kapasi, a Muslim couple from Leicester, felt this in a small way when they met Diana at a garden party at Buckingham Palace in 1992. A few years later, Jaffer fondly recalled the moment Diana approached his wife—who was wearing a "Muslim veil"—and said, "I like your outfit, that's why I've come to say hello"; not at all the "smack in the yashmak" that the *Sunday Express* thought Diana delivered in the presence of Muslims. "We meet people like that," Jaffer said about life in Britain, "who are kind enough to come and talk because we are different," though they too were accustomed to feeling invisible at times: "When we came to Leicester, for example, our neighbor didn't speak to us for nearly three years." Despite thriving in the UK and believing that "British people are very tolerant compared to all the other races in the world," he admitted that "I always have this feeling in my mind that I don't really belong here."

IN FEBRUARY 1992, Diana's sense of spiritual mission strengthened during time she spent at Mother Teresa's hospice in Kolkata, India. Paul Burrell gives his impression of the scene: "She went to each bedside, and offered everyone a box of chocolates. One man was so weak with tuberculosis that she placed a chocolate in his mouth for him." That moment was captured by the photographer Jayne Fincher—who was among the many representatives of the British press who followed Diana to the hospice—and reproduced in Fincher's book *Diana: Portrait of a Princess*. The princess's compassion and good intentions cannot be questioned. Even so, these are uncomfortable images, made all the more so by the accompanying text that suggests she was performing an act of heroic sacrifice: "Without regard for her designer pink dress, which was covered in dirt from the bare walls, she visited every one of the 50 patients." In another of Fincher's photographs, Diana is pictured in Hyderabad "warmly greeting India's lowest of the low, the Untouchables, who flung themselves at Diana's feet." In that shot, she is dressed in all-white and gold earrings, a similar outfit to that which she wore a year later when visiting a refugee camp in Zimbabwe; in front of the cameras, Diana doled out food to a line of waiting children. If looking simply at the photos in isolation, maybe one could argue that this is Diana, the People's Princess, transcending race, class, nationality, and all the other constructions of identity that we jam ourselves into. But the conjunction of the images and the purple prose—representative of so much media coverage of the royal family—gives us Diana the white savior: the heavenly princess illuminating benighted corners of the world with her magical luminescence.

To her friend and spiritual advisor Oonagh Shanley-Toffolo, Diana said her visit to Mother Teresa's hospice instilled in her a desire "to be part of all this on a global scale," a grand ambition she was still discussing with friends in the week of her own death. It was through Shanley-Toffolo that Diana met Hasnat Khan, the man with whom Diana enjoyed what was perhaps the deepest, most intimate—and, in many ways, the most conventional—romantic relationship she ever had. Khan was working as a heart surgeon at the Royal Brompton Hospital when Diana came to visit one of his patients, Shanley-Toffolo's husband, Joseph. Diana was instantly smitten, and in short order, the two began a secretive relationship which ran for roughly eighteen months between late 1995 and the beginning of the summer of 1997, and included—to

Khan's exasperation—a solo trip by Diana to meet his family in Pakistan where she hoped to convince them that she would make a suitable marriage match. It was a risky strategy which brought the relationship to public notice and sharpened Khan's focus. While Diana urged him to give up his job and join her in her mission to heal "those who suffer or . . . require light in their dark existences," Khan realized there was no way that he could live as the significant other of the world's most famous person—even if his rather conservative family were to give their blessing to the relationship.

For the British comedian Shazia Mirza, Diana's relationship with Khan seemed almost an inevitability, the final step in what was an impossibly glamorous, grandiloquent version of an existence with which she was intimately familiar. Mirza's father was raised in Rawalpindi, while her mother was born in India shortly before the Partition of India and grew up in Lahore. They married in the 1960s, after which they moved to the UK, settling in Birmingham. Among Pakistanis in the part of Birmingham in which she was raised, Mirza remembers that there was always strong interest in the royal family, which seemed to more closely resemble traditional family structures found in Pakistani, and other South Asian, communities than did the majority of families in wider white British society. In particular, Charles and Diana's wedding was a moment of celebration in her neighborhood: "It was great," she recalls, "really fun, people were really happy." And to the older generation, it seemed less like an outlandish fairytale and more like a lavish version of something that was familiar to their own lives: "having a white man and a white woman having an arranged marriage . . . it endorsed what they had always been doing," says Mirza. "It's okay now, because Diana's doing it." When the marriage frayed so utterly and so publicly, it reinforced the bond for a lot of women who recognized the pattern. Speaking to the journalist Unzela Khan in 2020, another British Asian woman said that seeing Diana go through "the emotional turmoil Asian women experience simply validated our own struggles. It was our reality being played out in a culture which is seen to be 'progressive'" and exposed the "backwardness of the higher class."

Surely, far from everyone from a Pakistani—or any other South Asian—background felt positively about either Diana or the Windsors. But Mirza talks as though many women in her orbit in the eighties and nineties were not just hugely interested in Diana but regarded her as someone who lived their lives in a parallel universe, and with whom they had a kind of personal relationship. Her mother, she says, had her hair styled like Diana, as did many of her peers, and they would look for "a green-and-white spotty dress, because that's what Diana had" or have shalwar kameez made using colors and designs that Diana had been seen wearing in her western wardrobe. They would read about the princess and her friend Jemima Khan, the British wife of the Pakistani cricketer and politician Imran Khan, in Urdu-language publications such as the *Daily Jang*, and when they learned of Diana's reliance on psychics and fortune tellers, this too struck a chord; Mirza's mother frequently visited a palm reader who apparently delivered spookily accurate readings. Among family and friends in Islamabad and Lahore, Diana's relationship with Hasnat Khan was known about relatively early on and became a topic of frequent discussion and speculation; "*everyone* knew and talked about it constantly." That Diana was seeing a Pakistani doctor was the ultimate confirmation that "she was one of us . . . she was doing what every Asian daughter was meant to do: marrying an Asian doctor."

THE PERIOD in which Diana's personal links with Pakistan deepened coincided with a moment when South Asian culture began to break into mainstream British popular culture in an unprecedented way, across television, film, pop music, and literature. At the vanguard was *Goodness Gracious Me*, a radio sketch show created by and starring a cast of British Indian actors that soon transferred, with huge success, to television. The title, which references a song from the film *The Millionairess* in which Peter Sellers plays an Indian doctor, set the tone for the series in which stereotypes are playfully skewered, prejudices ridiculed, and roles reversed. Around the same time there was also a trend for South Asian clothes, especially among women, for which Diana and Jemima Khan were contributing factors. "Shalwar kameez: how will you wear yours?" asked

Diana wearing shalwar kameez during a hospital visit in Lahore, Pakistan, May 1997.

The Independent newspaper in July 1996. "Jemima and Diana started it," the subhead announced. "Now Eastern clothes are working their way into everyone's wardrobe," though "everyone" might have been a bit of a stretch. The proprietor of one of the ritzy London shops featured in the article frankly admitted "I don't have Indian people shopping here. . . . They probably have their own designers."

Diana, of course, *did* have her own designers, including Ritu Kumar from whose Mayfair boutique she bought the blue shalwar kameez that she was photographed wearing on a trip to Pakistan in 1997. Yet her presence was felt in less exclusive places, too. A June 1997 edition of the *Ealing Leader* included an article promoting a shop in the modest London suburb of Hanwell that specialized in shalwar kameez. "Look like a princess," read the copy, which gave details about the shop and explained for the uninitiated what a shalwar kameez is. Next to it was a photograph of Diana wearing the blue outfit designed by Kumar. Here was Diana being used to steer suburban British women, of all ethnicities, toward South Asian fashion—yet it was also the opinion of Kiki Siddiqui, who ran Ritu Kumar's boutique, that by being seen wearing these garments Diana also "made a lot of Asian women take pride in their wardrobe."

Plenty of British Asian women would push back on that. Indeed, in the nineties many people expressed irritation and unease at the way London's rich and famous were wearing their cultural heritage as a means of exotifying themselves. In the edition of *The Face* that ran a tribute to Diana in September 1997, there was a letter from a young Asian man from Middlesex who took exception to the magazine's recent feature on the popularity of Asian dress. Seeing pop stars or princesses in bindis and shalwar kameez didn't gratify him at all: "It doesn't mean that society has become more tolerant," he argued, and it would not help people from backgrounds like his "become accepted." Britain was not in the midst of a cultural sea change, this letter writer felt, but messing about with fancy dress.

When it came to Diana, scorn of that kind was rarely found

in *Eastern Eye*, the country's foremost English-language newspaper for British South Asians, though undeniable notes of irony and skepticism accompanied the paper's coverage of what turned out to be the final weeks of her life. Her adventures that summer—from consoling victims of landmines in Angola and Bosnia to luxuriating aboard the yachts of billionaires—preoccupied every million-selling tabloid on the market, and most of the so-called quality papers, too. But the *Eastern Eye* perspective on Diana was unique.

August 1997 was a hugely significant month for the people of India and Pakistan, and their diasporas: the fifteenth of the month marked the fiftieth anniversary of the Partition of India, the moment in 1947 when the British Raj was formally dissolved and the two independent states of India and Pakistan came into being; a moment of joy and optimism—but also of rancor, dislocation, and bloodshed. All four of *Eastern Eye*'s August editions featured items that engaged with the legacies of the empire, partition, and independence. The monarchy was at the heart of various stories, such as a demand to remove the Koh-i-Noor diamond from the Queen Mother's crown and return it to India, and a call for Elizabeth to cancel her planned tour of India unless an apology was issued for the Amritsar massacre of 1919. Then there was the name that came up time and again: Mountbatten, the uncle of Prince Philip and Charles's beloved mentor who had personally overseen partition and who, many believe, had acted with such recklessness and incompetence that he hastened and exacerbated the dreadful violence that accompanied the birth of India and Pakistan as they are known today.

The soap opera of Diana's love affairs was dotted around these weighty stories, usually with a wry acknowledgment of how embarrassing it was for the Windsors to see Diana smooching her new boyfriend aboard a yacht and berating a group of photographers while astride a Jet Ski. In *Goodness Gracious Me* there is a recurring character who claims virtually everyone and everything—from Superman to Jesus—as Indian at heart. Nobody in *Eastern Eye* went quite that far, but the notion that Diana was living some form of South Asian life was often raised. For example, a week before the official anniversary arrived, a reader's tongue-in-cheek letter praised Diana for her sterling efforts in promoting India and Pakistan at this special time, thanks to her association with various men: Hasnat Khan, Gulu Lavlani (an Indian British businessman with whom Diana was romantically linked), and the Hinduja brothers, the UK's two wealthiest people. The correspondent said he was happy to report that he had consulted a fortune teller who assured him that this summer Diana would land herself a dashing "Eastern prince" and swap her Princess of Wales title for something with a much nicer ring: "Raj Kumari Diana ji of Southallpur."* When Dodi Fayed's ex-fiancée Kelly Fisher publicly denounced him for two-timing her with Diana and began legal proceedings for breach of promise, the acerbic columnist Thufayel Ahmed suggested we should stop calling the Diana saga a soap opera and start thinking of it as a Bollywood epic instead, with the lead role of Diana played by Madhuri Dixit, a superstar of Indian cinema. Ahmed also expressed disappointment that Diana had—so it seemed at the time—dumped Hasnat Khan for Dodi Fayed. Shazia Mirza remembers her Pakistani relatives feeling the same way. *She's wasting her time with this playboy; it's obvious that she really loves Hasnat.*

The first edition following Diana's fatal accident was published the day before her funeral. "United in grief" was how the paper summed up the British South Asian response. Quite how fairly this reflected the thoughts and feelings of what was, by definition, a very broad range of people and identities, is all but impossible to gauge. Nevertheless, the scenes depicted certainly suggest widespread sympathy and upset. A candlelit vigil in Southall Park attracted hundreds of residents; South Asian radio and TV stations were flooded with calls professing love for Diana, sorrow and out-

---

* The suffix "ji" is used in numerous South Asian languages as a term of respect. Southall, in west London, has long been home to a large South Asian community.

rage at the nature of her passing. "Diana genuinely cared for the Asian community" was the opinion of Avtar Lit, the head of Sunrise Radio; "she made us feel part of the wider British community." Again, Diana's life—and now her death—was interpreted as a story that had taken place within South Asian society: the queen was the demanding mother-in-law, and "the unseen auntiji was the media." *Eastern Eye* canvassed the opinions of eight prominent British South Asian women. Meera Syal, one of the stars of *Goodness Gracious Me*, noted how surprised she was by Diana's popularity in India; one women's magazine had named her "woman of the century." She too reckoned that Diana was so embraced by South Asian Britons because she was "essentially a 'daughter-in-law,'" but one who rebelled against familial tradition and the "out-dated commitments that come with it." That held a particular appeal to second-generation immigrants who may have felt caught between conflicting expectations of family and wider society. It was not only South Asians in nineties Britain who may have felt that way about her. When the *Royally Obsessed* podcast recently held a giveaway contest, they asked listeners to write in with an explanation of why they should receive one of the reissued black-sheep sweaters. The entries included one from a twenty-six-year-old woman who said that as a second-generation Indian Canadian she had always felt like a black sheep in her family, wanting to do right by her heritage, but also striving to build a niche for herself as an individual—just like Diana, she said.

But even amidst the eulogizing in *Eastern Eye*—one reader called Diana the "world's true Koh-i-Noor"—the paper found space for dissenting voices. Hard Kaur, the rapper and singer who moved from India to Britain as a child, was depressed that so many South Asian women in Britain looked to Diana and Jemima Khan as their guiding lights when they could be idolizing Benazir Bhutto and the legendary Indian singer Lata Mangeshkar instead. "If there's one thing we could learn from Diana," she said, "it's that you've got to be proud of who you are, even when there's people around you telling you you ain't good enough."

*   *   *

IN AUGUST 1997, the theatre director Jatinder Verma was touring the UK with "a tragic tale of love from India . . . about a princess who chooses to marry a commoner" and is then murdered by her father for bringing shame on the family. He wondered whether some of the British South Asian mourning for Diana was a legacy of empire, a susceptibility to the inherited notion of white, blonde, aristocratic superiority. Yet like so many others, he also thought the myth of Diana resonated with people who felt not entirely at home in the UK. "Being visible and invisible is inherent in the contemporary Asian experience in Britain," he explained. "Perhaps it was this ambivalence that we saw echoed in Diana: a princess, but not quite of the blue-blood Windsor variety." Then there were the Muslim boyfriends and, he pointed out, even Martin Bashir, the conduit for her televisual roasting of the royal family, was Asian.

When Verma and his colleagues first heard the news of Diana's death, their instinctive response was to assume that she had been bumped off by the Grey Men. The idea of a conspiracy took off across the world among communities with a deep distrust of the British establishment. Ultimately, the flag bearer of the conspiracy theories was Mohamed Al-Fayed, the father of Dodi, who died alongside Diana in the accident. Furious and grieving over the loss of his son, Al-Fayed felt insulted by the Windsors' attempts to distance their family from his in the weeks and months that followed the awful events in Paris. To Al-Fayed, it capped decades' worth of racist slights from the toffee-nosed elite who were happy to accept his cash but refused to accept him into their club. In 2008, he gave evidence at the inquest into Diana and Dodi's deaths and gave vent to his indignation that after decades of buying castles, and football clubs, and beloved department stores, of praising Her Majesty, and taking tea at four, he still found himself out in the cold: "I lived here for 40 years, I give my life to the country, I pay billions in taxes, I employ hundreds of thousands of people. . . . How can I be treated this way? . . . You think it is fair that you don't give me a passport? I do not need the passport. I am proud to be Egyptian, the cradle of civilization." He insisted throughout that not only had Diana been madly in love with his son, but that she was pregnant with his child, hence why the establishment wanted her dead. Hasnat Khan? "He was just a friend . . . how can she marry somebody like that, who lives in a council flat and has no money?" And what about Kelly Fisher, the woman Dodi cheated on when he was with Diana? "Just a hooker." Outbursts like that didn't do much to endear him to the public. Though here, too, some discern a deep-rooted prejudice: in the eyes of white Britain, Hasnat Khan was held up as the "good Muslim," quiet, humble, and invisible; Al-Fayed was the "bad Muslim," loud, brash, and unapologetically on display.

Al-Fayed confirmed in court that he believed Prince Philip was "not only a racist but is, in truth, a Nazi as well," and gave the impression that the Windsors—like every other branch of the establishment—were an active block on his attempts to be accepted as truly British. Nevertheless, the royal family have long been a locus of British identity for many immigrants. "Like a lot of immigrants that came over in the sixties and seventies," says Shazia Mirza of her parents, "they were obsessed with the royal family because they felt that's what made them British: the royal family." On Wellington Terrace, a stone's throw from Kensington Palace, Café Diana has become a local institution since it opened in 1989. In most ways, it's a very ordinary London "caff," to use the British term: a café serving a mixture of British greasy spoon fare (full English breakfasts, fried egg sandwiches, mugs of milky tea), American coffees, and falafel, halloumi, baba ghanoush, and other staple flavors of the Middle East. What makes Café Diana different is that its walls are plastered with pictures of Diana. No matter which of its red pleather benches you sit on, those famous doe eyes are watching. The place has had a makeover in recent years which gives it the bright countenance of a theme café—a quainter, camper Planet Hollywood, perhaps—but at the start of the century, it had the feel of something between a shrine and a stalker's dining room, so crowded was it with Diana's presence. The proprietor is Abdul Basit Daoud, originally from Iraq but proudly British for many years. Daoud moved to London not long before Diana did, as a student in 1977, the year of Elizabeth II's Silver Jubilee. He had always been very aware of the royal family; he believes that for most Iraqis of his generation, Elizabeth II defined how they viewed Britain. Support for the monarchy is fundamental to his sense of Britishness. "I am a royalist," he says. "I am patriotic. You live on the ground where you are, that is my philosophy on life. You can't have split loyalties."

Yet for Daoud, Diana represented something different. According to him, when he first planned to open his café, he had no idea that the princess lived so close; he was planning on calling the place after himself until he saw police stopping the traffic to allow Diana's car to pass on the way to dropping Harry and William off at school. When Diana learned that a new local eatery had been opened in her honor, she paid a visit and gifted a photograph of herself which Daoud hung on the wall. Over the years, he acquired one or two more photos; it was only after she died that he made the decision to cover every wall with her image. He concedes that naming the café after her was a smart business move. "Putting her name on the café has helped a lot, because between '89 and '90 there was a big recession. . . . Notting Hill became a ghost town; one shop after another was empty," but the café which bore Diana's name stayed open. Today, people come from all over the world to see the café; it's a spot on the unofficial Diana tours of the UK. Speaking in 2021, Daoud said it was his dream to expand the business internationally, opening cafés under Diana's name in much the same way that there are pubs named after Queen Victoria everywhere in the world where there are thirsty Anglophiles. Turning Diana into a global franchise would pose a few ethical questions, but it's a neat idea: the London caff of the 2020s captures something about modern Britain just as traditional pubs reflected the nation in the years immediately after Victoria's death.

The summer before Diana's funeral, England hosted the men's

European Football Championship, an event that is often looked back upon as an important moment in the fashioning of modern Englishness—though that's not how everyone felt about it. *The Sunday Telegraph* reported from a pub in south London, most of whose regulars were Black English people, many of whom felt so excluded from the flag-waving patriotism that was washing over much of the nation that they had chosen to support Germany instead. A year later, there was endless talk of how different the crowds at Kensington Palace were from those who had been at Wembley Stadium the previous summer. In his introduction to *Empire Windrush: Fifty Years of Writing About Black Britain*, published in 1998, Onyekachi Wambu bestowed upon Diana a transcendental power of sorts; her multiracial mourners "seemed genuinely to want to confront the past and liberate themselves from it . . . acknowledging that they were comfortable with the body suit, this new identity they had awkwardly and fitfully been trying on since the loss of Empire." Twenty-five years later—after the fractures caused by 9/11, the 7/7 London bombings, the Iraq War, and Brexit—a revised edition of the book appeared in which Wambu turned on his heel, stating "it is amazing to reflect on the shattering of the illusions" that Diana's death had actually or symbolically expunged bigoted, old-fashioned ideas about race and belonging in contemporary Britain.

Rather than the culmination of any kind of postimperial reckoning, Diana Week was only the start—and it set up camp right on the Windsors' doorstep. Accusations of racism from various quarters were riven through the Duke and Duchess of Sussex's relocation to America. Harry has said that in conversations among the most senior royals, "concerns" were raised about the color of his unborn son's skin; incongruously, he told interviewers that this was a case of "unconscious bias," though it sounds a lot like *conscious* bias, pretty much the definition of racism. Harry has vowed never to disclose precisely what was said by whom, thus allowing the people of fifteen realms to speculate whether or not any of its present or future heads of state racially discriminate against their own family members. Yet there's certainly evidence, including Harry's own past behavior, that the institution at the apex of British society is in an important sense disconnected from both the multiethnic population over which it reigns, and the Commonwealth to which so much of its energies are committed to preserving. Take this passage detailing the arrival of a Black colleague in the 2007 memoir of one of Charles's former staff members: "Elaine is only the second black girl—or, to use the correct phrase, 'only the second girl from an ethnic background'—to work here in the office. . . . Personally, the liberal in me is delighted. . . . I just wonder, though, how she will fit in. This is a fun office . . . [but] she does seem a bit solemn—politically very correct. I am therefore always scared of saying the wrong thing in front of her. The first black girl who worked here was the delightful Lizzy Norris. . . . In spite of her occasional temper, she fitted in well because she was so relaxed as well as amusing." There's no malice here, no intention to upset, exclude, or discriminate—but it does sound cringingly clueless, and underlines that historically the institution has been out of bounds to great swathes of society.

Among certain grand families, attempts are being made to exorcise the specter of empire. David Lascelles, the 8th Earl of Harewood, is a second cousin to the king and a co-founder of Heirs of Slavery, a group comprising people whose ancestors' wealth stemmed from involvement in the transatlantic slave trade, and who seek to make amends in the form of reparations. "They are researching their own history," says Lascelles of Diana's former in-laws, the royal family, "and they are talking openly about that." There isn't a stately home in the country that doesn't have difficult chapters to address, Althorp included. At the top of a grand staircase in the Spencer Gallery, hang portraits of recent and current Spencers, one of which is the Nelson Shanks painting of Diana looking lonely, melancholy, and vulnerable, the very image of the People's Princess that has the power to circumvent so many modern identities. Above the fireplace at the foot of the stairs, is a famous eighteenth-century portrait of John Spencer, the boy who would become the 1st Earl Spencer. On the canvas, John sits astride a horse just behind his father, who stands imposingly with gun in hand. Crouching beneath them, looking up, is a Black man named Caesar Shaw. In the Althorp visitors' booklet, he is referred to as a "page-boy" who lived and died on the estate. The depiction of Shaw is typical of its time: Black workers—enslaved or free—crouching in awe in the presence of their white masters is a staple of eighteenth-century aristocratic English portraiture. The front cover of the Althorp booklet describes the Spencers as "a unique family." Yet even this singular clan find themselves tied in the same messy knots that bind the rest of us to each other.

9

Don't Trust Anyone Who Doesn't Want to Be a Queen

Queen of Hearts. Diana in Manchester, October 1993.

O N 1 December 1993, George Michael stepped on stage at Wembley Arena for his first live performance in the UK in more than two years, with a special guest in the audience. Lately, Diana and Michael had become rather close in the way that the gigantically famous sometimes do, via phone calls in which they bonded over the isolation and strictures placed upon them by their social status and celebrity, very rarely meeting but trading exquisite gifts as a means of cementing their connection. The chats could be a little stilted: Diana's royalty put something of a barrier between them, and Michael was a bit concerned that the princess was infatuated with him. For a number of reasons, that could be tricky.

Diana had drawn upon every available shoulder to cry on during the last two years. The triumph of her first solo trip to Pakistan was followed by a visit to India, in February 1992, alongside her husband—although the defining moment of the trip was when Diana sat mired in sadness all alone outside the Taj Mahal, photographs of which were used the world over to paint the picture of a princess neglected by a cold, unfeeling husband. Conventional wisdom has suggested Diana orchestrated that moment, or at the least opportunistically seized the chance to make herself look as pitiful as possible. Others who were there on the day say Diana was unwittingly framed in a way that suited the tabloid narrative. Either way, the Taj Mahal moment was the first sally in a year of tumult, the fabled *annus horribilis*. In June, the Morton biography was published; later that summer came Squidgygate, leaked recordings of Diana's intimate conversation with James Gilbey (who repeatedly called Diana "Squidgy"), and Camillagate, Charles's even more intimate conversation with Camilla Parker Bowles. In the same year, the Duke and Duchess of York's marriage went up in flames, as did Windsor Castle. On 9 December 1992, the prime minister, John Major, announced in Parliament that Charles and Diana were to be officially separated.

Inevitably, media interest in Diana over the ensuing twelve months was higher than ever. Plenty of people, then and now, say Diana's behavior—tipping off journalists and planting stories in order to influence media depictions of her and her husband—only worsened her problems and deepened the animosity between her and the Windsors. Through the hullabaloo, she pressed ahead with promoting the causes that fitted her profile of the wounded healer; in April 1993 she gave a speech on the subject of eating disorders, which was interpreted as an indirect reference to her own experiences. Then, in December, she unexpectedly announced that she was stepping back from royal duties for a while to gain some respite from the media frenzy. In true, contradictory, Diana fashion, she made her announcement during a speech at an event for a mental health charity, in front of TV crews and press photographers, making it the top item on the evening news.

It was apt that her last high-profile event had come just two days earlier at Wembley, where she appeared in her capacity as patron of the National AIDS Trust to see George Michael headline the Concert for Hope, organized to mark World AIDS Day and televised across the globe. It was her ready embrace of the cause of HIV/AIDS several years earlier that had signaled to the public that Diana had designs on approaching royal charity work in a different way from the older generation. It had also forged an informal cultural association between her and gay men that has only strengthened and expanded since her death, in ways that perhaps don't tell us much about Diana as a person, but do illuminate how sexuality has shifted as a cultural concern since the days of Diana's public emergence, and how the memory of her has become entwined with a particular idea of gay experience, in which defiance and radical honesty are king and queen.

Diana's starter home was a spacious flat in Coleherne Court, an Edwardian apartment block situated on Old Brompton Road in the Earl's Court district of west London. The address is a well-established part of the Diana fairytale, the place where her flatmates discovered they were sharing a fridge and a cleaning rotation with the future queen, and where Diana first experienced the bottomless appetites of the news media: innumerable reporters, photographers, and camera operators have stories of staking out Flat 60, Coleherne Court, and pursuing its famous owner through the surrounding streets.

But Diana's home was also on the doorstep of what one chronicler of the capital's recent past has called "London's gay ghetto." A couple of hundred yards down the Old Brompton Road was the Coleherne Arms, one of the oldest gay pubs in the city and the epicenter of what was then the Earl's Court gay scene, known to some locals as Girls' Court; "not just pubs, bars and discos: there were queer hotels, saunas, shops, cafes and restaurants." A profile of the neighborhood in a 1987 edition of *The Pink Paper*, a British newspaper covering issues of interest to gay and lesbian readers, reckoned that on any given night Earl's Court Road—which ran perpendicular to the road on which Diana lived—was host to "a thousand men, dress coded, polished and continually on heat."

Grant Burnside was a bank worker in his early twenties when he first went to Earl's Court in the summer of Charles and Diana's wedding. He was astonished by what he found. "This was Sunset Strip for me: prostitutes—male and female—skinheads, bikers, rockers, you name it." It was also a place of both escape and community, especially the Coleherne Arms. Burnside recalls that "in the days when the pubs closed at 3:00 pm for four hours each day, the entire crowd (it was always packed to the rafters) hung out in Earl's Court, most notably in Brompton cemetery just along the road. It was a place to cruise, sunbathe and, if you dared, have full on sex if you hadn't quite managed to score whilst in the pub. The entire area was abundant with gay men, many of whom had flown in from around the world to discover and experience what was then a gay mecca." Diana probably never set foot in the Coleherne Arms, but she would have to have been spectacularly oblivious to her surroundings not to have noticed what was in her midst.

Burnside recalls plenty of famous faces from those days, some of whom would soon become part of Diana's story, including Freddie Mercury and the comedian and broadcaster Kenny Everett. But, he says, few of those well-known men were publicly "out" as we might understand that term today. At the start of the 1980s, gay men and women occupied an odd position in British culture. Camp had always played an important part in British entertainment, and gay people had long been among its most celebrated names. But now, a new generation of gay pop stars was achieving tremendous success whilst rejecting the stereotypes associated with older generations, sometimes explicitly engaging with the realities of living the life of a gay person in the 1980s; Bronski Beat's hit single "Smalltown Boy" is perhaps the definitive example. Yet this increasing, unapologetic visibility went hand in hand with extreme degrees of discrimination and vilification. For a time, the dichotomy of being celebrated and reviled defined the public existence of Boy George, the lead singer of Culture Club. After huge international success in the early eighties, George attracted scorn for his well-documented drug addiction and for talking publicly about having same-sex relationships. It was probably for that reason that he was asked by a Palace aide to remove himself from the line of people waiting to greet Diana at a charity function at the London Hippodrome in March 1987. "I was so embarrassed," says George, who had brought his mother with him with the express intention of introducing her to the princess. "I crept over to the bar and bought myself a piña colada. Diana spotted me and broke protocol to come and say hello . . . I asked her if she would meet my mum. She said 'I'd love to.' Mum was thrilled and I decided Diana was the nicest one out of the royals."

According to George's recollection, no photographs were taken of the meeting: "There was a huge scuffle when a photographer tried to take our picture. His film was ripped from his camera." But reports filed around the world stated that the princess and the pop star had apparently swapped sexes for the evening: Boy George was dressed in black tights and a white dress, while Diana was in a tuxedo and bowtie.

Androgyny was a huge part of Boy George's image; when he appeared alongside Annie Lennox on the cover of *Newsweek* in January 1984 as the faces of the "Second British Invasion" of America, genderbending and sexual ambiguity were identified as elements that distinguished this new breed of UK pop stars from their 1960s' forbears. And though it's rarely remarked upon now, Diana's image was sometimes edged with a touch of androgyny, too, despite the vast edifice of the fairytale princess that encased her. That evening when she met Boy George at the Hippodrome was one of several occasions when she was seen wearing a tuxedo, her height—five foot, ten in bare feet—underlining the hint of masculinity. Even during that very first stalking of Diana in Scotland back in 1980, it struck her observers that there was something about Diana's appearance that wasn't *entirely* female: "there was this girl," remembers Arthur Edwards of the moment he spotted her. "She was dressed like a man but you could tell." A famous photograph of her fully clothed on a beach in Australia among six male lifeguards—all shorter than her, all in Speedos—is like an inversion of those images familiar to us from Miss World and the like, of a high-status man, formally dressed, surrounded by young women wearing nothing but their swimming costumes and high heels. In the nineties, her exercise regime led to comments that she was allowing herself to become too muscular and masculine looking. Others delighted in messing with Diana's role as the feminine half of the ultimate "heteronormative" couple, to use the language of our own times. The artist Alfred Gescheidt reproduced Charles and Diana's official engagement photograph—the one where Charles stood on a step behind Diana to exaggerate his height, his hand clasped on her shoulder—but Gescheidt switched their heads, turning Charles into a beaming bride-to-be and Diana into a suit-wearing man, her bashful smile now a sly smirk of dominance.

On a few other occasions, Diana and Boy George found themselves lumped together on the basis of their appearance. When British hat sales soared in the mid-1980s, they were identified as the dual causes, and several newspapers compared and contrasted their respective taste in headwear, noting that one of Diana's milliners, Stephen Jones, was an old housemate of George's who also made numerous hats for him. Really, there was very little to link them sartorially: tuxedos weren't George's thing, and Diana wouldn't have been seen dead in one of his frocks. In any case, the issue of clothing was a triviality to those who alighted on far weightier concerns than who had been wearing the trousers when the princess met the pop star. In the *Burton Trader* in Staffordshire, the writer June Wall despaired not only that Fleet Street papers were giving time of day to this "transvestite homosexual junkie," but that the future queen was now making a special effort to be associated with him. "What chance do parents stand," she said of the royal endorsement, of "warning their children of . . . the degradation they could face if they chose to become homosexual?" Wall published her rant on 8 April 1987. Her response to what Diana got up to the very next day was not committed to print.

GAY MEN were hardly a rarity around the royal family. Princess Margaret had close personal connections with gay men, as did the Queen Mother, whose devoted servant William Tallon—"Backstairs Billy" as he was nicknamed—was in a long-term relationship with another royal servant, Reginald Wilcock. A third, Guy Hunting, wrote a memoir, *Adventures of a Gentleman's Gentleman*, that gave details about some of his homosexual experiences while in service to Elizabeth II. In past decades, domestic service to the royal family suited those in search of a chance to reinvent themselves away from the old ties of family and community in surroundings where discretion and secrecy were highly valued. As with so many aspects of royal life, the preponderance of gay men in the Windsors' midst was accepted in the very act of being ignored. This, of course, was not Diana's style.

Some of those who knew her say that Diana feared the potential impact of the HIV epidemic on the many gay men who worked at Buckingham Palace. She wasn't the only royal to be concerned about the devastating effects of the virus: London Lighthouse, a groundbreaking center for people with HIV/AIDS that Diana has become prominently associated with, was opened by Princess Margaret in 1988. However, that happened a year and a half after Diana had made what was widely seen as a startling intervention when, on 9 April 1987, she opened the Broderip Ward of the Middlesex Hospital in London, the UK's first dedicated facility for treating those with HIV/AIDS. Considering how much destructive misinformation and scaremongering surrounded what was often referred to as "the gay plague," and how reluctant world leaders had been to associate themselves with the issue —President Ronald Reagan was yet to make a public speech about it—Diana's presence at the Broderip Ward was thought of as a most un-royal thing to do, and for that reason hugely consequential. Famously, in keeping with her usual practice, she decided to forgo gloves when shaking hands with ten patients, a decision that caused a stir, even though it had been stated publicly over and again for years that HIV could not be transmitted through a handshake. Such was their fear of being identified, only one of the patients she shook hands with—a man later named as Ivan Cohen—allowed the moment to be photographed, and even then he insisted on having his back to the camera.

For the next several years, Diana met, shook hands with, and hugged HIV+ people around the world. Frequently, the visits were off duty; visiting the sick and the shunned became a central part of her private existence. Describing the intensity of her involvement in the final days of the art dealer Adrian Ward Jackson, who died with AIDS in 1991, Tina Brown observes that "It was as if the drama of other people's pain was the only thing sure to work in the assuaging of her own."

Staff at some of the institutions she regularly attended weren't always entirely comfortable with her presence. She got off on the wrong foot with Ricky Gellissen at London Lighthouse, when she made a tart comment about his weight: "the first words out of Princess Diana's lips, 'I see you've just managed to squeeze into those dungarees.'" It was an odd thing to say, coming as it did from someone who had publicly struggled with weight and body-image issues. Gellissen was one of those who thought that her visits were at least partially about comforting or healing something within herself. "I have to do it," she told her staff. "Nobody else understands the rejection they feel!" It was not only those with HIV she saw herself in. "I can talk to them because I am one of them" was her explanation for wanting to meet all manner of marginalized people, from drug addicts to leprosy sufferers. If she thought this was literally true—that their predicaments were a parallel of her own—she was obviously mistaken. Ultimately, though, it didn't much matter: almost all of those she visited in hospitals, hospices, and care homes were thrilled to see her—albeit those who were *not* excited about the prospect of meeting her were discreetly left off the itinerary. Ricky Gellissen concedes as much: "I might take the mickey at times, and there may have been some of her own personal needs tied up in that, but it was beneficial and there were people who really appreciated it." Likewise, Jane Burton, a ward sister at the Broderip Ward, says Diana's embodiment of "things that I find really difficult," such as celebrity and royalty, cannot obscure the fact that she had a marvelous impact on many patients. Her rare abilities were underlined when she visited the ward with Barbara Bush, a dual visit Burton was not at all happy about. The First Lady "was dreadful with the patients," remembers Burton, while Diana "was brilliant, I have to say," especially with one elderly royalist whose dying wish was to meet the princess.

The evidence is far too voluminous to doubt: by publicly embracing (in every sense of the word) those living with HIV and AIDS, Diana provided support to maligned minorities, much needed positive publicity for the cause, and joy to many of the individual patients she took the time to visit. Other, grander claims are harder to substantiate. Her youngest son has declared that his mother "changed the world" by shaking hands with those infected with HIV; Ken Wharfe states that "in one moment of compassion she had changed the world's perception of AIDS"; Arthur

Edwards of *The Sun* espouses that Diana "single-handedly took the stigma out of AIDS." There is certainly anecdotal evidence that Diana had a direct impact on some people's attitudes about HIV/AIDS and its sufferers. Not long after Diana's death, one gay man told researchers that his partner's mother "had been significantly influenced by Diana years before, when she shook hands with the bloke with AIDS. And that it must be alright if she did it." But there is nothing approaching empirical evidence to gauge precisely how and to what degree Diana affected public knowledge and behavior. In 1990, ignorance and hostility concerning HIV/AIDS was considered substantial enough in the UK for it to be challenged by the hugely popular soap opera *EastEnders*—one of Diana's favorite shows—in the form of a long-running storyline about the character Mark Fowler being disowned by his family and stigmatized by other members of the community. Fowler's plight became wrapped up in the mass media's coverage of HIV/AIDS; reports from the time suggest that the storyline coincided with a spike in HIV tests and a great increase in public understanding of the virus. In 2023, the Terrence Higgins Trust—a leading HIV/AIDS charity—reported that two-thirds of Britons aged forty-five to fifty-four still remember that Mark Fowler was HIV+, testament to the remarkable cultural impact that the character had on viewers in the nineties.

There was also a conspicuously measured reaction to Diana's work with HIV/AIDS in the British gay press of the 1980s. Her handshake at the Broderip Ward did not cause a great stir in publications such as *The Gay Times* and *The Pink Paper* at the time. Eight years later, Diana's admission on *Panorama* that she had told William and Harry that the very ill men she introduced them to actually had cancer, not AIDS, elicited a mixture of bemusement and eye-rolling. "Motto for the week," ran an article in *The Pink Paper*, "don't trust anyone who doesn't want to be a queen."

Nevertheless, the idea of Diana being principally responsible for tackling misconception and stigma around HIV/AIDS lives on in avenues of the Internet devoted to her, on clickbait "news," fan pages, and seemingly endless numbers of YouTube videos, many of which feature the same footage of Diana at the Broderip Ward in April 1987 and the still photograph of her shaking hands with Ivan Cohen. Rarely does the footage include the moment Diana shook hands with Shane Snape, a nurse on the ward who was also HIV+. On the TV news on the day of her visit, Diana appeared in silence, but Snape gave an interview on camera in which he explained what it was like trying to combat the misinformation surrounding the illness and caring for those living with a virus that he himself had. "I don't routinely tell all the patients I'm HIV; I don't think I have the right to actually burden them with it." But, Snape pointed out, if ever a patient claimed "you don't understand," he was in a position to assure them that "I too am positive."

Snape died in 1992, from an AIDS-related illness, at the age of thirty-two. His candor and resolve is remembered by most, if at all, as a footnote to Diana's visit, an event that has become a key moment in her mythological narrative. André Durand captured the moment of Diana's famous handshake on canvas in his painting *Votive Offering*, in which the princess is depicted as a saintly figure alongside St. George, St. Catherine, and St. Sebastian, deigning to

Votive Offering, André Durand. A mythological depiction of Diana's famous visit to the Broderip Ward of the Middlesex Hospital in London.

offer her royal touch to a patient. That kind of interpretation caused frustration among some of those who worked at facilities Diana visited. "It was the largesse of the beautiful princess with the poor suffering person," said Jane Anderson, a doctor who worked at the Broderip Ward, of the coverage of Diana's visits. Anderson had no words of censure for the princess and recognized that the publicity generated by Diana was very valuable. Yet she was discomfited that the media fixated on "her largesse rather than their wellbeing."

None of this is criticism of Diana, but a correction to the exaggerations written about her, and a clarification of what was distinctive and special about her contribution. Paul Gambaccini, the broadcaster and gay rights campaigner, draws an analogy between Diana and certain esteemed figures in British pop culture, such as David Bowie, who achieved colossal success by taking ideas from the margins and putting them into the mainstream. Diana offered nothing novel or groundbreaking in her message or her actions; even Norman Fowler, the UK's secretary of state for health, publicly shook hands with HIV+ people a year before Diana did so. What she had, however, was Bowie-like levels of charisma and star power that could disseminate the message formulated by others. "She was listening to that frequency," says Gambaccini. "She tuned in and got there first among the leading world figures." For instance, in 1991 Diana said "HIV does not make people dangerous to know. You can shake their hands and give them a hug. Heaven knows they need it." They echoed sentiments that had been voiced years earlier by activists such as Bobbi Campbell who, as a nurse who was also HIV+, gained a public profile by speaking out against the exclusion and emotional disregard that sufferers experienced as a kind of social death that preceded their physical one. Of course, Diana and Campbell—who passed away in 1984—were very different figures from very different worlds. Yet he and his peers provided a powerful example for many more high-profile people in years to come, the Princess of Wales included.

* * *

DIANA FOLDED visits to those she saw as marginalized and unloved into her unofficial schedule. Friends report that as her domestic situation worsened, she took to going out at night to make connections with those in need, motivated by both a desire to do good and her own need to feel needed. Usually, whoever she encountered was delighted to see her—though perhaps not always. One trip to a hostel for the homeless in January 1992 made its way into the newspapers when Diana was profanely harangued by one man for being royalty. An eyewitness reported that Diana stood up to him by telling him to "get your life sorted out" and commenting to others at the hostel that "people like that are just losers."

In Diana's mythology, furtive nocturnal activity plays an important role as moments when she secretly revealed hidden aspects of her true self. At boarding school, so she told others, she crept out of her dormitory either to perform a dare or to practice her dancing all alone in the school hall; at other times she raided kitchen fridges in search of the brief, fleeting comfort that binge eating brought. And nighttime offered the possibility of reinvention and anonymous adventure; the best-known example being the alleged occasion when Diana took a trip to one of London's most famous gay bars.

In her memoirs, the actress Cleo Rocos describes an evening she spent with Kenny Everett, Freddie Mercury, and Diana, who she had befriended in the late eighties. At some point in the evening, Rocos claims, Diana persuaded them to take her to the Royal Vauxhall Tavern, a place that Everett warned was "not for you . . . full of hairy gay men." Diana was insistent, however, so Everett helped her disguise herself in male drag: "a camouflage army jacket, hair tucked up into a leather cap and dark aviator sunglasses. Scrutinizing her in the half-light we decided that the most famous icon of the modern world might just . . . JUST, pass for a rather eccentrically dressed gay male model." It seemed to work. "It was fabulously and so bizarrely exciting . . . no one, absolutely no one, recognised Diana." They stayed for one drink and left. Diana returned to Kensington Palace and sent back Everett's clothes the following day.

The story sounds far-fetched, like one of the many apocryphal yarns of royal transformation that litter folklore and fairytales. Equally, Diana at the gay bar could be said to have a Shakespearean quality, with a girl dressed as a boy slipping into an enchanted world. Yet there are other, slightly less fantastical, tales about Diana disguising herself on nights out, such as when she accompanied Hasnat Khan to Ronnie Scott's jazz bar in Camden, the princess obscuring her true self beneath a wig and glasses. These are very Diana updates of old tropes about royal and aristocratic women discovering themselves while in disguise in the strange surroundings of London at night. Even Elizabeth II has such a tale attached to her, the time when she and Margaret ventured out into the city crowds celebrating the end of the Second World War, vastly fictionalized as a journey into London's illicit underworld in the 2015 film *A Royal Night Out*.

Irrespective of its veracity, the story of Diana in drag at the Royal Vauxhall Tavern has been taken up as an illustration of her connection with the gay community and a metaphor for her own search for a family in which she felt truly accepted. Jacob James (aka Scarlet Envy) dressed as Diana for a shoot for *Harper's Bazaar* in 2017. It was, he claimed, a way of thanking her for the support she gave to "the community that I call home." He finds her "inspirational in subtle ways . . . just good to her core." Diana's public prolife "lends itself to drag," James thinks: "Not always putting forward what is really going on under the surface." That sentiment is shared by Desmond O'Connor who wrote *Royal Vauxhall*, a cabaret musical based on the tale of Diana's night out. The writing of O'Connor's musical, in the mid-2010s, coincided with a spate of famous London gay venues going out of business, and it was feared that the Royal Vauxhall Tavern might also be at risk. It struck O'Connor as a powerful theme that united Diana's life with the experiences of London's gay community: both needed places to go where they could be themselves. Diana may have had the luxurious residences of Kensington Palace, Highgrove, and Althorp at her disposal but, *Royal Vauxhall* contends, each of them was a gilded cage where only her material needs could be fully met. It was in the guise of a different person that, for at least one night, she could discover herself.

The legendary Soho drag artist David Hodge, who performed as The Very Miss Dusty O, was working on reception at London Lighthouse one morning in 1996—"feeling like shit, my eye make-up still on from the night before"—when Diana turned up for one of her impromptu visits. As he found himself flustered and unusually togue-tied by her presence, she took the initiative to start a conversation, commenting on the book he was reading, *Mapp & Lucia* by E. F. Benson. "Oh, yes, I've read that," she said. "It's *very* camp isn't it." She was absolutely correct, but Hodge was "amazed that a real-life princess actually knew what 'camp' was." In fact, Diana was ensconced in campness. Camp can be found in filling daily life with unnecessary, oversized grandeur—see Princess Margaret. Yet it also exists in the opposite of this, in flamboyantly undermining anything grand and self-important, such as the monarchy. A princess who made scatological jokes while on duty; who arrived at official functions wearing a royal heirloom converted into a headband; who made herself up like a soap opera widow in order to dish the dirt on her cheating husband, the heir to the throne—much of Diana's public life could be read as camp performance.

It is for that reason that Linus Karp's enormously camp take on Diana in his show *Diana: The Untold and Untrue Story* is effective. Karp, a Swedish actor based in the UK, plays Diana in a (largely) one-man show that tells an alternative version of Diana's life story. "Untrue is the key word in the title," he said in 2023 of his attempt at "giving her the life she wished she had rather than how it actually played out." Karp is an unabashed Diana fan who adores her for the support she showed gay people. But he also acknowledges that "maybe for all generations she has become a myth, a meme. . . . People don't treat her like a real person." Thus, in his show Karp both celebrates Diana and, with maximum campness, sends up the tinseled mythology that surrounds her. "I love the gays!" his Diana exclaims at one point; at another moment, she dances with a rainbow flag around her neck to the accompaniment of a rousing song that includes the lines: "You're a friend of Di, whether gay, trans or bi. . . . She'll hug you if you have AIDS!"

There have been other attempts to tell Diana's story through the medium of a stage show; their relative lack of success might be because, unlike Karp's version, they play it straight, failing to acknowledge the inherent campness in Diana's public image, her theatricality and her extravagant flourishes of mawkish sincerity, such as telling the world she wanted to be known as the "queen of people's hearts," as she did in her *Panorama* interview. Simply put, a stage musical celebrating the People's Princess is an overload of campness. *Diana: The Untold and Untrue Story* addresses the elephant in the room, injects silliness and irony into the telling of Diana's tale, and as a result captures something truthful about her public reputation.

In this alternative narrative of Diana's life, her dreams—and those of the Dianaist audience—come true. She dumps Charles and beats up Camilla Parker Bowles, represented on stage by a huge rag doll with a mophead for hair. When Diana learns that the queen has tried to bump her off, she puts on her revenge dress (a gun nested in the cleavage) with a plan to get her own back—but being the saintly figure that she is, Diana turns the other cheek and lets her mother-in-law live.

THOUGH HE thinks "people are very quick to call basically any popstar or any woman who does anything a 'gay icon,'" Karp is certain that Diana deserves the label. Half a century ago, a gay icon was likely to be a sparkling figure brought low by a tragic flaw—Judy Garland being the textbook example—reflective of a time when gay lives were still saddled with the expectation of loneliness and isolation. Diana represents something different: "she did the work," says Karp. "She did so much for our community." To those generations for whom "doing the work"—the business of activism, allyship, calling out, and stepping up—is ingrained within the idea of minority identity, Diana seems to have been a gold-standard prototype for a twenty-first-century vision of a gay icon. New gay icons needn't necessarily be "kitsch or camp, smart-mouthed or bitter, tragic or grotesque," explains the writer Tim Benzie. "Rather, they must be in some way political/friendly, but still provide necessary key definitions of identification for gay men. Diana provided all of these."

Among those key definitions were her expressive physical presentation and her perceived bravery in putting her head above the parapet to bellow "I am what I am." Or to quote an audience member at "Dirty Di's Tunnel of Love," a mordantly camp Soho cabaret night from 2019 that featured the drag queen Fagulous as the princess, Diana "was a bad bitch, she owned what she was about." She may not have stepped out of the closet, but she did claw her way out of the fairytale castle—or so it appeared to much of the world—in a way that enhanced her iconicity, happening as it did around the same time that many celebrated pop culture figures told the world they were gay.

In particular, Diana's journey into the daylight of truth rhymed with that of George Michael's. At one point as half of the 1980s pop duo Wham!, Michael resembled Diana so much that he could be listed as another of those Diana doppelgangers. Odd as it seems now, at the time of their first album in 1983, Wham! had a reputation for being incorrigible womanizers, which Michael worried could scare off the teenage girls who had the power to make or break them. So in advance of the second album—*Make It Big* (1984), the record that catapulted Wham! to global fame—he cultivated something remarkably similar to the "original" Diana haircut, the one tended to by Kevin Shanley, "a blown-out, layered shag with blond tinting" in the words of Michael's biographer James Gavin. The Dianaesque restyle gave Michael a distinct image: a feminized machismo that was glamorous yet everyday, mimicking the atmosphere of Wham!'s records. As the writer Mark Simpson argues, it also carved out for Michael a unique spot in pop culture: more than anyone, it was he who provided the blueprint for the modern metrosexual, making tinting and tanning and pierced ears acceptable to working-class lads across the country. If Diana's look is still evident in the female fashions on British high streets, then, Simpson suggests, there's more than a little George Michael looking back in the mirror at millions of today's young men, straight, gay, and anything else.

Even before they first met, Diana was unwittingly folded into the fiction of George Michael the lady-killer; press articles reported that Diana was a huge Wham! fan, often in a way that portrayed her as a charming schoolgirl with a hopeless crush on a pop-star heartthrob, the quintessential male pinup of the day. The sad irony is that the red-blooded ladies' man was no less a fictional construct than the fairytale princess: for years Michael lived in constant dread that his homosexuality would become public knowledge.

As a metaphor for a person acknowledging their sexuality to themselves and others, "coming out" appears to have first been used roughly a century ago. Back then, there was no implication that anybody was emerging bravely from a closet; rather the notion was that one was stepping into a special—if secretive and proscribed—environment that was both dangerous and enchanted. It was only in the 1970s that "coming out" acquired its modern connotation of emerging from the darkness of lies into the light of truth. Diana could be thought to have come out in both senses. The first happened on the day of her wedding. The moment she descended from the carriage, her fantastical dress splaying in every direction, she entered a world of role-playing, symbolism, and coded meanings. The second coming out was her *Panorama* interview in 1995. We now know all about Martin Bashir's extreme dishonesty in obtaining access to Diana for that interview: he preyed on her vulnerabilities by forging bank statements to make it appear that royal staff were being paid to spy on her and setting himself up as someone who was on her side. Yet Diana's decision to have spoken out in the way she did slots so perfectly into the narrative shape of her myth that it feels inevitable that she would have launched an Exocet missile at the Windsors at some point, with or without the conniving Bashir. The interview is sometimes placed into a tradition of confessional TV broadcasts that hit its stride in the 1990s, such as Bill Clinton's admission about his affair with Monica Lewinsky or Hugh Grant discussing his encounter with Divine Brown. But it fits more neatly alongside certain high-profile coming-out interviews in the US and the UK that began with Ellen DeGeneres in 1997. Diana didn't really confess anything to Bashir. Rather, she gave the impression that she was liberating herself of past lies, whether they were ones told to her, about her, or by her. In 2021, Oprah Winfrey's interview with Prince Harry and Meghan Markle understandably drew a lot of comparisons with Diana's *Panorama* twenty-six years earlier; both, after all, were intended as salvos in public relations wars against the Palace. Yet Winfrey's other big interview of that year, in which Elliot Page came out as transgender, also evoked memories of Diana's blockbuster, both of them telling the watching public the truth about who they really were and the trials they had been through.

The year after Diana died, George Michael finally had his unambiguous coming-out moment. Having been arrested for soliciting in a public toilet in Los Angeles, Michael appeared on CNN and, to the shock of many of those watching, was steadfastly unapologetic; when he was interviewed on *Parkinson* later that year in London, he insisted on seeing the humor in every aspect of the situation: "Almost immediately I saw the funny side of it. . . . If you can't laugh when everyone else is laughing, you're in trouble." Diana ultimately followed up her *Panorama* revelations with the public show of defiance that was the last year of her life; Michael did so with the single "Outside" and a promo video in which he dressed as a police officer and danced in a public lavatory that turned into a disco. To borrow a line once used to describe Diana, Michael had become a mouse that roared: a man who once went to great lengths to shield his sexuality from the public had suddenly become the most gleefully "out" figure in mainstream popular culture. Opprobrium came from the usual sources. Several years later, Kelvin MacKenzie, one of Diana's old tabloid tormentors, seethed at Michael's continued refusal to hate himself: "every time he tries to laugh off another vile gay sex exploit I dislike him a little more . . . I'd like to give him a good kick in the balls."

In a previous life, the Reverend Richard Coles was a peer of George Michael and Boy George, one of those young gay men who revitalized British pop in the 1980s as one half of the Communards. Not long before Diana died, Coles found himself in her company at a HIV charity function. As she joked with the gay men present—"there's only one Princess around here, honey," etc.—it occurred to him that "Diana was a gay man." Or at the very least, her "coming out" was the central pillar in what was her "complex identification with the narratives which shape contemporary gay identity," right down to the fact that "coming out is not living happily ever after, as happens in stories." As both she and George Michael could attest, "It is work-in-progress, not the showstopper."

CHRISTMAS DAY, 1996. At 3:00 pm sharp, Queen Elizabeth II arrived on BBC and ITV television, as she had every year since 1957, overflowing with festive non-cheer. Even in wishing the Commonwealth a happy Christmas, it was impossible to tell what she was thinking or feeling. At the very same moment, Diana broadcast her own Christmas message on Channel 4. Or rather, a man dressed as her was doing so—Rory Bremner, the satirist and impressionist who had got a lot of mileage out of Diana in recent times, spoofing her *Panorama* interview and her recent appearance at the Harefield hospital where she had watched open-heart surgery in front of photographers, an episode that was mercilessly mocked in print and on screen.

Bremner as Diana was performing Channel 4's "alternative" Christmas message, now a longstanding tradition but then still a relatively new addition to the schedules. The inaugural message in 1993 was delivered by Quentin Crisp who encouraged everybody watching to leave the sinking ship of Britain and move to America. Like Bremner, Crisp was experienced in dressing as female royalty, having played Elizabeth I in the film *Orlando* the previous year.

The director Sally Potter hailed him as "the Queen of Queens, the true royal of England," but Crisp baulked at the idea that the People's Princess might have been an icon to gay people, or anyone else. "I don't know how she became a saint," he commented not long after her death. Having lived as an aristocrat before becoming a princess, Diana "knew the racket," Crisp said. "You stand beside your spouse and you wave and for that you never have a financial worry until the day you die and you are photographed whenever you go out . . . what more could she want?" In his one-man shows from around the same time, he described Diana as "trash" and elsewhere lamented that "Princess Diana died at the same moment that Mother Teresa died, and somehow it all got muddled up and they both became saints at the same moment. Had Diana died on a different day there might have been a more sensible assessment of her character."

Something Diana and Crisp had in common was that their roles as princess and queen both involved a lot of performing. Just as Diana knew that her audience craved her mixture of dazzling glamour and Lady Bountiful tenderness, Crisp knew he was expected to live up to his persona of the outrageous, unconventional, incorrigible bon vivant. Perhaps, then, his expression of distaste for Diana didn't precisely match his feelings for her—or maybe they did. In any event, he was far from the only person to voice doubt about whether Diana's status as a gay icon was deserved, or even made sense.

The 5 September 1997 edition of *The Pink Paper* interviewed a number of gay people mourning Diana outside Kensington Palace "who all spoke of a deep spiritual identification with the Princess. . . . For them, she was a feisty woman who had fought their corner with humour, vivacity and style." The next week's edition quoted Peter Ritchie, who said the bar he worked in had been "mobbed by gays and lesbians" on the day of the funeral. "We blacked out our windows and put up posters of Di as a mark of respect." However, in the letters section of the paper, readers complained of "the lack of respect shown in certain gay pubs." A couple said they had been to several London gay venues, asking for "Candle in the Wind" to be played. "We were often met with sarcasm and were humiliated." One landlord was so annoyed by the request that he played "Dirty Diana" by Michael Jackson instead. Other readers got in touch to mock and question what they thought was a rush to claim Diana as a spiritual leader of gay Britain. "A statue in the village or Canal Street to be renamed Diana Street?" asked one incredulous correspondent, referring to suggestions that key sites associated with gay communities be dedicated to Diana's memory. "Isn't this all going a bit far?" Voices of dissent had been aired even before Diana's death. Two days before her accident in Paris, the letters page featured concerns about Diana's inclusion on the "Pink 500" list of the most important figures in gay life. "The Princess of Wales. What has she done?" asked one woman, exasperated at the number of females on the list who were popular with gay men but had no experience of living a gay life. These tensions were mirrored elsewhere. In Australia, the magazine *Lesbians on the Loose* ran an article challenging the amount of unquestioning praise heaped on Diana, which led to some irate responses. "I found the article an insult," complained one reader. "My lesbian friends and gay men are all mourning the loss of the Princess of Wales."

Peter Tatchell, a prominent figure in the gay rights movement in the UK and beyond, was scathing when it was revealed that Diana had made no provision in her will for any charity. "She was very happy to do charity work for people with AIDS, providing it didn't cost her anything," wrote Tatchell, who suggested that a person of Diana's means was more than able to leave a few thousand pounds to those "charities she claimed to 'really care about', including London Lighthouse and the National AIDS Trust." Tatchell's criticism cuts to the core of what it means to be a good ally. Perhaps, though, being an ally and being an icon are rather separate things. The notion that Diana was significant to gay people appeared to astound several of those who recorded their feelings about her for the National Lesbian and Gay Survey, a project inspired by Mass Observation, that contacted its participants with a special directive after the events of September 1997. Only thirteen people responded to the directive, and the majority of those seem to have been politically left of center, but even so the wide range of opinions expressed is fascinating. Some people declared themselves astonished to have been contacted. "My immediate reaction on opening this directive was to be annoyed that even in the lesbian and gay environment this event was being assumed to have some personal significance for me," wrote one respondent, who thought that "because Diana seemed to be such a classically heterosexual icon, I had expected lesbians and gays to have something more of a sense of proportion about it." Another flatly rejected the idea "that this event will seem to future historians like a key date in lesbian and gay history."

A third, who watched the funeral and stood observantly for the minute's silence, was adamant that "Diana did nothing for gay issues. She had been rebuked in the past for speaking at a convention supporting 'family values,'" perhaps a reference to a speech she gave at Barnardo's fiftieth annual conference in 1988 in which she urged a resurgence of traditional family life, a statement that was applauded by ministers in the Conservative government that had just introduced legislation to "prohibit the promotion of homosexuality." Recognizing Diana's broad, protean appeal, the respondent believed that

> If she had gay friends—Elton and Gianni—then that was not a statement to the world, in my view. It was a private friendship between seemingly extraordinary people; unreal people; people who cannot be like the "poofter down the road." I can imagine gay-bashing thugs sweeping through the streets holding posters of "We love you Diana" in one hand and beating the crap out of gays with the other, never thinking that the person they are brutalising is like the friends of the woman these thugs profess to love.

Another respondent was "absolutely certain that front-page photos of her shaking hands with PWAs [people with AIDS] had no lasting effect on the public intolerance of AIDS . . . far from dispelling they did as much to <u>reinforce</u> the disgust and fear that many people still feel."

Others, of course, felt the passing of a beloved champion whose very exit from the world seemed to strengthen their bond with her: "She was too young to die. How many times have our families heard that over the past few years. . . . Her car crash / our HIV diagnoses—Another parallel with our community" wrote one HIV+ respondent. Then there were those who found their sexuality had little, if any, bearing on how they made sense of Diana and the disorienting whirl of emotion and spectacle that her demise precipitated. "Maybe I'm too English or too male but I found the whole thing very embarrassing," ventured one man living in Edinburgh who was baffled by the outpouring of grief around him. A woman who had also been in Edinburgh on the day the princess died found some of the core parts of her social identity in complete conflict with her emotional response, in a way that she felt adhered her to millions of others she would never meet, each of them nothing more, or less, than a fellow human being:

> I am a socialist, a feminist, a lesbian woman, anti monarchy etc.
> I spent the days of Royal Weddings on remote Welsh beaches!
> I spent the day of Diana's funeral enthralled and absorbed by
> the T.V. coverage. I have to say that I <u>would not have missed</u>
> <u>this event for anything</u>. . . . There was a definite sense of being
> part of history—history in the making—a history that people,
> ordinary people were making—despite the obvious feeling
> that lurked beneath the surface that we were being manipu-
> lated. But I really didn't feel manipulated—I wanted what hap-
> pened before my eyes <u>to happen</u>. . . . Maybe that is what we
> were all doing at some level—celebrating the anti-hero in each
> of us—collectively.

❧ 10 ❧

Whatever "In Love" Means

Diana at the Palace of Versailles, France. November 1994.

WHEN DIANA ANNOUNCED her decision to temporarily step back from public life in December 1993, she cited the immense intrusion into her privacy as a dominant reason. But several months later, on 29 June 1994, she arrived for a fundraising dinner at the Serpentine Gallery in a way guaranteed to fix the public gaze on her private life as only she could. When the invitation had first been issued, Diana declined it. She changed her mind when she learned that on that same evening a pre-recorded interview with her estranged husband would air on ITV, in which the heir to the throne admitted his adultery. Not famed for her inclination to turn the other cheek, Diana took the opportunity of the Serpentine dinner to underline her status as the wronged woman, betrayed but unbowed, by wearing what was dubbed by others as the "Revenge Dress," an eye-catching black silk evening gown designed by Christina Stambolian that drew all eyes to Diana and supposedly showed the prince what he was missing. The photographs of her that appeared in the next day's newspapers drew a definitive end to Diana's period of reclusion and set in train what has become the popular narrative about the remaining three years of her life: the princess's intense, and thwarted, search for love.

In the following weeks and months, there came a steady flow of rumor and revelation about her love interests. The publication of *Princess in Love* in the autumn of 1994 purported to tell the story of Diana's own infidelity, a five-year involvement with the soldier James Hewitt. The book broke dubious new ground: the first in-depth account of how a future king or queen conducted an extramarital affair. A year later, Diana gave a measured, tactical reply, conceding to the affair in a way that underlined what was said to be her greatest virtue— her capacity for unconditional love—and Hewitt's caddish vices. "Yes, I adored him. Yes, I was in love with him. But I was terribly let down." It was around this same time that Diana began her relationship with Hasnat Khan, the man who was possibly the love of her life—though the relationship became the prelude to her romance with Dodi Fayed, during which her life came to an end, in a Paris underpass in August 1997.

The meaning of Diana—the public figure and the mythological character—began and ended with love. Whom she loved and who loved her, were, and are, topics of perennial, global interest. But they have never been as important to her public as *how* she loved and how others loved her in return. As the fairytale princess at the center of an archetypal romantic fantasy and later as a representative woman trying to balance a yearning for coupledom with a need for autonomy, Diana has been loaded with other people's ideas about love for close to half a century. And in her, "love" found a walking evocation as a force for social good—though for both her and us, the destructive power of obsession sometimes seemed more powerful.

"THE DIANAMEN." This is the collective noun given by some inhabitants of Dianaworld to the men romantically linked to the princess from the late 1980s on. As Tina Brown explains in her biography, *The Diana Chronicles*, the first of this group were Sloanes such as James Gilbey (of Squidgygate fame) and other affable chaps from the social worlds familiar to Diana since childhood, many of whom were on hand to provide companionship and fawning devotion, and probably harbored no serious design on any physical or deeply emotional involvement with the Princess of Wales. Over the last thirty years, the category of Diana's reputed love interests has expanded to incorporate, among others, the international rugby player Will Carling, the private equity billionaire Teddy Forstmann, Bryan Adams, and John F. Kennedy Jr. It is often alleged that her bodyguard Barry Manakee was reassigned from his duties in 1986 because of concerns that he had grown too close to his principal; Diana was distraught to learn of his death in a motorcycle accident around a year later.

All things considered, this is a relatively diverse sample of masculinity, though back in the mid-1990s, both critics and supporters feared that by knocking around with men who had no inherited title she was debasing herself and demeaning her position in much the same way she was said to have done by wearing her white jeans and chunky gold jewelry. Ignoring all the other men she was associated with, not least the philosopher prince she spent fifteen years married to, the psychiatrist Dr. Sidney Crown—who does not appear to have ever met the princess—told the authors of the book *Diana on the Edge: Inside the Mind of the Princess of Wales*, that in his opinion Diana's interest in soldiers, bodyguards, and rugby players was evidence that she "cannot deal adequately in emotional terms with people who arc her peers and reflect her background." That all but her in-laws could be considered her social inferiors didn't seem to figure in Dr. Crown's thinking. Bolstering Diana's association with gay men, he suggested that the princess was imitating a dynamic he observed among London's non-royal queens: "Incredibly sensitive, marvelous people, who must . . . make relationships with the toughest, roughest trade." For very different reasons Lucia Flecha de Lima, one of Diana's most loyal friends, also disapproved of the princess dating beneath herself. She recognized that Hasnat Khan was "a very kind man. . . . I saw why they were in love." Yet she told Diana to forget any idea that the two of them could be together long-term. "You are not a middle-class Princess," she bluntly, but realistically, told her friend, "and can't dream of leading a middle-class life." De Lima was just as dismissive of the supremely rich Dodi Fayed. "I did not think that was a proper thing to do," she said of Diana's decision to spend the summer of 1997 aboard the Fayed yacht; "she is a Royal Princess of England. She could be among her peers."

Though Khan was perhaps her most serious involvement other than Charles, and Fayed is the man with whom her mythology will always be entwined, it is James Hewitt who is in many senses the archetypal Dianaman, one who had a foothold in the establishment world, but also offered Diana a glimpse of a life away from the royal bubble, and who had a tabloid caricature created around himself. They met in 1986 at a cocktail party hosted by Diana's lady-in-waiting Hazel West, though they had admired each other from a seemly distance. As a captain in the Life Guards, part of the monarch's official bodyguard, he was often in the vicinity of Buckingham Palace around the time of special events; while preparing for the wedding of Prince Andrew and Sarah Ferguson, Hewitt—a dashing Harlequin Romance cavalry officer come to life—caught Diana's eye. He, of course, had known of her for years, though seeing her in the flesh in the summer of 1986 had a particular impact. There are various stories in Diana biographies that paint the same essential picture: Diana, beaming, animated, and, most significant, barefoot, a physical detail noted in myriad descriptions of her to evoke the naturalness and joie de vivre that her admirers found so attractive.

Taking a shine to Hewitt, Diana bonded with him as she so often did with people, by sharing an emotional truth early on in their conversation. To Hewitt, she offered just a little of her fractured childhood: the occasion when she fell from a horse and broke her arm, which instilled in her an aversion to riding ever since. The affable Hewitt naturally offered his services as an instructor to her and her two sons. Very soon after began a five-year-long affair with frequent weekend tristes at Highgrove and at Hewitt's mother's home in Devon. The relationship was an open secret: Diana's protection officers knew about it, as did the staff at Highgrove and Hewitt's colleagues, while gossip columnists wrote about it. Even Prince Charles was aware of it. Supported by details in Hewitt's autobiography (published after Diana's death), the princess's biographer Sarah Bradford writes that "Charles and Diana had come to some accommodation, comparing diaries to avoid the risk of one being caught by the other, or, at the very least, to avoid meeting each other" in the company of their respective lovers. Some royal watchers theorize that more than turning a willingly blind eye to the relationship, Charles and the Palace might have actively encouraged it, in an effort to engineer something close to domestic contentment in a dreadfully unhappy marriage.

Extensive details of the affair were made public three years after its conclusion in 1994, when the writer Anna Pasternak published a book about it based on interviews with Hewitt and sixty-four letters Diana had sent him while he was serving in the Gulf War. *Princess in Love* was widely taken as a frightful betrayal on Hewitt's part, though Pasternak has claimed that both the book and earlier articles that she had written about the affair had been undertaken with Diana's blessing, hoping to "control the narrative" before it became detailed by other authors, especially a forthcoming book by Andrew Morton. "The brief I got from Hewitt was to write a love story in four weeks, to be published ahead of Morton's offering," says Pasternak, who was only twenty-six at the time. "I knew nothing of love but wrote my best gushing account." *Princess in Love* was ridiculed and parodied for its florid romanticism; "I regret that I used so many adjectives," is Pasternak's measured self-critique.

Regardless of its literary merits, the book is an important contribution to the Diana mythology, explicitly fusing the idea of Diana's search for love in her private life with her calling to serve the people, whose essence she personified. "Just as she was desperate for love and affection . . . so she knew that they [the public] must be. . . . Her needs were their needs." In Pasternak's telling, Captain Hewitt is both a lover and a fighter, who stepped up to do his patriotic duty in Challenger tanks and in the princess's arms. "This was why he had come into her life," Pasternak says of Hewitt's mission to help Diana feel love, to understand "how exquisite she was. . . . For, after all, by helping Diana . . . he was helping the country and the Crown." Two years after the publication of her book, Pasternak claimed mission accomplished: "He has shown the world that Diana is a wholly loving and lovable woman." Surely, most of those who read the book had already come to that conclusion a long time ago.

FROM THE outset, Diana was publicly associated with the idea of love as both an emotional experience and an important civic value. Her official introduction to the world came on a brief tele-vised interview alongside Charles on the day of their engagement announcement. That interview is now notorious for Charles's "whatever 'in love' means" remark. Studiedly ignored at the time, those words have since been resurrected and often misremem-bered as "whatever love means," a tiny but crucial distinction that was used to malign Charles not as someone who rushed into a marriage he was never sure about, but as a cold, cruel man who—unlike his emotionally expressive bride—hadn't a loving bone in his body.

The wedding was talked of not simply as the union of two peo-ple, but a moment of emotional indulgence for Britain. Two days before the ceremony, Charles said he hoped that the whole nation would have "a marvellous musical and emotional experience." On the evening of the big day, one broadcaster looked back at the event and declared that it had indeed been a very British love-in. "Just like you can feel violence in a football crowd," said the radio host John Junkin, "the feeling of goodwill, even love, was tangible." Diana was identified as the source of this effusion of feeling. This girl who was quick to tears and lived with her emotions always on display hadn't been born to royalty; she had chosen to enter it, for love—love of the Prince, and of the people.

Charles mightn't have known what it meant to be in love with Diana, but the public did. That, at least, was the message of the mass media, which disseminated the public's crush on Diana in an endless variety of ways. Among the staple features of the local news coverage of Diana in the UK were stories about young women or girls who had amassed a cornucopia of Diana ephemera. Eleven-year-old Caroline Melia from Bishop's Stortford, for instance, was photographed by the *Herts & Essex Observer* in 1984 with her collection, the centerpiece of which were twenty-six scrapbooks clogged with photos of her heroine. This was nothing compared to the archive compiled by twenty-three-year-old Julie Turner from Reading, which included 118 scrapbooks and, unusually, fifty Diana-themed spoons. Local papers also ran stories about Diana flirting with elderly men in residential care homes and schoolboys who asked to kiss her hand.

For those who loved the idea of Diana, James Hewitt (via Anna Pasternak) gave an unprecedented insight into what it was like to love the real woman, a task that was complicated for him by what is presented to the reader as Diana's intense emotional existence, which variously scares and baffles her lover. It could be said that there were three of them in this affair: Diana, Hewitt, and the stiff upper lip. Sometimes the Anglo-British froideur is admired as "that marvellous stoical manner that only the British can muster"; other times, it is lamented as a barrier between Hewitt and his princess in love: "He was coming face to face with this irrational emotion and he did not know what to do with it." When Hewitt's mother received the news of her son's relationship with the future queen, "her lip had not so much as quivered," Pasternak tells us. Though "a true aristocrat" from a world of rigid tradition, Diana could not have been more different: Hewitt first saw her in person at a polo match in 1981, when she cried in full view of everyone present. Throughout their relationship, so Pasternak informs us, Diana could barely stop expressing herself, splattering unruly emotion onto the canvas of Hewitt's orderly life.

Diana's way of expressing her feelings was frowned upon as letting the side down among some of those who admired her the most. Felicity Clark, the beauty editor at British *Vogue* who had instigated Diana's styling as the definitive modern English rose, was asked what she made of the tit-for-tat media war between Diana and Charles. "I thought it was terribly un-English," she replied, especially Diana's appearance on *Panorama* when she talked about her emotional struggles and her love for Hewitt. Then she checked herself: "probably I'm naïve to say it was a very un-English thing to do."

Clark was right to add that qualification: the evidence tells us that the extreme reserve and sangfroid for which the British were famed across the world during the twentieth century was, like so many other facets of supposedly bred-in-the-bone Britishness, a rather recent innovation. As Thomas Dixon explains in *Weeping Britannia: Portrait of a Nation in Tears*, before the Victorian era, Britain—and most especially England—was renowned throughout Europe as a place of unchecked emotional display. In particular, the English had a reputation for unselfconscious public crying. "Every period in British history was more tearful, and more approving of tears, than the middle decades of the twentieth century," Dixon tells us. Various historical factors are at play here, but in Dixon's view the growth of empire and the shock of the French Revolution played a huge part in spreading the idea that crying and other forms of emotional expression were not only un-British, but anti-British, a threat to national greatness. When Diana was so frequently seen to cry, it was a further instance of her acting as a bridge to a pre-imperial past, though it seemed to many more like a portal to a future Britain of emotional openness, full of tears and hugs, and profusions of love—liberating to some Britons, utterly terrifying to others. A man quoted in *The Guardian* documented an instance in September 1997 when his eighty-four-year-old father was spontaneously hugged by someone who was very upset by the princess's recent death. Being embraced in this way apparently proved almost as distressing for this gentleman as receiving the news about Diana had been.

In September 1991, Diana urged her compatriots to follow her lead and unbottle their emotions. "It does not harm people to cry," she said. "But there seems to be a curious conspiracy in adults to suppress this emotion. People keep trying to stop others from crying as though it will harm them." She wasn't the only member of her generation sending out the message. A little more than a year earlier, the footballer Paul Gascoigne—another English folk hero with childhood trauma at the center of his lore, often loved because of his flaws rather than in spite of them—had cried on the pitch during the World Cup. His tears immortalized him; seemingly, he had hit a wellspring of deeply buried memories of a time when Englishmen were known to weep in public without shame. In 1996, with the soap opera of Gascoigne's life rivalling that of

Diana's, an ad for a cable TV channel run by Kelvin MacKenzie featured a mocked-up picture of the two of them as newlyweds, Britain's most famous criers, from opposite social worlds, united by the public's love for them and a shared conviction that there was never a bad time to show the world how you feel.

THE DIANA of *Princess in Love* is obsessional. Whereas Hewitt's mother was "not emotionally open enough to tell him that she loved him," Diana had "a childish need to hear these words, to have constant confirmation." When apart, she telephoned Hewitt dozens of times a day. This comports with the stories of Diana's other love affairs. At the end of her relationship with the art dealer Oliver Hoare the police were called in to investigate a complaint from Hoare's wife about three hundred or so silent phone calls being made to her home which, the authorities discovered, had been made from inside Kensington Palace. Once their relationship began, Hasnat Khan received numerous calls at work from Diana, too, and she developed an intense interest in his specialty of cardiology. This was similar to the passion for outdoor pursuits she exhibited while courting Charles, and taking the trouble to dress her sons in little army uniforms when they were with Hewitt, and rugby kits when she took them to meet Will Carling.

Diana's propensity for such behavior mirrors the way she was treated by others. At the extreme end of the scale were the stalkers, among whom Diana considered certain paparazzi. In August 1996, just days before her divorce was finalized, Diana gained a court injunction against the paparazzo Martin Stenning, banning him from getting within three hundred meters of her. As horrid as some of their conduct was, the paparazzi who tailed her probably shouldn't be described as stalkers; if they had a fixation, it wasn't with the person of Diana or any of their other targets, but with the thrill of breaking societal norms. There were others, however, whose obsessive tracking of Diana was fueled by an intense emotional connection. As her public tussles with Stenning demonstrate, Diana's susceptibility to unwanted, up-close attention had increased following her post-separation decision to forgo personal protection when she wasn't engaged in official duties. Inevitably, however, she had been prone to such attention from the moment she became a fixture in the mass media, a situation faced by many members of the royal family in the modern era. As the scholar Mandy Merck points out, it was the case of a woman who stalked George V that the psychiatrist Gaëtan Gatian de Clérambault cited in defining his concept of erotomania. Among Jacques Lacan's best-known psychoanalytic studies is that of a woman known as Aimee, whom he diagnosed with an erotomaniac fixation on George V's son, the future Edward VIII.

Six weeks after Diana won her injunction against Stenning, Channel 4 aired *I'm Your Number One Fan*, a documentary that follows four people with an obsessive interest in a different celebrity. One of them is Klaus Wagner, a doctor who not only adores Diana, but has become enraged by Fleet Street's treatment of her, "the lies and slander, and also the ruthless invasion of her privacy," he says: "I decided I would stop the abuse." The filmmakers follow him as he makes repeated attempts to contact Diana, turning up at events she attended, waiting outside the gym she was known to use, bombarding her staff, family, friends, and her psychotherapist with documents. When interviewed on camera, his wife says, "He doesn't talk about anything else. . . . He'd be up all night looking through papers he got from the recycling bin to see if there was anything about Diana." It's a fascinating but disturbing period piece, exploitative and insightful. From Diana's perspective, it is a stark, albeit extreme, illustration of how frightening the intensity of the public interest in her must have been at times—especially once she decided to lose the round-the-clock security. One scene shows Wagner placing a bundle of papers under her windshield wipers. "That's it," he tells the camera, "my mission is accomplished now." It wasn't: eight days later he was apprehended by the police when he tried to make personal contact with Diana at an event in London.

Hotel worker Ian Jackman was a more benign variety of super-fan. His adoration of Diana also led him to shadow her around the country, arranging the whole of his life around her schedule. His was a platonic but unconditional love; his intentions were utterly innocuous: to wave at his princess from behind a barrier, take a few photos, and give her little presents. That Diana came to recognize him and frequently took the time to greet him and engage in a bit of conversation meant the world to him. He considered his handheld camera "a magic wand" with which he could "summon her to my side, to come to me and converse in an open, warm and plain manner." He remembers the excitement he felt when collecting those first photos of Diana from the pharmacy; "I paid the bill and almost dropped the coins all over the counter." Whenever he had a fresh batch of photos, he would take them back to his studio flat, spread them out on the kitchen worktop, and absorb himself in the magic of Diana. "I spent many hours in the kitchen, sometimes making toast on the grill, and replaying in my mind the 'motion pictures' of the moments just a few hours prior, when I had been standing with and talking to the Princess of Wales in a 'close-up' scene." He is certain that he and the princess formed a friendship that was as significant for her as it was for him. In a way, perhaps it was. Diana absorbed the emotions of others; their love and adoration powered and propelled her. The property developer and art collector Peter Palumbo is one of numerous people who has a story about Diana's mood being transformed by a sudden shower of attention, in this case at Notre Dame when she was spotted by a few dozen people who quickly gathered excitedly around her. Diana's previous bad mood evaporated "as though the spotlight had gone on and she became animated and full of laughter."

Another variety of Diana fan were the wealthy, powerful men who admired her from afar in deluded belief that they stood a chance with her. General Mustafa Tlass, the infamous Syrian minister of defense between 1972 and 2004 is the most conspicuous in this category. In 1984, Garth Gibbs, one of James Whitaker's fellow royal watchers at the *Daily Mirror*, reported that Tlass had the world's largest collection of books about Diana. Tlass had recently spoken to German interviewers about his fascination with Diana and his plan to include a poem he had written about her in an anthology of his own work. British diplomats recall being made aware of Tlass's obsession: he contacted the British embassy in Damascus, requesting that certain gifts from him be forwarded to the princess, including an oil painting of her, and a horse. None of those concerned can recall how these unusual requests were dealt with, but it's highly unlikely Diana ever received her presents. In 2009, Tlass welcomed a camera crew from RT into his trove of weird memorabilia. He didn't display the library of Diana books he was reputed to have but he did show off a gold-plated submachine gun that he said had been gifted to him by Prince Charles. Diana, said Tlass, sent him "letters of love and appreciation," and once offered to spend four days with him in Syria in exchange for twenty-eight million dollars. It's utter nonsense, of course; the lurid imaginings of a career fabulist. But in the mind of the Assad family's long-serving henchman, Diana was the point where his maddest fantasies about love, sex, and power collided.

Clive James was another poet who found his muse in Diana. Perhaps an unlikely devotee of the People's Princess, James was a left-leaning, satirical Australian renaissance man—poet, linguist, and literary critic by day, entertainment TV host by night. He once said, "Achievement without fame can be a good life. Fame without achievement is no life at all," an observation that one might think pertinent to understanding several members of the royal family, though in his panegyrics about her, he described Diana's very existence as the most remarkable achievement imaginable. Diana enjoyed James's work on television, and she must have known of his admiration for her. For a while, he was inducted as a member of her fragmented court of wise heads; filmmakers David Putnam and Richard Attenborough were part of this group, as was the historian Paul Johnson. Diana tended to keep such courtiers in tiny siloes, frequently seeking their advice, which she then usually ignored, though she did follow James's prompting to learn a few words of Japanese ahead of her trip there in 1995. Judging by his account of the several lunches they shared in the 1990s, James's main role was to boost Diana with garrulous devotion, which she consolidated in her customary way by sharing details of childhood upset. Like Diana, James experienced a life-shaping upheaval at the age of six, when his father died. As he told the princess this, she "touched my wrist, and that was it: we were both six years old." There was no way back from there. Twenty years after she died, he sounded every bit as besotted: "She was like the sun coming up when she was enthusiastic about something," he explained.

As a committed Dianaist, James was unusual in that he rarely commented on Diana's body, which was often located as the source of her magnetism. Colin Campbell begins her biography with five paragraphs of anatomical examination, parsing Diana's allure feature by feature, her famous eyes, of course, as well as her "slender build, narrow trunk, almost flat chest, boyish hips, long legs and arms." In Judy Wade's biography, a worker on the Sandringham estate is quoted as recalling that Diana's legs were "the best I've ever seen on a baby," which must rank among the strangest observations made about Diana's uniqueness. When James indulged in such scrutiny he mused on Diana's perfect imperfections—a pretty clear sign that he was in the grips of hopeless, unrequited love. Of the photographer Tim Graham, who James thought captured Diana better than anyone else, he wrote that "He even knows about that single incipient spot right in the middle of her chin which starts feeling like Vesuvius if she so much as looks at an ice-cream." Such flaws, James said, were the very things that defined Diana's unmatched beauty, "unearned, unjustifiable, a pure accident"—much like her royalty, one might add. "Beauty," sighed the lovelorn James, "it's a bit of a joke."

The joke, said others, was that Diana was ever thought beautiful at all: the obsessive attention paid to her was the symptom of a mass delusion. Two stories that appeared in Irish newspapers illustrate the conviction. One was about a sports reporter who was suspended from his job on a radio station in Wolverhampton after he described Diana as "a bit of a dog," who was only considered beautiful because she had married the Prince of Wales. The writer Mark Smith made the same argument in Dublin's *Sunday Independent*. Diana, he declared, was "an attractive, if rather gangly woman with a large nose . . . the day the people of Britain can bring themselves to admit that fact is the day the Royal mystique is finally peeled away."

A shifting combination of all these conflicting feelings about Diana—love, lust, and scorn—suffuse Woodrow Wyatt's observations of her in his journals. A former MP and a passionate royalist, Wyatt embodied a particular type of upper-class man for whom the Queen Mother was the epitome of womanhood. His earliest mentions of Diana rather suggest that he saw her as a modern incarnation of his favorite royal lady, all demure elegance, charming and chaste. In 1990, he recorded that the Iraqi government had unfairly besmirched Diana's morals, and he sympathized with her for having to live with the ice king that was Charles. "Poor child," he wrote, "It must be hell." In early 1992, his entries praised her for her compassion, her vitality, her naturalness. But in the summer, when Andrew Morton's book was published, his picture of Diana as a latter-day Queen Mother was quickly replaced by Diana the femme fatale, a deranged, volatile, and predatory woman whom he loathed. And at the peak of Wyatt's disdain for "the poor child" who had now become "that vixen," he explicitly mentioned her sexual attractiveness. In April 1996, he found himself sitting behind Diana at a classical recital at the South Bank Centre, feeling rather awkward because of all the unflattering things he had written about her in recent newspaper columns. He didn't speak to the princess, but stared at her from behind, noting her beautiful hair and her skin "free of blemish and very sexy. I resisted the temptation to touch it." It's a small, but significant, shift in tone. The scene reads like the moment in Alfred Hitchcock's *Vertigo*, that eerie film about the thrill and danger of male voyeurism, when James Stewart's character finds himself troubled and transfixed by the bare neck of Judy, played by Kim Novak, as she lingers in front of a painting in a gallery. No longer required to revere Diana as the English rose, Wyatt—and many others like him—was now free to despise her and desire her, the nasty twin impulses that had always hovered in the backdrop of the soft-focus princess worship of earlier, more innocent, less honest times.

Fellow monarchist and professional nostalgist Auberon Waugh stated the appeal in rather different terms. In 1981, he too considered Diana the purest specimen of aristocratic femininity: "Even if I could think of a single unkind thing to say about our new Princess of Wales I would refuse to say it in deference to her beauty, birth and obvious amiability," he wrote in *The Spectator* at the time of the wedding. Thirteen years later, he revealed that his admiration for her had only intensified following the stories about her various entanglements. For Waugh—who had previously met and been charmed by Diana—it boiled down to this: "is she a mad, sexless, manipulative monster or is she a sincere woman? If the former, it is time to put her in the dustbin." If, however, "she is sincere and delivers the goods to whatever man or assortment of men she chooses," then Waugh declared himself ready "to love her unconditionally" and "happy to die for her."

ELTON JOHN had numerous opportunities to witness what he terms "the Diana Effect," the phenomenon whereby straight men "seemed to completely lose their minds in her presence." One such incident occurred at a house party, thrown sometime in the mid-1990s when Diana and Charles were already separated. If John's memory serves him well, Sylvester Stallone arrived "with the express intention of picking Diana up" and was infuriated to see her "in rapt conversation" with Richard Gere. At some point in the evening, John's husband, David Furnish, came upon Stallone and Gere "squaring up to each other, apparently about to settle their differences over Diana by having a fist-fight." Stallone said he wouldn't have bothered turning up if he'd known that "Prince fucking Charming was gonna be here." Tessa Baring of the Barnardo's children's charity recounted that at a lunch in London, Stallone was thwarted in getting next to Diana not by a fellow silver-screen silverback but by a little girl called Tracy. Stallone "really, really wanted to come and sit next to the Princess of Wales," said Baring. "We didn't let him do that, but we did let him sit next to a child who was sitting next to the Princess of Wales." Baring remembered the occasion because she thought Diana hit upon an effective way of placating the film star, making the child feel included, and indulging her own desire to find out the latest gossip, by leaning over and asking Stallone questions about his love life as though she were asking them on Tracy's behalf: "Tracy and I want to know if you're married," and the like.

Part of Diana's attraction to Hasnat Khan seems to have been his apparent immunity to the Diana Effect. When they met for the first time at the Royal Brompton Hospital, Khan was treating the husband of Diana's friend in his capacity as a heart surgeon, and displayed no obvious sign of attempting to impress her or of being impressed by her. This Diana found very attractive; desire of all kinds tends to be inflamed by the obstacle of unobtainability. Khan's apparent lack of concern for Diana's status in that first encounter set the tone for the rest of their relationship, which rumbled along in relative secrecy throughout 1996 and into the summer of 1997. Journalists first got wind of the relationship early on, in late 1995, though the story was overshadowed by Diana's surprise appearance on *Panorama,* during which she presented herself as the performer of a "unique role" as "a queen of people's hearts," no longer merely the focus of public love, but its source. In answering Bashir's questions about her travails, she ran in tandem the story of her futile efforts to receive love in her private life with her quest to project it wherever she saw it lacking. She spoke of her commitment to battle "the disease of people feeling unloved, and I know that I can give love for a minute, for half an hour, for a day, for a month." Hers was a calling to make her compatriots "feel important, to support them, to give them light in their dark tunnels," all the things, in fact, so the unspoken subtext stated, that she had only fleetingly enjoyed in her own life.

On the one hand, she longed to love like everyone else did. On the other, she pledged to love as no one else could. The disparity was immense, though in the following eighteen months she got as close as she ever did to balancing both sides of the equation. With Khan, she developed a relationship that was more mundane, uneventful, and enriching than any that she ever had. There were rare, discreet evenings out, when Diana would disguise herself with a wig, though very often they enjoyed quiet nights in. She relished time spent with Khan's family, too. According to Kate Snell—the author of a book about Diana's relationship with Khan—Diana once went to a supermarket with some of Khan's relatives from Stratford-upon-Avon, and sprinted up and down an aisle while pushing a shopping cart, knocking over a stack of tin cans, one of them smashing open as it hit the floor. It sounds odd in a way that several stories about Diana in moments of supposed normality do, as if transcribed from something seen in a formulaic television show. One man who claims to have been approached by Diana in a gym says the princess introduced herself to him by saying "What does a girl have to do to get a guy to buy her a cup of coffee around here?" as though speaking a line from a bad American romcom. Perhaps such things didn't happen entirely as recalled, or perhaps they evince that Diana drew a lot of pointers about real life from what she witnessed of it on TV. Either way, she was delighted to have these moments of living and loving normally, respite from the self-imposed challenge of reigning in the hearts of a nation.

Real life, however, was the very thing that brought the relationship to an end. Khan had no taste for the glare of global publicity in which Diana lived and that she was attempting to harness to create a new post-royal life as a champion of the world's ignored and afflicted. He was exasperated by her attempts to engineer solutions to the couple's problems. Without his knowledge, she attempted to land him a job with the acclaimed cardiologist Christiaan Barnard in South Africa, where she believed they could start a new life. As Khan tells it, the split was instigated by Diana soon after she came back from a holiday with Mohamed Al-Fayed's family in the South of France in July 1997. He says that he had no idea that Diana had formed a connection with Dodi, but suspected she had met someone else and told her that deepening her association with Al-Fayed was a huge misstep. "I remember saying to her at the time 'You are dead', meaning her reputation was dead," he says. "I genuinely thought it was downhill now for Diana and I thought I would just sit on the sidelines and watch."

Mohamed Al-Fayed had been floating around Diana for years. He had been a friend of her father's and in 1996 Raine was appointed to the board of Harrods. Raine says that Diana had jokingly suggested to Al-Fayed that he needed to find Raine something to keep her occupied, and Al-Fayed responded by making her a director of Harrods International Limited, despite the fact that Raine claimed she "never went shopping in Harrods because I was too busy." Diana, however, "went to Harrods endlessly . . . she used to see Mohamed quite a lot there." Not half as much as he saw her: Al-Fayed instructed members of staff to track Diana around the shop whenever she went in, allowing him to run into her accidentally on purpose. This was one manifestation of the vast intelligence and security operation he created around himself—just the thing, Diana thought, to protect her from the likes of Martin Stenning and Klaus Wagner. "Diana finally realised that Al-Fayed could give her all the things I could not," says Khan. This might not have included her dream of ordinary love, but she may well have thought that Al-Fayed could help her deliver on loving people in the way that the Queen of Hearts should: she discussed with friends the idea of using his money to fund an international network of hospices bearing her name. Allying herself to Al-Fayed in this way allowed him to inch closer to dreams of his own. During Diana's first trip to Al-Fayed's properties, he made sure that Dodi paid them a visit. A friendship quickly developed, which soon turned into something more involved.

Across two further week-long jaunts on Al-Fayed's yacht the *Jonikal* in August, Diana and Dodi pursued a romance that was the tabloid story of the summer. Floating in the middle of the Mediterranean, they were hosed by the lenses of the paparazzi; at one point Diana took a Jet Ski to remonstrate with the photographers and reporters who were constantly circling, snapping merrily away whenever the princess was in sight. Diana's search for love with her latest boyfriend was the lead, though a compelling B-story soon presented itself involving the American model Kelly Fisher, who believed herself to have been Dodi's fiancée. In mid-July, Fisher and Dodi had been on the Fayed yacht the *Cujo*, a stone's throw from the *Jonikal* where, unbeknownst to Fisher, Diana was relaxing with Dodi's family. During the day, Dodi absented himself, claiming he had business to attend to; in fact, he was dashing off to spend time with Diana at his father's behest, before scuttling back to the *Cujo* at night. It was only when she returned to America in August and saw the paparazzi photos that Fisher put the pieces together. She sold her story to *The Sun* and held a press conference alongside her lawyer, Gloria Allred, announcing her intention to sue Dodi for breach of promise, popularizing a notion that Diana was caught up with an indolent man-child who treated women like dirt.

Whatever the truth about Dodi and his father, the consensus among Diana biographers—and among those who were closest to her in the summer of 1997—is that Fayed junior was only a summer fling, and perhaps a tactical device to nudge Khan into the commitment Diana wanted from him. While Myriah Daniels, a member of the Al-Fayed staff, swears that during those few days on the *Jonikal* "I held the Princess in my arms while she cried in gut-wrenching pain to not be able to just enjoy a moment's peace without tabloid assault," the paparazzo Jason Fraser insists that not only did Diana want herself photographed that summer, she was in frequent contact with him to keep him updated on her movements. "I think overall, she was happy with all the pictures taken that summer," claims Fraser, who also claims he felt morally conflicted about selling the famous photo of Diana and Dodi kissing as he didn't want her reputation to be tarnished.

Until his death in 2023, Mohamed Al-Fayed insisted that his son and the princess were soulmates who spent their final weeks wrapped up in a romance for the ages. Really, the story of that Mediterranean summer looks more like a tale of the rich, famous, and influential publicly exploiting each other for their own gain.

CLIVE JAMES was floored by Diana's death. "Some men knew her intimately," James wrote in his requiem for Diana, a testament to his love for a woman he conceded he barely knew. "Now, at last, I do not envy them, because what they have in their memories must make loss feel like death." In *Princess in Love*, Anna Pasternak had speculated the opposite on James Hewitt's behalf. "It seemed so difficult to be mourning the lost love of someone who was alive," she wrote in 1994 of Hewitt's feelings after his relationship with Diana ended. "He wondered if it would be easier if Diana was dead. Then at least he would know that he could never repeat that love; eventually, he might learn to accept his fate." His fate, as it transpired, was to live with the love he had for Diana playing in the background on an endless loop. Hewitt's was one of those whose life was turned upside down when Diana sailed right through it and out the other side. Castigated by the tabloids as a "love rat," at moments he seems to have done his best to live down to the caricature. Among various reported attempts to sell the letters Diana wrote to him, he once appeared on *Larry King Live* and stated that he might be prepared to part with them for the right money. Like other former denizens of Dianaworld, his coda has also featured the reputational graveyard of reality TV. In 2004, he was crowned the winner of *Back to Reality*, a contest among those who had previously appeared on other reality shows.

In a very different way, Clive James remained tied to Diana, too. Twenty years after her death, and while facing the prospect of his own, James wrote the neatest articulation of a sentiment repeatedly expressed in the archives of Mass Observation and the Great Diary Project about the events of the start of September 1997—not the sadness of Diana's passing, but the topsy-turvy oddness of it, the mad absurdity that the ubiquitous figuration of vitality, youth, and love was gone, stolen while the country was asleep, never to return:

> *we all sit silent where*
> *She, only, was not sighing for the waste*
> *Of youth, health, beauty*

Those lines appear in "Choral Service in Westminster Abbey," his experience of a global cultural happening that was also the funeral of someone he loved.

Of Diana's former lovers, only Hasnat Khan received an invitation to her funeral. He attended, discreetly, and has kept largely distant from the public gaze ever since. One of his few appearances came in the form of a statement that was read out during the inquest into Diana's death in 2008. Mr. Wonderful, as Diana had called him, was predictably circumspect. "It is impossible to tell whether we would have got together again," he said in evidence that was far more sober than much of what was heard throughout the inquest. When the film *Diana*, starring Naomi Watts, about his relationship with her was released in 2013, Khan criticized it as fiction based on gossip and speculation. Asked to reflect on what could have been, he played it, as ever, with a straight bat: "I try not to think about these things. I can't change anything now."

Ian Jackman, the superfan who followed Diana around Britain, was present at one of Diana's final official engagements, at Northwick Park Hospital in London, where he handed her a birthday present: a CD compilation album titled *Love and Affection*. "Oh my goodness," he remembers her saying to him, "How topical." He found out about Diana's death in the early hours of 31 August, when a fellow Diana follower from the United States woke him with a phone call that left him devastated. The next day he was sent home early from work, too tired and upset, he says, to focus. In his published account of his experience of Diana Week, Jackman writes that he planned to claim a spot on Finchley Road on the day of the funeral, hoping to see the hearse drive past. Instead, Kensington Palace called to offer him a seat in Westminster Abbey. On the day, he tells us, he sat on the tenth row, the Spencers in front of him, the Windsors to his right, Hollywood stars and global statesmen dotted all around.

Jackman was, in effect, an emissary of the loving public Diana had romanced for seventeen years. For the previous week they had crowded the streets around London, expressing their emotions in precisely the way Diana had been encouraging them to do for as long as she'd occupied a space in their collective consciousness. Great seas of flowers were laid outside Kensington Palace and other locations associated with Diana, along with teddy bears, children's drawings, and handwritten poems. Throughout the country, people gathered in their hundreds and thousands for vigils. Many of them did what the cultural stereotype of the stiff upper lip disallows: they held hands, they hugged, and they cried. The wave of feeling that crashed upon British shores was matched by an equally powerful disbelief at this viral "emotional incontinence," to use a term that crops up often in discussions about Diana Week. Aside from the fact that it seemed incomprehensible that anyone could be upset by the death of a stranger, a portion of the public felt Diana was a self-involved exhibitionist who was fundamentally unworthy of all this sentimental hokum. There is too much compelling testimony to doubt Diana's capacity for kindness, compassion, and friendship. But irrespective of the truth about her true qualities, she had become a cipher for love and emotional openness. To some degree, the mourning for Diana was an affirmation of that which she had successfully left behind. And in any case, it seems that she loved others in private in the way that her public loved her— lavishly and inconstantly, stiflingly and adoringly, tyrannically and needily, all or nothing. Perhaps this is why the more her public learned about Diana's caprices, the more they seemed to bond with her: as Clive James wrote, "The more you know she was never perfect, the less you, who are not perfect either, are able to detach the loss of her from the loss of yourself."

Was this loving Britain a land of the future or of a distant, half-remembered history? Was the stiff upper lip quivering into oblivion and along with it the connective tissue of the imperial past? Or was the phenomenon of the mass mourning a novel reinforcement of tradition? Most likely, it was a cut-and-shut amalgam of the two. Many of the same people who praised the crowds in London for letting it all hang out were most affected by the sight of Diana's sons being blankly stoic as they walked through central London behind their mother's coffin, adult strangers around them weeping and crying out for their beloved princess. It was much like how Thomas Dixon describes the fandom surrounding the classic 1940s film *Brief Encounter*: "a very modern and very British phenomenon—weeping over the stiff upper lip, crying at people not crying." Watching the funeral on television in Northamptonshire, one member of the public wrote in his diary that he had been moved by the emotion of the mourners but proud of the uncrying princes: "the boys gained their spurs."

In her contribution to the Mass Observation record of that week of public tactility, one woman suggested that Diana constituted a great British anomaly. "Princess Diana did touch and hold people but the strange thing is not many of us do much touching and holding of our own family. We accept this from a nurse but would find anyone touching us to be a bit worrying"—an observation that pretty much holds true more than a quarter of a century later. "Princess Diana could get away with it," of course. Perhaps more than anything, it was that for which she was loved.

Do You Think
They'll Give Me a Job
When the Revolution Comes?

The People's Princess. Diana in Washington, lending her voice
to the Red Cross anti-landmines campaign, June 1997.

OUGLAS HURD IS very open about it: he was as suscepti-
ble to the Diana Effect as anyone who ever met her. Two
days after the announcement of the Waleses' separation in
1992, Hurd met Diana in his capacity as foreign secretary in John
Major's cabinet. "There the Princess was," says the Tory grandee,
sounding like a lovestruck undergraduate, "bestowing that special mixture of beauty and charm which melted men's bones." He
knew that other international statesmen felt as he did when in her
company, "content to bask for an hour or two in an extraordinary radiance." In his various encounters with her between 1989
and 1995, Hurd came to the conclusion that "she was not in the
least interested in politics," a fact that chimes with the withering
assessment of the Irish ambassador who stated in an official communication to Dublin that Diana's understanding of British politics was so remedial that she seemingly didn't know that Northern
Ireland and the Republic of Ireland were not of the same country. Nevertheless, Hurd was taken by the fact that despite—or,
perhaps, because of—her shifting position with the royal family,
Diana remained "almost painfully anxious to continue her over-
seas visits with our blessing." Naturally, "I was glad, or more accurately, enchanted, to give it."

Hurd's six-year tenure at the Foreign Office had ended a few
months before Diana was given an award for Humanitarian of
the Year at a glitzy ceremony in New York at the end of 1995,
among a who's who of selfless lovers of humanity, including Henry
Kissinger and Donald Trump. Neither did Hurd have to deal with
the furor caused in January 1997, when Diana—now divorced from
Charles and no longer an official Royal Highness—performed a
photo opportunity like no other, as she walked through a minefield in Angola in support of the Red Cross campaign to institute
a worldwide ban on landmines. Diana had alighted on an important cause, and one that was fiendishly difficult to take issue with.

Except, however, that ministers within the Major government felt she was treading on their toes and publicly contradicting its policy of a multilateral rather than unilateral disavowal of landmines. Earl Howe at the Ministry of Defence referred to Diana as "a loose cannon"—an unfortunate choice of words, given the subject matter—and suggested her ill-informed contributions to government policy were not welcome. Diana responded that "I am not a political figure, I am a humanitarian figure."

Setting aside the tricky business of defining who or what constitutes a humanitarian—is it, for instance, a label that can be applied to overworked, underpaid nurses or only world-famous millionaires?—what Diana did in Angola was bold, admirable, and groundbreaking. In the venue of celebrity activism, her nearest predecessors were Audrey Hepburn and Elizabeth Taylor, two other women known at first for a performance of a demure type of Englishness that morphed into something different when they went stellar in the United States. But Diana had something those two did not: the mythological power of royalty. In the decade between her handshake with HIV patients in London and her trip to Angola, Diana burnished the field of celebrity activism, giving it an august figurehead.

Her activities had an impact in the other direction, too. In the wake of her death in 1997, Douglas Hurd cited her as the outstanding example of the post-1945 monarchy's recalibrated purpose, that being to fill the holes revealed by the Thatcher overhaul of the welfare state. "Voluntary and charitable effort on a massive scale is needed to rescue those who fall through the gaps between commercial and state provision, to sustain minority groups or causes, to experiment with new forms of service, and to stimulate artistic creation," Hurd wrote, and it was the royal family who took on the mantle, with Diana at the fore. Hurd doesn't say so, but in reimagining the role of the monarchy in this fashion, Diana was surely fulfilling a political function. Her involvement in the landmines issue was political in nature not because she meddled with government policy but because it was the highwater mark of the monar-

chy's renewed purpose, one that had significant ramifications for
the conduct of public life in the UK. The fact that she was no longer an official HRH is by the by. She was still the Princess of Wales,
the woman whose self-attested role was to shape British kingship
for the twenty-first century.

From 1980 onwards, Diana was catnip to politicians, in Britain
and elsewhere, a variety of whom tried hard to be associated with
her, though her political identification was perceived, accurately or
not, to shift over time. In framing her own identity as an important
national figure, she also established a style of public engagement
that reflects a change in the conduct of British politics, acting, yet
again, as a bridge between ancient British tradition and American
innovation. For generations, right up until the start of the twentieth century, the Spencers had been crucial players in British politics. In the unlikely form of Diana, they reasserted their presence.

For several diarists of the Great Diary Project, mentions of the
royal family are as close as they get to discussing politics or current affairs. Amid Betty Allen's catalogue of everyday happenings,
there is next to no mention of the world that pulses beyond her
circle of family and friends, except when a moment in the domestic
affairs of a Windsor bustles in. "David Wilkinson was singing—
quite good," she notes of her visit to church on 24 February 1981,
in an entry evocative for British people of a certain age. "David
collected me + we got home in time to watch *Pot Black*. Prince
Charles got engaged." Nigh on twelve years later, she itemized the
things that had occupied her on 9 December 1992—making three
dozen mince pies; getting a quote for repaving the driveway—
before finishing with the news of Charles and Diana's separation.
"I don't think she should ever be crowned Queen—feel very sorry
for Her Majesty + the Duke."

With Tony Benn, the opposite was true: he only spoke of the
Windsors when he had no choice. Benn was a Marxist aristocrat
who renounced his title of the 2nd Viscount Stansgate in order to

serve as a Labour MP between 1950 and 2001, an era recorded in his absorbing diaries. For many of those years, Benn was probably the most prominent republican in the UK, so dedicated to the cause that he wrote and published a draft constitution for a Britain without a monarch. In his view, to ignore royalty and its media coverage, as so many British republicans do, was to inadvertently strengthen the monarchist cause, hence the occasional mention of palace intrigue in his diaries—though always with a caveat for future readers. "I put it down in case it comes up later," he added to his June 1991 entry about a bit of gossip he had heard regarding Diana and her alleged affair with a man on her staff.

His entry of 20 November 1995, featured no such indemnity. On that evening, he sat alone in his parliamentary office to watch Diana's interview with Martin Bashir and was alarmed and depressed by what he saw. "It is the end of politics," he concluded. That the private lives of one couple could command so much attention—including from one of the BBC's premier current-affairs outlets—was proof to Benn that the nation was in deep trouble. Democracy was being cheapened, Parliament was being undermined, and socialism—his life's cause—was withering on the vine. Britain was a post-politics place, "a gossiping nation," obsessed with princes, princesses, and queens of hearts. In Benn's mind, Diana wasn't merely nonpolitical, as she asserted, but anti-political.

Benn glided over parts of what Diana said that surely were political in character, addressing as they did the functioning of the monarchy and its relationship with the people over whom it reigned. She spoke of the institution striking a new pact with the people, offering consolation, hope, and guidance, "light in their dark tunnels." Though her words are almost always interpreted as a call for the royals to bring themselves up to date, they could just as easily be viewed as a pitch to wind the clock back three hundred years to a premodern ideal of monarchy which in certain ways was (literally) more in touch with ordinary people, yet more magical—capable of a more spiritual, intimate connection with people and therefore a far larger presence in their lives. She urged her in-laws to get closer to the problems that affect society (by closely observing them, that is, not by actually experiencing them) yet swatted away the possibility of curbing the magnificence of the institution as modern constitutional monarchies in the Netherlands and Scandinavia have done, "riding round bicycles and things like that." It was a populist monarchy, a monarchy of the people and for the people—though, of course, never embodied by the people.

At the time of the broadcast, Diana's talk of bringing the monarchy closer to the people, allowing them to "walk hand in hand" into the future, sounded a lot like the "modernization" rhetoric of Tony Blair, then the leader of the Labour Party which aimed to oust John Major's Conservative government and, so Blair assured the electorate, guide Britain into an exciting new era. If the republican campaigner Anthony Barnett is correct in saying that Diana "saw that only a populist monarchy could be the personification of today's cruder, grasping nation," Tony Benn might have said something comparable about Blair and his idea of turning Labour into New Labour, filleting its socialist principles in favor of "third-way" liberalism as a means of navigating the realities of British life at the start of the twenty-first century.

Blair entered Parliament in 1983, the nadir of Labour's electoral history. Superficially, his situation resembled that in which Diana found herself at that moment: a shiny young face enmeshed within a grand institution that was strongly criticized for a sclerotic adherence to tradition that kept it remote from swathes of the population. Eleven years later, he became party leader after his predecessor John Smith died of a heart attack, in May 1994. Smith had enjoyed a fair degree of popularity, and his death struck a chord among the public. Diana's antennae told her that his funeral was the kind of event that she should be seen at, in her de facto role of guardian of the nation's heart strings. Royal protocol, however, forbade it. "It may not have been a full state occasion," she told Peter Stothard, former editor of *The Times*, shortly after Smith's death, "but it became a powerful public event and no one from the

Royal Family was there." During the same conversation with Stothard she commented waspishly that the current prime minister, John Major, and Prince Charles were "very much alike, quite BFs these days, always seeing each other." If, as Diana saw it, the Tories were the old-guard batting for the queen and her heir, Diana would look elsewhere for Westminster allies.

New Labour gave voice to a New Britain, said Blair, "in which ambition for oneself and compassion for others can live easily together." A Britain of equal parts Margaret Thatcher and Princess Diana is how some at the time translated that—though, perhaps Diana actually fulfilled both sides of the equation herself, something Blair recognized, admired, and attempted to emulate. In the 1990s, the scandals surrounding the royal family ran in parallel to those of the Conservative government; where Diana managed to position herself as the whistleblower on Windsor dysfunction, Blair pitched himself as the vanquisher of "Tory sleaze." Her approach to royal duty resonated with an apparent shift in attitudes among the general public, something "less deferential, more liberal on social issues, less class-bound, more meritocratic," said Blair, though it's puzzling to think that a Spencer who became a Windsor could be held up as the poster child for a classless meritocracy. He goes as far as to suggest that his modernization of Labour was designed in the princess's image: "Whatever New Labour had in part, she had in whole."

In the spring of 1995, she and the buoyant New Labour leadership began a mutual flirtation that continued for the remaining two years of her life. Blair was rapt by her shrewdness and savvy; "if she were ever in politics, even Clinton would have to watch out." Sharing her insights into the art of image making one evening, she baldly urged him to "touch people in pictures"; in the words of Blair's spin doctor, Alastair Campbell, who was also present, photos taken with "down-and-outs" and "children with no hair" were especially effective, Diana felt, in curating a reputation for compassion. A hint of that had popped up in her chat with Stothard, when she told him a story, the precise details of which he didn't quite believe, about "how she had helped a tramp who had fallen in Regent's Park canal" and was heading off to visit him in the hospital later that day. Realizing that Stothard wasn't interested in the lede, Diana seems to have taken it elsewhere; the story appeared in various newspapers the next day. "She spoke in fairly calculating terms of how she had 'gone for the caring angle,'" Alastair Campbell remembered of Diana's tutorial on how to wage a PR war. What some would understandably interpret as cynicism and shallowness, Campbell took as necessary hardheadedness in a brutal, image-led media environment. "She also saw it as her work," Campbell explained, "to make people feel happier and better, and to support causes which didn't always get strong support."

More than the populist exhortation, the pop culture sheen, and the shrewd use of the visual image, Blair's connection with Diana had a personal element, too; something connected to a sense of not being one of the gang. An irony of Diana and Charles's marriage was that this hopelessly unsuited couple had an awful lot in common, including the deep-seated feeling that each of them had of being an outcast, misunderstood and underappreciated. In the decades since their marriage publicly disintegrated, this interpretation has dominated sympathetic profiles of them: the Charles of Jonathan Dimbleby and the Diana of Andrew Morton are each the ultimate insider revealed to be the ultimate outsider. Dianaworld teems with fellow self-declared outsiders. From biographers to domestic staff, the paparazzi who pursued her, the men who romanced her, and the designers who made her exquisite clothes, Diana was surrounded by people who thought themselves to have their nose perpetually pressed against the glass. Blair is one of them. The princess "throbbed with non-conformity," he says, a quality he recognizes in himself. "I am not a great one for the Establishment," writes the former prime minister, now a knight of the realm, in his memoirs, while presenting his interactions with Palace officials in the week leading up to Diana's funeral as a clash between a convention-busting outsider (him) and archaic insiders (the Grey Men). Had he been either upper class or working class, things might have been different, he says, explaining how his middle-class origins perplexed those aristocratic stuffed shirts who caused Diana so much strife. "People like me were a bit nouveau riche, a bit arriviste, a bit confusing and therefore suspect."

Perhaps Blair's sense of middle-class outsiderness simply reflects the logic and character of the New Labour project: "a bit nouveau riche, a bit arriviste, a bit confusing and therefore suspect" is essentially what much of Old Labour thought of him, too. Or maybe it's just an example of the growing tendency in post-sixties Britain for public figures to identify as members of an impeded minority, even if that means recasting good fortune as misfortune. The actor Dominic West, for example, has claimed that his status as an Old Etonian carries with it a "stigma that is slightly above 'paedophile' in the media in a gallery of infamy." *The Crown*, the show in which West plays the role of Prince Charles, presents the entire royal family as a clan held together by loneliness and disaffection, whose status has cruelly separated each of them from the life they should have lived. Whatever the case, on Blair's run-up to Downing Street, he was another Diana doppelganger, an insider-outsider on a mission to excite and captivate the public.

BLAIR'S RELATIONSHIP with Diana was not the first time that Labour had been beguiled by royalty, a surface contradiction that reveals a characteristic strain of the British left as well as the deep roots of British monarchism. Clive James was a leftist monarchist: he argued that the UK, and his native Australia, "benefitted from having a head of state from a family which had no interests beyond preserving its own continuity." Richard Crossman, a left-wing member of Harold Wilson's Labour government in the 1960s, noted that "The nearer the Queen they get the more the working-class members of the Cabinet love her and she loves them." Thirty years earlier, Labour had latched on to Edward VIII who was—not quite accurately—quoted as saying "something must be done" about unemployment, a tiny gesture that involved no effort on the king's part but was considered to be earthshakingly consequential, rather like Diana's handshake of 1987.

Even so, when she first stepped into the royal limelight, Diana was rarely a figure actively celebrated by Labour, which was led at the time by Michael Foot, who, although considered to the right of Tony Benn, was undoubtedly to the left of his immediate predecessors. Labour's manifesto for the 1983 election—when Blair became an MP—vowed to nationalize banks, withdraw from the European Economic Community (the precursor of the European Union), and abolish the House of Lords, which, of course, would have seen the Spencer family lose its centuries-long presence in Parliament. Foot expressed scant enthusiasm for Charles and Diana's wedding, ditto the Labour leadership in London. Ken Livingstone, the socialist leader of the Greater London Council, invited journalists into his office on the big day to let the city know that he was ignoring the event and getting on with representing the people. "I haven't been able to do as much as I would have liked because it seems that about fifty percent of London's journalists who haven't been covering the Royal Wedding have been in here," he said Eeyore-ishly to Capital Radio, in an ironic foreshadow of a future Diana, grousing about journalistic intrusion in the middle of a scheduled interview. Livingstone spoke of his distaste for the fervid celebrations of the monarchy, especially at a time when Irish republicans imprisoned at Her Majesty's pleasure were dying during their hunger strikes. Similar sentiments were issued in Moscow, where Soviet television claimed that the "People of London hope the sound of wedding bells will drown out the rioting in Ulster and the shouts of young people being beaten mercilessly in Liverpool."

Unsurprisingly, the young Diana was cheered by Conservatives across the board as a brilliant affirmation of tradition. In newspapers of the 1980s, various stories bubble to the surface in which some or other male Conservative MP had defended the princess's honor; some surely felt it their obligation to the Crown, but in other cases it was a manifestation of Diana as an object of romantic fantasy that took some into decidedly weird territory. In a crowded field, Alan Clark won the gold medal: this minister in the Thatcher government spoke of Diana as a "goddess" and alleged that "this up-front crusading thing about AIDS" was the horrible price she'd been forced to pay to keep the homosexual clique that dominated the Palace off her back.

Clark resigned from government in 1992, the same year that he admitted to having been "economical with the *actualité*" regarding an arms deal, a uniquely louche way of saying he'd lied through his teeth. It was also in this year that Diana began to generate real antipathy on the right, following the publication of the Morton biography and the ructions it caused. In the immediate aftermath of Diana's November 1995 *Panorama* interview, Nicholas Soames—a Conservative minister and Winston Churchill's grandson—rode into battle for his good pal Charles and accused Diana of extreme paranoia. Alastair Campbell had Labour MP Andrew McKinlay "attack him" in response. Then, in the early weeks of 1996, Labour's top Welsh MP took it upon himself to join in the pile-on of the Prince of Wales, and on St. David's Day, no less. Ron Davies called Charles a hypocrite who wasn't cut out for the top job, echoing things Diana had intimated on *Panorama*. Then he went an explicit step further: "You can't divorce from the continuation of the monarchy the individuals who are likely to succeed to the monarchy." On the same day that Davies's comments were aired, Alastair Campbell was told by a *Daily Mail* journalist that Conservative MPs were fearful that Diana was being lined up as a Labour candidate for the next election.

This was not the case. Blair had Davies walk back his sally against Charles, not least because, as Blair has stated, Charles projected ideas and rhetoric—interfaith dialogue, environmentalism, healing social division—that were very much in-step with New Labour. Like Blair, Charles even publicly declares himself a renegade at odds with the establishment. "This is a call to revolution," begins his 2010 book *Harmony*, a grab bag of ideas about how to bloody-well-do-things-properly-for-goodness'-sake, which advocates doing away with just about everything other than the monarchy.

Diana also had instances of publicly indulging in such talk of rebellion. On a trip around a toffee factory in South Wales in 1984, she asked workers there, "Do you think they'll give me a job when the revolution comes?" This was in jest, of course—but by the time the Waleses' divorce came through in the summer of 1996, a popular idea had been seeded that the Tory top brass was Team Charles, making those opposed to them Team Diana. Further, an association between Diana and the end of the monarchy had entered public discourse. Throughout 1997, for the first time in living memory, something approaching serious debate was being had in prominent, mainstream venues about whether the UK should become a republic. It started on 7 January when ITV aired a live show titled *Monarchy: The Nation Decides,* which, at the time, was the biggest phone poll in British history: more than two and a half million viewers called in, a third of whom voted to ditch the royals. Among the Great Diary Project contributors for whom politics and current affairs barely intrude on their record of daily life was a woman from Littlehampton in West Sussex, whose precise identity is unclear. Her diaries record the workaday details of her domestic and social routines but in 1997 even she found space among details of a night at the bingo and the grief she'd been getting from her hip to mention that she'd had a conversation with her friend Doris about the prospect of jettisoning the monarchy. Doris, it turned out, shared the diarist's regard for the queen, though another friend of theirs revealed that she'd far sooner have a president than a monarch.

In the buildup to the general election of May 1997, it was Blair who was doing all the running in his meetings with Diana. During a dinner in January, Blair had talked about the importance of the royal family reforming itself—as always, the idea was that the horse should find its own way to the water and not be led there—and becoming part of the New Labour vision of a modern, unbuttoned Britain. This was intended as an unsubtle hint about Diana "taking on a new role," says Campbell, "but she didn't bite." Blair says that this was because Diana was "too smart to give her support to any political party," suggesting that to have done so would have been impolitic because of her status as Princess of Wales. Yet Diana had shown very little interest in constitutional matters before; it's as likely that she didn't want to get too close to Labour before May 1997 in case they didn't win. With a seat in the Lords on one side of the family and a throne on the other, elections were very much not part of her world; competing and losing was not something Spencers or Windsors knew much about.

Labour didn't lose, of course. Indeed, its victory was of historic proportions, a colossal 179-seat majority. Diana was delighted with the result and expected to get down to business, shaping the globe-trotting ambassadorial role that she had let Blair know she was interested in fulfilling, a kind of brand ambassador for Blair's New Britain—although nobody, including Diana, really knew what such a position might entail, especially if she was to maintain her existence as a humanitarian, not political, figure. But the dynamics had changed. With so much power and political capital, Blair no longer felt the need to chase any explicit association with Diana. Besides, no sooner had he got his feet under the table than the newspapers were filled with stories of Diana's relationship with Dodi Fayed, the kept son of a man whose alleged bribery of two MPs had been one of the biggest British political scandals of recent times. Blair raised this difficulty with Diana; "She didn't like it and I could feel the wilful side of her bridling." Though never having had a democratic mandate—and no longer in possession of a royal title—Diana believed her unique identity entitled her to unique treatment. The woman who expressed her desire to be a "queen of people's hearts" felt she should be accountable only to the hearts of the people, and she was certain she knew those better than any vote-grabbing politician.

Tony Benn did not vote for Blair to be the leader of the Labour Party in 1994, but he did identify him as "the spokesperson for a new generation." Four weeks after Labour's gigantic victory in May

1997, Blair stood next to Bill Clinton in the garden of 10 Downing Street and announced the end of old left-right divisions; "the radical centre" was the exciting new venue of political change. "It was all crap," said Benn.

Spokesperson for a generation and spouter of crap: those two interpretations of Blair pretty much summed up the different takes on his address to the nation, and the world beyond, on the morning Diana died. Appearing before the television cameras, brows knitted, voice wavering, he declared Diana to have been "the people's princess." It was repeatedly said that Blair had perfectly captured the national mood—though plenty detected a performance of emotion that Diana herself was sometimes accused of. Not only did he declare, as though by government decree, Britain to be "in a state of shock, in mourning, in grief that is so deeply painful for us," he underlined that he felt "like everyone else in this country today. I am utterly devastated." The evidence from Mass Observation, the Great Diary Project, and the British Library's oral history interviews suggests this was a sizable exaggeration: shock and sadness abounded, but a majority of the nation was probably not in any meaningful sense "devastated" by the news. Yet Blair's speaking in such emotional terms, in the very style that Diana had ushered into public life, in itself resonated with an exceptionally large constituency.

Diana's ambition of being Britain's roving ambassador without portfolio—whatever that meant—was left unfulfilled, although it might be said that in death she increased Britain's visibility abroad in a way that even a living Diana would have struggled to achieve. As James Thomas details in *Diana's Mourning: A People's History*, his detailed study of public attitudes to the week of mourning, there were many among the general population whose hearts swelled with national pride, knowing that the UK was front and center of news coverage the world over. One Mass Observation respondent quoted by Thomas said he'd been eager to watch the funeral because he knew "the world would be watching," and that he felt "proud that 'we British would do it properly.'" Thomas also draws our attention to *The Princess's People*, a BBC documentary about Diana Week, in which another man who had come to London for the funeral fizzed with patriotism: "It's been absolutely marvellous. You'll never ever see anything like this again in the history of mankind. . . . It's a fairytale." Those words were the very kind of thing said of Diana's wedding, the other great ceremonial that bookended her public life. Several weeks after the event, the chief executive of the British Tourist Authority said that the funeral had boosted the UK's profile in Asia, serving as "a wonderful advertisement for Britain's grandeur in terms of its traditional values."

Some found the week of mourning—or, at least, the versions of it presented to them by the media—not only excessively emotional but profoundly sinister. This seemed especially the case when certain newspapers voiced "the people's" anger that flags at Buckingham Palace were not being flown at half-mast. Helena Kennedy, one of the nation's leading lawyers, surmised that Diana Week was the symbolic beginning of an era in which the public had lost its capacity for rational thought. Others thought it portended totalitarianism. Harry and Joan Bygate, a married couple from Kemnay in Scotland and committed socialists born in the 1930s, told an interviewer that they found in the atmosphere of that week a reminder of Nazi Germany. "The emotion's there," said Harry. "A certain leadership can turn that emotion. It's very dangerous. . . . When we're singing the Red Flag at rallies, I enjoy that a wee bit, but at the same time at the back of my head I'm thinking, 'am I just one of these . . . doing the same thing at a different political spectrum'?" Interviewed in 1999, Norman Docherty, a fellow Scot born in 1928, said he was old enough to remember how Hitler "managed to persuade a large number of people in a civilised country to behave like lunatics . . . and I thought with the Diana things, 'well, if somebody wants to brainwash the public . . . they can do it'. . . . Do we think it couldn't happen here? It's very disturbing." As James Thomas lays out, several Mass Observation respondents similarly likened the Dianaists of 1997 to spellbound Nazis in 1930s Berlin. Such responses seem as overwrought as some of the more extreme displays of upset witnessed among the mourners. Anthony Barnett puts it well in saying that had some charismatic totalitarian turned up to lead the Dianaists in a republican revolution, they would have been "offered sympathy for being so upset at the death of a Princess, and possibly a cup of tea from the Harrods catering vans . . . [T]he mood was quiet and self-contained." Watching the footage of the funeral underlines this: the occasional audible cries and shouts from the crowd are conspicuous for how they pierce a silence as total as one you're likely to hear in a rush-hour London Underground train. New Britain, after all, was still Britain.

Yet both the mourners and "those who felt differently" frequently framed their criticisms of the other lot as the appearance of something not truly British. If the Dianaists crying in public were like the brainwashed mob at the Nuremberg rallies, then by not grieving in public, the Windsors were displaying their true Teutonic colors, stiff and cold and alien. For decades, the queen's aloofness, inscrutability, and restraint had been hailed as the epitome of a distinctively British attitude to life. Now, those same qualities were reviled as horribly out of touch with modern Britain.* In the *Princess's People* documentary, a coach driver who's just dropped off a large group of mourners in London tells the camera that he feels sad for Diana and has had a bellyful of the queen and her husband: "They're Germans, anyway."

"A Latin American carnival of grief," is how Boris Johnson described what he saw throughout London. Johnson was a political columnist back then, having previously made his name as a peddler of fake news about the European Commission, claiming that euro banknotes caused impotence and that penpushers in Brussels wanted to ban curvy bananas from British supermarkets. His articles reflected centuries of British anxiety about the perils posed to Britain and Britishness by engaging too closely with the Con-

---

* After Elizabeth's death, her self-possession was once again listed as one of her great qualities. "How we will miss not knowing what she thought," wrote Tina Brown in *The New York Times*.

tinent. His observations of Diana Week likewise communicated a real concern that it wasn't just social change that was evident in the mourning, but a fundamental erosion of national identity, a foreignization of the British soul happening before our very eyes. He was far from the only Eurosceptic to express this. One of them, David Starkey, then one of the best-known historians in the country, thought London had turned itself into Sicily. Various others despaired that scenes in London could have been mistaken for those somewhere in France, or Spain, or North Africa, or North Korea—just about anywhere other than Great Britain.

Combing through magazines and newspapers that chronicled Diana Week, one can't help but notice how often the issue of Europe crops up, as it did more widely in the 1990s when discussing the significance of Diana and the future of the monarchy. So often, it was unquestioningly assumed that Britain was becoming increasingly European—socially, culturally, and politically—and Diana was cited as representative of this change. Anthony Holden provides a good example of the trend in his 1993 book *The Tarnished Crown*, in which he cites Diana as the modernizing example that the Windsors must follow to have any hope of surviving the nation's inevitable future in a federal Europe. "So long as the monarchy remains redolent of Britain's lost empire," writes Holden in his concluding chapter, "it will compound rather than amend Britain's failure to face its future as a European nation-state." He quotes the Labour MP Clive Soley saying, "With the move towards a federal Europe, I think it is inevitable that we will become a republic." Famously, Thatcher had been a splenetic opponent of anything that looked or smelt vaguely like British affiliation with a United States of Europe, but enthusiastic participation in the European project was utterly central to Blair's New Labour vision of New Britain. Center-left press coverage of Diana Week shows it was commonly assumed that the young, modern nation represented by Diana's mourners in London was largely pro-European, too—even though focusing on this faction distorted the very diversity among the mourners that so many found noteworthy.

What Diana thought about Britain's membership of the European project is utterly unclear. There's a good chance that she didn't have strong opinions on it one way or the other—in the 1990s, relatively few people did. However, we do know that Dianaworld's connection to Europe was as complex as one might have expected of an issue that cuts across traditional right-left divides. For instance, Alan Clark, the Conservative MP and Diana's adoring cheerleader, shared an antipathy for European institutions with Tony Benn, who lamented Diana's prominence and found the mourning for her "ghoulish." Among the considerable chunk of the general public who suspected that Charles and Diana's problems had been exacerbated by shadowy republican figures aiming to damage the Windsors, there were those who saw the conniving hand of Europe. In *With Love from Diana*, her 1995 account of her time as Diana's friend and astrologer, Penny Thornton claims to have had dreams that revealed to her the secretive work being done to bring Britain—or England, as she often refers to it—into the European fold by robbing it of its royal family, which is "still the envy and admiration of the peoples of the world." Thornton hails her home nation, rather oddly, as "at once a sceptred isle in a silver sea and a sore thumb in the seat of Europe," but, she continues, "Since the early 1970s England has been in the process of being swallowed up by Europe." She praises Thatcher who assumed the "mantle of Britannia and endeavoured to keep Britain as independent a nation as possible." The effort, however, seems futile: Diana's misery and the wreckage of her marriage betray a "stage management of the monarchy's demise . . . the unfoldment of a global plan."

A feverish notion, perhaps—though these are the same anti-European sentiments which Boris Johnson eventually rode all the way to 10 Downing Street. Did Diana personify New Britain with the promise of its greatness restored as a leading member of a federal Europe? Or when Elton John sang "Goodbye, England's rose," was she a reminder of her nation's enduring uniqueness? This is Diana we're talking about; the answer could be *jawohl* on both counts.

*   *   *

SEEING DIANA'S personal strife in the context of a globalist plot has occurred to many people other than Penny Thornton. In the minds of those who claim to have communicated with Diana after her death, from her spirit plain she urges us to wake up to the evil of chemtrails, mass migration, vaccines, pesticides, the EU, and all manner of dastardly schemes orchestrated by a secret cabal intent on enslaving humanity. There appears to be a split on whether she thinks climate change is an impending apocalypse or a hoax perpetrated by Mossad and the Chinese Communist Party. The one thing she seems consistently emphatic about is the ills of fast food, despite the earthbound Diana's storied love of Big Macs and Diet Coke. To one of her supposed interlocutors, Diana endorsed David Icke, the vehemently anti-EU conspiracy theorist who believes the royal family are shape-shifting space lizards. On the other hand, Stewart Pearce (the man who helped Diana enhance her speaking voice) frames Diana as the ultimate liberal who can soothe us all "in this seething world of Trump and Brexit." Her spiritual force, he believes, was evident in #MeToo, the tenure of New Zealand prime minister Jacinda Arden, and Christine Blasey Ford's testimony against US Supreme Court nominee Brett Kavanaugh.

As esoteric as these viewpoints are, they hint at an overlap between public discourse in Britain in very recent years and that which surrounded Diana at the time of her passing. For those who have lived through Brexit and COVID, the experience of social polarization, of the apparent—though perhaps not actual—existence of two parallel Britains, neither of which really comprehends the other, has been inescapable. With less ferocity, something similar punches through the contemporary accounts of Diana Week.

The caricature of these two different worlds would posit the lachrymose mob—the princess's people—versus an out-of-touch elite, headed by the stone-cold Windsors. The diarist James Lees-Milne was proud to consider himself among the latter. He looked askance at the mourners, feeling as though he no longer understood the country he was living in. Friends of his who lived in London brought news from the capital that one "risks being lynched" should they be heard saying anything critical of the princess. Londoner James Malpas, an art historian, might have agreed. "You'd think a deity had died," he wrote in his diary the day after the accident. Over the coming week, he grew increasingly annoyed by the mourners who seemed to be captivated by mass groupthink led by the "cynical canting hypocrisy of the British press." On the day of the funeral he staged a little protest, playing Berlioz "very loudly, when we were all supposed to be quiet, according to the dictates of the tabloids." Pondering exactly who these people crying and hugging in public were, the historian Dorothy Thompson said, "No one I know bought flowers, wrote a condolence message or joined the crowds in the streets; few watched the televised funeral. Most people I know blessed *Private Eye*," the satirical magazine that made jokes about Diana and the response to her death.

The Scottish artist Ian Hamilton Finlay took delight in the discombobulation of these "smarty-pants" when confronted by what, in his estimation, was an authentic expression of general will. In particular, he enjoyed reading *The Scotsman* newspaper that week. "They could not write about this thing that was happening with their usual cynical distance, with their usual psychological interpretation of everything, with their usual superiority." A zealous student of the French Revolution, Finlay was exhilarated to see and feel something he had never witnessed in Britain in all his seventy-one years: "there it was: you could see 'the people.'" Yet as with the Brexit referendum, clean lines of division between "them and us" were only fleetingly visible. In the *Princess's People* documentary two women talk on camera after the funeral has ended, quietly fuming about their fellow mourners, whom they regard as an embarrassment to the nation and an insult to Diana's memory. "I felt like I was in a bloody zoo," said one of them without fully explaining why. "When I looked at the kinds of people we were around; I'm not being prejudiced . . . Diana *was* the English rose, she was a jewel. And then you've got these ugly males and these ugly opinions . . . I'm sure the royal family don't like half of you out there," she continued, apparently certain that she was among the 50 percent they did like. "I'm really, really angry at the people today."

Clearly, Diana's death did not lead to Brexit. Yet her existence in the 1990s and the responses to her death did inject into the mainstream of British public life a strain of populism that had usually existed only on the fringes. "I do things differently, because I don't go by a rule book," she said on *Panorama*. "Someone's got to go out there and love people," she said of the "unique role" that only she was in a position to perform. She spoke of her strength, a strength she drew from and gave back to the people, and which baffled her enemies. "Why is she strong? Why do the public still support her?" Diana asked, speaking about herself in the third person while pointing out that she continued to draw large crowds wherever she went. To her most ardent fans she made a vow: "I want to reassure all those people who have loved me and supported me throughout the last fifteen years that I'd never let them down." If these things had been said by a public figure seeking a democratic mandate from their adoring base they could possibly be described as Trumpian—and certainly Johnsonian. After all, Diana cast herself as a people's tribune who refused to be silenced by a bullying, elitist establishment, just as those two men do. She held the torch for her "constituency of the rejected," to quote her brother, and vowed to restore the dignity of a beloved British institution and return it to the people.

If Diana was—as has often been suggested and explored—a significant figure in the way modern Britons engage with religion and spirituality, it seems reasonable to suggest that the same could be true of her impact on politics, irrespective of her insistence on not being in any way a political figure. Ian Jackman, the man who regards himself to have been Diana's biggest fan, says that the key lesson from Diana's life and death is that "the people should be heard, and listened to, and respected. . . . I hope that with her passing, that the English government understands that message and continues to listen to the will of the people." Her populist presence, the sentiments she engendered, the vocabulary she used and the vocabulary that was used about her helped make possible not only the phenomenon of Tony Blair, but perhaps Boris Johnson, too. Certainly, it's difficult to think of a high-ranking public figure in postwar Britain before Johnson who made such play of being an ill-disciplined rule breaker, a troublemaking member of the elite who charmed so many by appearing to be both unbelievably posh and "one of us," and who turned their moments of dishonesty into a reason for them to be celebrated as the people's champion, fighting against a cold, sinister establishment that sought to bring them low. Despite his bemusement at the thoroughly un-British weeping masses of September 1997, once Johnson's political career began, he made sure the nation knew that he could bawl with the best of them. At the London Olympics opening ceremony of 2012—arguably the most Dianaist public event since her funeral—Johnson was the city's mayor and pronounced himself deeply moved by this New Britain update of that old national genius for pomp and pageantry. "People say it was all leftie stuff," he remarked of the ceremony's eclectic content which had been attacked by some Tories for being socialist "multicultural crap," and anti-British propaganda. "That is nonsense. I'm a Conservative and I had hot tears of patriotic pride from the beginning. I was blubbing like Andy Murray," referring to the British tennis champion who once cried on court following defeat at Wimbledon.*

Diana's influence on the way British politicians try to engage with the public has been plentifully evident over the last thirty years. Three weeks before Diana died, the new Conservative leader, William Hague, attempted to modernize his party's image by going

---

* In a further parallel with Diana's mythology, biographers have suggested that Johnson's career in public life has been fueled by his need to fix damage done to him in childhood, especially by his father's alleged treatment of his mother and her subsequent sudden absence from the family home.

on water rides at a theme park: the cringeworthy photos that were plastered all over the papers are an unwittingly funny recreation of photos of Diana doing the same with her sons in 1993. Years later, when David Cameron was making his pitch for "compassionate Conservatism" by urging us to, as his critics put it, "hug a hoodie," he struck a very similar note to Diana imploring us to hug those living with HIV, to show compassion for people with eating disorders, or to understand the difficulties faced by the homeless. Tony Blair's legacy on the style of British political leadership is endlessly discussed; Diana's example is less noted but pivotal nonetheless. In his memoirs, published in 2010, Blair expressed some regret about the sobriquet he famously endowed upon Diana on the morning of her death. "The phrase 'people's princess' now seems like something from another age." In the 2020s, it seems more fitting than ever.

WITH DIANA'S funeral less than a month behind him, Tony Blair addressed the Labour Party Conference on 30 September 1997, rhapsodizing about New Labour's birthing of a New Britain. Diana was never named but her presence was palpable. Blair used the word "compassion" seven times; among the seventeen references to "the people" he vowed to address "the people's priorities," reminding us all that "the people have spoken." He banged the drum for Britain's membership of "a people's Europe," intimating that it's what the woman he had just dubbed the People's Princess would have wanted. Consciously or not, Blair's sketch of New Britain drew on Diana's cut-and-shut mythology: change and modernity would dovetail with continuity and tradition; fervent patriotism would inform outward-looking internationalism; the UK would make peace with its more modest role in world affairs yet at the same time transform the planet. Even New Britain's compassion would be "compassion with a hard edge." Blair once told an interviewer that Diana invented a "new way to be British." It might be more accurate to say that through Diana, the British invented a new way of fantasizing about themselves.

Assuming his role as mourner in chief, Blair was accused by some of exploiting Diana's memory for political gain. In the main, however, Blair's public standing was enormously enhanced during Diana Week when he appeared to be a national leader in Diana's image, the opposite of the aloof Windsors. One poll taken that autumn had his approval rating at 93 percent, the kind of number usually reserved for dictators and absolute monarchs. It didn't last. When Blair resigned in 2007, he was still considered a rarely gifted politician but one dreadfully tarnished by the Iraq War. Today, many hold him to be the epitome of the sort of slippery, egomaniacal careerist they'd end up with in Buckingham Palace should Britain ever ditch the monarchy. Among the numerous reasons given for the monarchy's survival in the democratic age, this is one of the most common. One Mass Observation respondent summed it up well when watching Diana marry Charles just a few months after the former B-movie star Ronald Reagan became leader of the free world in 1981: "Although I am a leftist, I believe it is cheaper to breed heads of state than elect them, they cost no more to keep, and you don't get lumbered with geriatric actors."

Halfway through Diana Week, there was talk of a "Floral Revolution"; the British were so furious with the way the cold, callous Windsors had treated Diana—in life, and now in death—they would demand an end to the institution. The fact that the popular antagonism was subdued by the queen making a short announcement on the telly and lowering the flag outside Buckingham Palace rather suggested that, actually, there never had been any incipient revolution, just overheated talk from Fleet Street papers eager to shift the focus of fury and blame for Diana's accident elsewhere. This kind of misidentification is a common theme in the modern history of the monarchy—criticism of a particular monarch labelled as republicanism when it is nothing of the sort. The historian Antony Taylor says that "It is almost as if the British monarchy has a life cycle, during the course of which criticism is incurred at regular intervals, addressed and rapidly defused." That pretty much describes the twenty-year period after the *annus horribilis*. Taking on board some of the things Diana urged about bringing the monarchy nearer to the people, the queen made a noticeable shift in the kinds of events in which she participated. In his compendious biography of Elizabeth II, Ben Pimlott gives the example of school visits. Before Diana's death, Elizabeth would stand in the doorway and observe a lesson; after September 1997, she would enter the classroom, approach children at their desks, and talk with them. In this Dianaist revamp of royal meet and greets, Elizabeth also cropped up in places she had never been seen in before, including a McDonald's—where her Rolls-Royce became momentarily stuck as Her Majesty's driver tried to navigate the narrow drive-thru lane.

These seem like meagre changes. Yet they appear to have helped put the queen back in the nation's good books. It might be that her standing was also boosted by the inadequate attempts at constitutional and electoral reforms that the Blair government made to the House of Lords. Though the place is now largely clear of hereditary peers—Diana's brother included—it is instead bulging with cronies; there are nearly eight hundred unelected people with lifetime membership of the country's upper chamber, a truly embarrassing state of affairs. People's champion Boris Johnson even elevated his little brother, now Baron Johnson of Marylebone, in recognition of the nine unremarkable years he spent as an MP in one of the safest Conservative seats in the land. Set against this, the late queen undoubtedly looks like a model of integrity, far above the grubby dealings of career politicians.

Diana once said that the biggest risk to the monarchy was public indifference; that the monarchy no longer sparkled and shone as a focus of national pride. It seems more likely that public indifference is the thing that will keep it afloat. Ian Hislop, the editor of *Private Eye* and a man who has perhaps made more jokes at the royal family's expense than anyone else alive, articulated common feelings when in 1993, at the depth of the royal family's difficulties, he described his monarchism as "reluctant at best. I would much rather be a disloyal subject of a monarchy than a loyal citizen of whatever alternatives have been proposed to date . . . a rotating presidency taken up by some Tory businessman or some ghastly ex-TUC [Trades Union Congress] man who's been kicked upstairs." Theoretically, the Brexit referendum might have been a cue for fundamental changes to the way Britain is governed, starting with the monarchy. Yet withdrawal from the European Union could have the effect of strengthening the monarchy's standing as something indispensably British. If the historian Linda Colley is correct in saying that Great Britain has, since its moment of inception in 1707, always been defined by a strong sense of what it is not—that is, Catholic, European, and American—then the fact of it *not* being a republic could be considered a crucial part of whatever the *new* New Britain is going to be. Moreover, the political process triggered by the vote to leave the EU has been so shambolic and painful that it might have turned a generation off sweeping constitutional reform. True, young adults voice very low levels of support for the monarchy. But there is no serious mainstream advocate for republicanism, no 2020s version of Tony Benn, who is willing to get into the weeds about what a British republic would look like, and who has the capacity to engage an audience of many millions in doing so. In this cut-and-shut nation so thoroughly bound up in historic ambiguity, contradiction, and paradox, one sometimes wonders if that's even possible.

Two days after Britain's star-crossed princess met her end, Julie Burchill wrote in *The Guardian* that Diana was "the greatest force for republicanism since Oliver Cromwell." In one sense, that's obviously false: Diana gave the Windsors the kit they needed to survive in the twenty-first century. It is true, however, that those who wish to do away with the monarchy long for a Dianaist figurehead for their cause. Republicans crave establishment voices who can stir the emotions as well as make reasoned arguments. Roundheads in Cavaliers' clothing is what's needed: flamboyant, entertaining characters who can induce a broad constituency of the British public to think the unthinkable, much as Johnson did on the matter of the EU. The danger, of course, is that such people tend to disdain the dull, vital business of planning and preparation without which the dream of change turns dreadfully sour. Details are for the Grey Men, they say; we can worry about how on earth we get to dry land once we've sunk the raft. It's the kind of strategy that Diana herself often employed.

❧ 12 ❧

Dianarama

Diana waves goodbye to her fans
at the end of a visit to Chicago, June 1996.

LATE IN THE evening of 30 August 1997, Alan Light was at home in Iowa trying out his new camcorder, filming friends playing Uno around the dining table. CNN was on in the background reporting the breaking news that Princess Diana had been seriously injured in a car crash.

Earlier that day, Diana and Dodi Fayed had disembarked from the *Jonikal* and flown from Sardinia to Paris. Their plan had been to have dinner at the Ritz—owned by Fayed's father—before spending the night at the Villa Windsor, the former home of the Duke and Duchess of Windsor during their decades of self-exile, and now owned by Mohamed Al-Fayed. On leaving the Ritz, the car carrying Dodi and Diana was pursued by a gaggle of overexcited paparazzi through the streets of central Paris. Shortly after midnight, Diana's car entered the Pont de l'Alma underpass, collided with a concrete pillar, then the tunnel wall. Dodi and the car's driver, Henri Paul, were both killed instantly. Bodyguard Trevor Rees-Jones was terribly injured but survived. Diana was still alive when emergency services arrived at the scene and was taken to the Pitié-Salpêtrière hospital.

"They just keep breaking the news over and over again," said Ken, one of Alan Light's friends, directly to the camera as he shuffled the next hand of cards. "*Seriously injured.*"

At length, there was an update: "Princess Diana dead." Ken screamed, while the others gasped and looked in astonishment at the CNN chyron. Alan kept filming, recording not what was on the television screen, but his friends' response to it: quiet, sad, and absorbed in the rolling news coverage which had nothing to add to the headline. Unwittingly, he created an early, authentic, and illuminating example of the "reaction video" genre, bridging the gap between the camcorder and the camera phone generations.

Other denizens of Dianaworld responded differently. The journalist and biographer Michael Wolff reports that Rupert Murdoch was so concerned by the prospect of the tabloid news media being blamed for Diana's death that on the day the news broke he went to the bar of the Dorchester and drank so much that he had to be physically carried out of the building. Murdoch's *News of the World* expressed itself furious about the behavior of the paparazzi and vowed never again to buy images from those who engaged in "merciless stalking and pursuing of people in the news." The *Daily Mirror* said much the same, suggesting it was their way of preserving the memory of the People's Princess: "It is what Diana would have wanted."

Fleet Street might have temporarily turned its back on the paparazzi, but there were enterprising people eager to fill the void. Enter Benjamin Pell, aka Benji the Binman, a cleaner who was responsible for numerous scoops in the late nineties and early aughts thanks to his practice of taking bags of rubbish from outside various London office buildings, spreading their contents over his parents' kitchen floor, and panning for paydirt. "The day of Diana's death was quite a revolutionary day in my life," he explained when telling the story of how he came across his first big scoop while rifling through someone else's garbage: heated correspondence between Richard Branson and Elton John's manager, John Reid, regarding John's refusal to allow "Candle in the Wind" to be included on a compilation album that Branson put together in tribute to Diana in late 1997. Pell sold his information for thousands of pounds to Piers Morgan at the *Daily Mirror* who printed parts of the stolen letters in January 1998. Morgan, who today vociferously rejects the suggestion that he had any knowledge that his reporters ever hacked into Prince Harry's voicemails, has said that his involvement with Pell's news gathering was "on the cusp of unethical."

Branson's album and John's single were just two of the commercial products that were marketed as tributes to Diana in late 1997 and 1998, with proceeds of their sales going to the Diana, Princess of Wales Memorial Fund. In that period, the fund received two hundred applications for Diana-related product licenses per week.

Among the successful applications were a limited-edition Beanie Baby, packs of margarine, and lottery scratchcards. Franklin Mint was denied a license to make and sell Diana dolls but did so anyway, allowing fans to dress up a perma-smiling fifteen-inch People's Princess in a variety of outfits, including her wedding dress and the clothes she wore during her walk through the Angolan minefield. These were the opening sallies in the battle to claim and define Diana's memory, an endeavor that has enveloped the broadest sweep of Dianaworld and continues to the present day.

IN THE aftermath, it seemed everyone had something to say about Diana's death, its meaning, and how best to remember her. Articles appeared not only in newspapers of record and supermarket tabloids, but in organs such as *Tobacco Control*, the *Canadian Medical Association Journal*, and *Rhetoric Society Quarterly*. In Los Angeles, George Clooney called a news conference to berate the tabloid media; the Libertarian Party responded by saying "the legacy of Princess Diana's death should not be new laws which infringe on the First Amendment." When blood analysis suggested that the deceased driver, Henri Paul, had elevated levels of alcohol in his system at the time of the crash, Warsaw traffic police ignored the paparazzi element and cited Diana's accident as a reminder of the dangers of driving under the influence, as did Mothers Against Drunk Driving in the US. "We've seen too many princesses die," read a statement from the group, followed by a list of one hundred women killed by drunk drivers. Even in the manner of her death, people around the world discovered proof that Diana was on their side.

A week after the funeral the Dutch newspaper *Volkskrant* began a new feature, "Dianarama," which ran for seventy-three separate instalments over the following twelve months, cataloguing the strangest, crassest, and most unsettling developments in the unfolding story of how the world responded to the end of Diana's life. Updates included various attempts by entrepreneurs to trademark her name and a Saudi businessman who had supposedly offered millions to buy the wreckage of the car in which she had died. It was also reported that when floral tributes to the princess had been scattered into the Pacific Ocean a school of dolphins had leapt out of the water. The subject of what to do with all the flowers—that ephemeral first wave of memorializing Diana—came up several times in "Dianarama," fittingly considering what a vast proportion of the estimated fifteen thousand tons of flowers bought by the British mourners came via the horticultural markets of the Netherlands. Absent was any mention of one aspect of the flowers for Diana that cropped up repeatedly in British discussion of the phenomenon: cellophane. For much of the twentieth century, British highbrows fixated upon materials they believed summed up the mindless vulgarity of the consumerist masses that undermined traditional virtues of British civilization. At the start of the century it had been tin cans—"Tinned fruit, tinned meat, tinned milk. . . . Tinned minds," to quote the poet John Betjeman. During the mourning for Diana, the offending material was the cellophane that the flowers were wrapped in by florists. That many mourners did not remove the cellophane before placing them at the gates of the various London palaces was, according to some, a metaphorical and literal sign of the falseness of the feelings being expressed: plastic, superficial, and disposable. Some journalists—sounding like caricatures of the out-of-touch chattering classes—believed it to be a means by which the masses demonstrated among themselves that their flowers had been bought and not stolen from someone's garden or grave.

To those who had been paying attention, however, cellophane-wrapped flowers were a widespread, if relatively new, convention in such situations: they proliferated in the vast tributes created in Liverpool for the victims of the Hillsborough disaster of April 1989, when dozens of spectators at a football match had been killed. The month before Hillsborough, Mass Observation received an unsolicited submission from a member of the public who recorded how he had witnessed the very recent emergence of roadside shrines at the

site of traffic accidents across the southeast of England, a phenomenon which he first noted in 1985, and which were distinguished
by the very type of floral tributes that would later be seen at the
mourning for Diana—"florist's funeral sprays, bunches from the
garden in jam jars, flowering pot plants and . . . red roses in special
packs nailed to the tree." Such rituals are so commonplace today
it's strange to think of a moment in the near past when they were
regarded as noteworthy. But they were—and it's evidence of how a
postwar consumerist folk culture, which had already transformed
art and entertainment in so many ways, was doing the same to
rituals around death and dying. The impoverished mourning rites
that characterized Britain during the twentieth century were being
challenged. These new practices perhaps offered a return to the
more demonstrative Victorian traditions that had been the norm
before the wall-to-wall devastation of two world wars engendered
a more stolid attitude to death. The Mass Observation correspondent pointed out that "When one considers the overgrown and
neglected state of most churchyards and cemetaries [sic] which is
often blamed on the uncaring young: it seems strange that at least
some of them are prepared to set up 'unofficial?' memorials at the
site of the death rather than the place of burial."

Diana's car accident, of course, occurred in Paris, not Kensington, but the mammoth shrines that emerged in London were
the apogee of this new folk custom. It is sometimes claimed that
Diana's funeral was unlike anything ever seen in modern Britain.
True, Winston Churchill's farewell in 1965 had the ceremonial
grandness. The spirit of popular expression, however, was more
reminiscent of the funeral of the East End gangster Ronnie Kray
in 1995, another event noted for being simultaneously as British
as could be and startlingly un-British, traditional Cockney ritual
transformed by the post-*Godfather* mythology of the Italian American mafia. Mourners packed the streets of East London for Kray's
send-off; hundreds of elaborate wreaths accompanied his horse-
drawn coffin to the church; men who prided themselves on their
masculine mastery of emotion publicly embraced each other in the

churchyard. While Diana's funeral featured Elton John as well as Bach and Dvořák, there was a similar mixture of tradition and pop culture during Kray's service: Sinatra's "My Way," the pop anthem of late-twentieth-century American individualism, abutted Henley's "Invictus," a late-nineteenth-century verse that encapsulates the stiff upper lip and that gave Prince Harry a name for his charitable foundation for wounded military veterans.

A good deal of the emotion invested in remembering Diana was borrowed or refracted from other experiences. Radio phone-ins and newspaper letters pages furnished testimonies from members of the public who claimed to have cried more about Diana than they had at the death of their own loved ones. One diarist whose record of the 1990s she donated to the Great Diary Project had no interest in Diana at all. Yet she noted how the news of the princess's death affected her, bringing back memories of a few years earlier when her daughter had also died in a car accident in the early hours of an August morning. Speaking in 1998, the British trade unionist Chanda Parmar recalled how Diana's funeral had stirred surprisingly strong emotions in her father, reminding him of his own experiences of bereavement. "It was never approached in the home," said Parmar about how her Hindu family addressed the subject of mortality during her childhood. "I don't remember one occasion where we'd talked about it"—except when Diana died, shortly before Parmar's father also passed away.

That was a time that drew us all quite close together and there were tears and there was sadness. . . . I remember my brother saying to my dad at the time, "Dad, why are you crying? You didn't even know her" . . . and I remember something that will never leave me: my dad said "when people die you don't just think of that individual that's dead, you think of all the people that were special that have died before them" . . . I thought to myself, "I wonder why my dad has thought this? I wonder who he's thinking about." But I never asked him because he was quite emotional.

Six months into "Dianarama," *Volkskrant* reported that British psychotherapists had noted a conspicuously high volume of clients who wanted to talk about Diana's death. In 2000, research that involved Professor Keith Hawton of the University of Oxford Centre for Suicide Research found that in the month following Diana's funeral there was a 17.4 percent increase in suicides in England and Wales, and a 45.1 percent increase among women aged twenty-five to forty-four. The memory of Diana's death has repeatedly been compared to that of JFK's, in that everyone remembers where they were when they heard the news. The authors of this study put a sad spin on the comparison: "The increase in suicides contrasts with the reported reduction in suicides in the USA following the assassination of President Kennedy." In the week following Diana's death, so the researchers claimed, there had also been a 65.1 percent increase in recorded cases of deliberate self-harm among women. According to the researchers, case notes of the women concerned indicated that where Diana's death was cited as a contributing factor it was "largely through amplification of personal losses or exacerbation of existing distress." For better or worse, Diana was doing what she had always inadvertently done: giving people an avatar through whom to lead a second life, one that was otherworldly, yet contained something of themselves within it.

"Dianarama" came to an end exactly one year after Diana's death. In the UK, the first anniversary was widely noted for the lack of fuss that attended it. There was no replication of the mass mourning; floral tributes laid outside those places most associated with Diana were a fraction of those amassed twelve months earlier. Candlelit vigils, teddy bears tied to railings, handwritten poems— all were conspicuous by their rarity. The weeping masses had dried up. It was proof, some said, that Diana Week had been nothing but cellophane, or perhaps a moment of collective hysteria, inflamed and magnified by the self-interested organs of the media. Considering the saturation coverage of the mourning, it's hard to dismiss that idea completely, though it's impossible to say to what extent the people took their cue from the media and vice versa, to clearly distinguish between authenticity and manipulation.

Regardless, that September 1998 was very different from September 1997 could just as easily be seen as evidence that the mourning had done its job. It's rare that any of us grieve a year after a loss as we do in the days and weeks immediately following it. Rather than demonstrating falseness and hysteria, the muted response of Diana's public in 1998 suggests that most of them had always had their heads screwed on. In 1952, Joan Thwaites noted in her diary how sad the world seemed on the day of George VI's funeral. Forty-six years later, she felt much the same when she heard about Diana's death. "Everyone devastated . . . a bad day of shock + grief," she wrote. Two days later, she still felt sad, but chose to incorporate it into the churn of daily life. "Walk round park. Washed kitchen tiles. Life goes on."

ALONGSIDE THE Diana, Princess of Wales Memorial Fund was a committee that sought to establish a range of lasting tributes; Diana's sister Sarah, Paul Burrell, Richard Attenborough, Gordon Brown, and the children's TV presenter Diane-Louise Jordan were among its eclectic membership. The committee established a number of "living memorials," such as an initiative to develop children's nursing teams to care for seriously ill children in their own homes. Physical memorials aimed to be immersive, experiential, and inclusive in a way that was said to have been reflective of Diana's life and her connection with the public. A playground within Kensington Gardens was constructed in her name, as well as a seven-mile walkway within central London. In 2004, a 210-meter oval fountain was opened in Hyde Park, designed by Kathryn Gustafson to be a family-friendly place for people to paddle and cool their feet. The fountain's contours were meant to mimic the course of Diana's story; Gustafson intended for the water to "run, tumble, cascade, curl and bubble" around the fountain's horizontal surface "before coming to rest in a large tranquil pool." The design was criticized by art critics, and some of Diana's friends, as a milquetoast tribute that kept Diana invisible and expressed nothing of her personality, though the drama that surrounded the project was certainly in keeping with her life. Soon after the memorial opened—late and over budget—it was temporarily shut: three people, including a child, were hospitalized with injuries caused by slipping on the wet, smooth stone. Just seven years after the ceremony of Diana's funeral had British chests bursting with pride, Diana's water hazard memorial had managed to unite media outlets left and right in feeling embarrassed at the country's decline. It was the nation's "latest Great Endeavour Gone Wrong," said *The Observer*, referring to recent similar problems with the Millennium Dome and Millennium Bridge projects. "Other countries do national memorials," said the *Daily Mail*, "Britain does national debacles."

A common bugbear was that the committee seemed willing to sanction anything other than a statue of Diana, which to many of her admirers was considered the best form of tribute, placing Diana among the greats of British history who had all been immortalized in grand works of lifelike sculpture. Yet attempting to carve Diana's memory into the national consciousness in that way was complicated. When he spoke at length about Diana's cultural impact in September 1997, just days after her funeral, Ian Hamilton Finlay lamented that there was little chance of Diana being commemorated in high-quality figurative sculpture. The issue, he said, was partly that so few modern sculptors had the requisite skill, but also because it would be all but impossible to agree on where such a work should be placed. Finlay also feared that people had lost the feel for figurative art, especially as memorial. Though he considered classical sculpture to be the perfect form through which to express Diana's textured, powerful, cultural significance, he suspected that for generations of the public who had grown up suffused in modern art, too much would be lost in translation.

In the absence of an official figurative commemoration of Diana, a glut of unofficial ones filled the space. Between September

1997 and the start of the new millennium, a huge number of artistic depictions of Diana were created and publicized, a great many of which could be classed as outsider art, pieces made by those with only the slightest connection to the recognized art world. Among this grand production of non-establishment artworks are two pieces of figurative sculpture that in their strangeness, flaws, and troubled biographies are as perfect a memorialization of Diana and her meaning as anything that the official guardians of her memory could manage.

John Houlston was a sculptor from Faversham in Kent who claimed to have sketched Diana in her apartment at Kensington Palace in 1996, preparatory drawings for a giant bust that he was working on at the very moment she was killed. Houlston had previously made busts of Archbishop Desmond Tutu that were displayed at Kings College, London, and later at the University of Western Cape in South Africa, both of which Tutu posed with for photographs during official visits. If Houlston did gain access to the princess, the Tutu connection might have been the reason. Some Faversham residents remember Houlston, who died in 2002, as a highly eccentric man whose claims about his work—especially regarding their commercial value and critical standing—were clearly fanciful. Nevertheless, the story of the last artwork for which Diana posed caught the attention of the press as Houlston attempted to finish it. In November 1997, he told *Faversham News* that his sculpture was to be a nine-foot, two-ton work of metal and resin designed to withstand the elements and to be placed on permanent display outside the London headquarters of the National AIDS Trust. By March, the same paper reported that the statue would be thirteen feet high and possibly made from carbon fiber. Houlston said that the news of his monument to Diana's memory had piqued interest around the world: photographs of him and the work in progress had appeared in multiple newspapers, two television news crews had filmed with him, and he'd been interviewed on American radio stations. His story had also been featured on the long-running BBC religious program *Songs of Praise*. In May, a third article quoted Houlston as saying that he was attempting to imbue his rendering of Diana with some of the qualities of Leonardo's Virgin Mary, as well as "the look of a classical Greek goddess." The fly in the ointment was that a family of thrushes had taken up residency in Diana's left ear; Houlston said he would leave off for six to eight weeks until the birds had moved on. When the national papers got hold of the story, they addressed the elephant in the room (now weighing in at eight tons, apparently) that the local papers had been too charitable to mention: Houlston's sculpture looked nothing like Diana at all. "It's Diabolical," wrote the *Daily Mirror*, which suggested the bust more resembled the football pundit Jimmy Hill than the People's Princess. "I'm not bothered what the critics say," Houlston was quoted as saying by reporter Jane Kerr. "It's a piece of sculpture for ordinary people." A year later, the *Sunday Mirror* delivered a sad update: ill-health and a lack of time and funds had forced Houlston to give up on the project. It now sat moldering in a builder's yard. After the article was published, the National AIDS Trust wrote a letter to clarify that it had never commissioned the piece; Houlston had offered it as a donation and nothing more. A local resident took the last known snap of the bust before the yard was cleared to make way for a new housing development.

The backstory to Andrew Walsh's sculpture of Diana is similarly odd. Walsh was a stonemason from Warwickshire who specialized in funeral memorials, and it was at the Funeral Services Exhibition in Birmingham, in May 2000, that he first displayed his life-size statue of Diana made from granite with a jet-black veneer applied to the face, arms, and chest. When the Spencer family complained, the statue was removed from the exhibition, after which various efforts were made to find it a new home. But the "Black Diana," as it became nicknamed, was prevented from being displayed at a local art gallery, and a plan to place it at Walsall bus station was scrapped when the queen objected. Clearly, some were aghast at the prospect of the statue being displayed in any prominent public place. One councillor described its look as "demonic"; an MP crudely remarked that it was "more like Diana Ross" than Diana, Princess of Wales. Walsh removed the veneer, but it didn't help the statue find a permanent home—so he decided to put it proudly outside his own premises, an all-female firm of funeral directors in Bloxwich where it stands to this day, its appearance hovering somewhere between a heartfelt tribute, a de facto company mascot, and a patron saint of modern British mourning.

The statue encountered the very problems that Ian Hamilton Finlay had predicted any figurative sculpture of Diana would face: an inability to render a strikingly realistic image of her, together with intractable public debate about where and how it should be displayed. Yet Walsh's work was created with genuine love and care; the oddness of the piece makes it a quintessential memorial to the People's Princess. The emotional honesty, the ridicule it attracted from establishment figures, its blithe breach of protocol, its unexpected appearance in incongruous locations, its blurring of the lines between traditional decorum and popular taste—these are the very qualities that Diana projected and for which so many love her. Neither the Houlston nor the Walsh sculpture is the most accomplished tribute, nor in many senses the most accurate— but both are weirdly apposite. Each of them offers an insight into Dianaworld—its hyperbole, drama, and bracing rejection of convention—as well as that strange, special moment occasioned when its queen departed.

THE FEELING that Diana's memory needed to be protected from the establishment was the prime motivation for the founding of the Diana Circle, a group of committed Dianaists who feared that Diana was being "airbrushed from history." According to its own lore, the group formed at the gates of Kensington Palace in 1999, when mourners were even sparser than at the first anniversary. "There were seven of us standing in a circle," one of those present recounts, "and we all said 'we've got to do something to keep this young girl's memory alive.'" Among the group's earliest objectives was to establish a fitting official memorial. They certainly didn't consider "a piece of granite in Hyde Park" remotely adequate. Nothing less than a statue placed in a prominent place closely associated with Diana, permanently visible and accessible to the public, would do. Diana Circle founding member Josephine Dobson says that on one day outside Kensington Palace she collected five hundred signatures which were included in a petition submitted to Parliament requesting that such a statue be commissioned. The efforts came to nothing; "we have enough statues in London," she says was the response.

Dobson is the closest thing the organization has to a public face. Her popularity with journalists rests partly on the front room of her suburban home in Gloucestershire which is a virtual shrine to Diana, every wall and surface covered with images of the princess and memorabilia devoted to her. In interviews she often wears a T-shirt with Diana's face on it along with the words "JO DOBSON DIANA CIRCLE UK FOUNDER MEMBER." When the then Prince of Wales announced in 2005 that he was to remarry, Dobson and her cohorts were incensed. Diana Circle members wrote to newspaper editors, various MPs, and the registrar general to protest the marriage, vowing that they would never accept "Cowmilla" as their queen. She was in their sights again in 2007, the tenth anniversary of Diana's death, when they wrote to Camilla to ask her to stay away from a Diana memorial service being held that year. It had been reported that William and Harry had asked Camilla to attend; eventually, she decided not to. Dobson publicly stated her view that whether Camilla attended or not, a single service was a paltry commemoration. She wanted a day of thanksgiving to Diana, a public holiday every year on her birthday.

The Dianaists of the Diana Circle believe that the late princess embodied the purest essence of true royalty, and that her reputation has been sullied by other royals who were threatened by her wonderful human qualities and her principled commitment to the people. It echoes the stance of the Ricardians of the Richard III Society, the group dedicated to rehabilitating the memory of that

Josephine Dobson, founding member of the Diana Circle, at home with her collection of Diana memorabilia, August 2017.

most infamous of English kings. In many ways, Diana's and Richard's stories are opposites. For centuries Richard's mythology has painted him as a black-hearted, physically unappealing man whose great crime was murdering the Princes in the Tower, whereas the beautiful, compassionate Diana's love of her young princes is thought to have been her crowning achievement. Ardent supporters of both insist that their cause was the victim of a gigantic conspiracy against them. "She was definitely murdered," says Dobson, who claims to have a source in the upper echelons of the British police who confirms that the seatbelts in Diana's Mercedes had been "done up so they didn't work."

That Diana had been killed by a vast conspiracy encompassing many of the world's most powerful people was a belief that took root around the globe from the very moment that the news of her death was confirmed. The predominant hunch was that some configuration of the establishment had killed Diana to prevent her from marrying, and having children with, a Muslim. It was the first big conspiracy theory of the Internet age; it spread and splintered faster than anyone was then accustomed to. In the process, it united several conspiracist genres, from *The Da Vinci Code*–style fantasies about ancient bloodlines and secret societies to the role of US intelligence in the deaths of JFK, MLK, and Marilyn Monroe, via Zionists, Muslim fundamentalists, British imperialists, American capitalists, the military-industrial complex, and international pedophile rings, the latter apparently enraged at Diana's protection of vulnerable children. All kinds of people and institutions were accused of having murdered the princess: the Windsors, MI6, the CIA, the EU, the UN. For years after her death, opinion polls revealed that between a third and a half of the British public were persuaded by the idea that the truth about Diana's death had been covered up by the establishment; around one in four thought she had died as a result of an ordered hit.

An impressive range of these beliefs was exhibited on "Diana Conspiracies," an episode of *For the Love Of . . .* Hosted by the writer and filmmaker Jon Ronson, it aired in 1998, once the initial wave of extreme public sensitivity about Diana's death had passed but when the topic still captivated mainstream attention. The show has the look and tone of a precursor to certain popular podcasts of the 2020s: Ronson's half a dozen guests sit on comfy sofas and leather armchairs and talk fantastical rubbish for an hour, stating with bulletproof confidence things they cannot prove. A couple of commenters on the program's posting on YouTube conclude that Ronson and co. must themselves be part of the conspiracy, plants to make serious, genuine experts on the matter sound ridiculous. Manifold aspects of Dianaworld find a place in the various alternative truths outlined in the program. Diana was not only of royal blood, but a direct descendent of Jesus and Solomon. Not only did she die at the hospital where Jean-Martin Charcot had long ago treated hysterical women, but the psychological techniques Charcot developed there were used to hypnotize Henri Paul into causing the accident. Diana's death was faked with the help of one of her many doppelgangers. Even the tension between New Britain and the old stiff upper lip is brought into the conversation. One contributor thinks the fact that Prince Harry walked behind his mother's coffin without shedding a tear tells us that Diana's death was faked and that the princes were in on the con. "Well, no," another contributor immediately responds, "he showed so much emotion by trying to keep in his pain. That was the whole point about it: he was a brave little chap."

One of the contributors is Simon Regan, a journalist associated with the first known interception of Diana's phone calls, something that became a conspicuous theme in her later life and that rumbles along in the lives of her sons. In May 1981, back when she was still Lady Diana Spencer, Regan sold to the German publication *Die Aktuelle* transcripts of what he alleged were recorded calls between Charles and Diana. In the UK, the Palace had a legal injunction placed on the publication of the transcripts which it insisted were fabricated. No great scandal emerged from the transcripts; perhaps they were most consequential for seeding the belief in Diana's mind, even before the wedding, that she was subject to constant surveillance by hostile forces. Regan's theory was that British and French intelligence turned a blind eye to a Muslim fundamentalist plot to take out Dodi Fayed in which Diana was probably collateral damage. In keeping with his earlier activities, this idea of his also rested on contested information from an unnamed eavesdropper: "a radio buff," he told Jon Ronson, "a voyeur, who was actually sitting under the Eiffel Tower," attempting to listen in on private conversations on the night of Diana's accident.

Another of Ronson's guests was Jeffrey Steinberg, an editor of *Executive Intelligence Review* (*EIR*), a magazine founded by Lyndon LaRouche, neatly labelled by the writer David Aaronovitch as "an American cultist who might be best described as the Reverend Moon of politics." The Diana conspiracy theories expounded by *EIR* fed into Mohamed Al-Fayed's campaign to prove that Diana and Dodi had been murdered on the orders of Prince Philip, a campaign that came to a head at an inquest led by Lord Justice Scott Baker in 2007 and 2008. Al-Fayed—who was, of course, a dreadfully hurt and grieving father—claimed to be fulfilling a solemn promise he had made to Diana that should she be assassinated he would fight to reveal the truth and protect her memory. It was a similar claim made by several of those who went to print with books about their time in Diana's company, though in his testimony Al-Fayed insisted that "nearly for twenty years" he had been "the closest friend to Diana," an obvious untruth. "What I am doing is not for myself," he told the inquest, imitating Diana's populist rhetoric, but "the ordinary people." His astonishing claims were given artistic expression in "Innocent Victims," a sculpture he commissioned that depicted Diana and Dodi as two angelic soulmates brutally murdered by the establishment and that he displayed at Harrods between 2005 and 2018. In those years, this was surely the most famous figurative dedication to Diana, a testament to that part of her reputation as a kind of Robin Hood figure, as well as a public reminder that a vast chunk of the public never trusted the official version of Diana's death.

That version was formalized in April 2008, when Lord Baker concluded the inquest and gave his verdict that Diana's death was accidental, echoing the conclusion of a report published by Lord Stevens two years earlier. Some observers refused to accept it. What about the white Fiat that had been seen at the scene of the crash, then mysteriously vanished? What about the CCTV cameras that hadn't furnished any footage of any of the vehicles involved? The Stevens Report and the Baker inquest had answered these questions, but a stubborn core of conspiracists refused to be swayed. However, for most people the inquest verdict drew a formal line under the matter. In any event, by this point Internet conspiracy theorists had moved on to 9/11, and in just a few weeks a global financial crash would give impetus to a fresh batch of ideas about the hidden hands guiding our fates.

For millions of people, Diana died as she lived, a whistleblower exposing the filthy secrets of the establishment. Identifying exactly what those secrets were was less important than confirming that they existed; if Diana could be undone by the Grey Men and the "dark forces," then so could the rest of us. Perhaps it was the final act of comfort that the People's Princess was able to offer. "Does it matter what type of conspiracy?" asked a contributor on Jon Ronson's show when addressing the huge areas of discrepancy between the competing ideas about what *really* happened on 31 August 1997. "The fact that we're discussing it here and now is because we're very unhappy with being told that it was an accident."

BETWEEN 1998 and 2014, one hundred and fifty of Diana's personal possessions were displayed at Althorp, the centerpiece of an exhibition called "Diana: A Celebration." For most of that period, in the months when Althorp was closed to the public, the exhibition went on tour around the world. The first destination was Japan, after which the collection spent much of its time shuttling between a variety of venues in the United States, though not the sorts of places Diana was used to visiting: Davenport, Iowa; Grand Rapids, Michigan; Bloomington, Minnesota. When it arrived in Bloomington, the exhibition was housed in the Mall of America. In Connecticut, it did great business at the Foxwoods Resort Casino. In Davenport, its arrival sparked ancillary events such as "A Royal Affair" and "A Toast to Diana," both sponsored by the Bling Bling Sisters, a local costume jewelry store. Precisely why the decision was made to bring "Diana: A Celebration" to an end has never been publicly articulated, but it seems a fair bet that William and Harry thought it time to take their mother's memory off the circuit. Under the conditions of her will, Diana's possessions came into her sons' control when Harry turned thirty, the very year in which the exhibition closed.

The winding down of the Diana touring exhibition coincided with the era of Diana reimagined. Diana's story had been harvested by artists, writers, and filmmakers from practically the moment she died, but usually she was conspicuous by her absence, often cast as the invisible instigator of events. She dominated the Oscar-winning *The Queen*, for instance, but was kept respectfully off-stage. She's likewise absent but ever present in David Baddiel's 1999 novel *Whatever Love Means*, in which her death provides the catalyst for a knotted mess of doomed love affairs, as the lecherous male protagonist exploits the strange emotional atmosphere of the times to put a notch on his bedpost. "Vic fucked her first the day Princess Diana died" is Baddiel's provocative opening line. Even on the front cover, she is the only thing the reader sees, yet manages to be not quite present, an illustration of "those eyes" pulsing through a yellow background like the unmistakable smile of the vanishing Cheshire Cat.

A shift in depictions of Diana began in 2011, around the time when she returned more strongly on the world's cultural radar than she had for several years, when William's wedding to Kate Middleton induced reminders of Diana's own wedding thirty years earlier. Enough time had passed, enough of the royal story had moved along, for fictional Dianas to be brought into the world. Among the deluge of coverage around what would have been Diana's fiftieth birthday, about two months after William's wedding, *Newsweek* ran a piece by Tina Brown which speculated upon what Diana would have looked like were she still alive, with the visual assistance of a computer-generated image. A decade later, the British daytime television show *This Morning* would mark Diana's sixtieth with one of Diana's former lookalikes modelling styles that its hosts reckoned Diana would be wearing had she not died a quarter of a century earlier. By that time, the world was once again used to women pretending to be Princess Diana, mainly thanks to *The Crown*, *Spencer*, and before them *Diana*, the 2013 film about Diana's relationship with Hasnat Khan. Upon the latter's release, Josephine Dobson surfaced to lodge her disapproval. She hadn't seen the film and had no intention of doing so, but that was beside the point. It was "sixteen years on" from Diana's death, Dobson complained, "and that young girl could not be laid to rest." Although letting Diana rest seemed to be the last thing Dobson herself wanted. As the twentieth anniversary of the accident in Paris approached, Dobson, still publicly campaigning for a statue, donated her collection of Diana memorabilia to the Gloucester Folk Museum. She was interviewed on the topic on live television, in national British newspapers, and was quoted in a *New York Times* article about Diana's standing in the UK. A physical, permanent tribute to Diana was necessary to stop her sliding from national consciousness, argued Dobson, who made a very good point in observing that a bronze statue of the queen's late mother on the Mall had been rustled up less than seven years after her passing. Surely it was only just that the adored mother of the future king be respected in the same way.

Eventually Dobson's hope was fulfilled when a statue of Diana, commissioned by her sons, was unveiled at Kensington Palace in 2021. The Diana Circle's leading advocate did the media rounds again, expressing her delight that at last Diana was to be memorialized in the correct manner—though she was upset that William and Harry had not extended an invitation to the event to her or her fellow hardcore Dianaists who had kept the faith for so long. The unveiling took place at an inopportune moment, which strengthened the argument that classical statuary was a dreadfully inapt way of capturing Diana's significance to the country. A year earlier, statues in various cities in the UK had been assailed by protesters in the wake of similar activities in the United States after the death of George Floyd. In Bristol, a statue of the eighteenth-century slave trader Edward Colston was toppled and hauled into Bristol Harbour. On the empty plinth, various unofficial replacements were briefly erected, such as a mannequin depicting the notorious sexual predator Jimmy Savile, an effigy of a Black Lives Matter protester, and a figurine of Darth Vader. In the same week that Diana's statue went up, one of Elizabeth II was torn down in Winnipeg, Canada.

Sculpted by Ian Rank-Broadley, the statue depicts Diana flanked by three children, her arms draped protectively across their shoulders. This is Diana as a quasi-religious figure, a Mary of the multifaith age, which reminded the art critic Jonathan Jones of Pietro della Francesca's fifteenth-century painting of Christ's mother as the Virgin of Mercy, shielding the vulnerable within her cloak. As with the Hyde Park fountain, Rank-Broadley's statue attracted negative comment for presenting Diana as the bland, flawless creature she was definitively not—but also because it was said to be a poor likeness of its subject. As with portraits of Diana, the sculpture at Kensington Palace suffers because so much of Diana's mythology is bound up in the profusion of photographs that made her the most recognizable face on the planet. Rosalind Jana makes the further argument that statues are ill-suited to rendering modern clothing; while the qualities of stiff military uniforms or nineteenth-century formal dress are enhanced by statues of bronze or stone, the clothing of a late-twentieth-century woman is intended "to be viewed in motion. Just as a smile line rendered in bronze becomes heavy and sinister, a stilled pleat in fabric feels devoid of life." To make matters worse, the sculptor chose to model Diana in conspicuously plain clothes, negating the dazzling impact that she had on just about everybody she met in the flesh. "Of the many hundreds of outfits she wore," asks Jana, "why pick one that looks so secretarial?"

SHORTLY BEFORE "Diana: A Celebration" made its American debut, Earl Spencer was asked how he felt about those who made money by exploiting their connection with his sister. "There will always be people making money from her in an unworthy way," he answered. Some might query whether the exhibition had itself been entirely worthy. Still, one can see his point: today, in the less-than-hallowed halls of the National Enquirer Live! tourist attraction, one can survey the circumstances of Diana's death via a 3D model of the Paris streets where her accident happened. When misleading reports in 2019 suggested the attraction actually featured a theme park ride that recreated the experience of the crash, a spokesman said that National Enquirer Live! offered nothing so crass as that but admitted that the exaggerations had been good for business: "Speaking as a marketing guy, it was a great thing to happen to us."

For those hoping to see material objects associated with Diana, the best place to go now is the Princess Diana Museum, an online museum that offers the chance to examine more than twelve hundred objects (around three hundred of them in 3D) connected to Diana. The museum is run by Renae Plant via her Princess and the Platypus Foundation, named after her experience of picking up a tiny clay platypus that she says Diana accidentally dropped in the dirt during her visit to Australia in 1983. Plant, who was twelve at the time, picked up the platypus with the intention of giving it back to the princess. But a police officer blocked her path and told her that if Diana had dropped it, "she must have dropped it to give it to you." The way Plant speaks, it's as though the object has a cosmic power, imbued with Diana's philanthropic spirit that was passed to her like a baton. The hundreds of objects she has amassed in recent years are all viewed in that same way: the museum is a virtual reliquary.

Since the Diana exhibition at Althorp closed, there is much less evidence of her, or, at least, her presence no longer overshadows the estate's other former residents. The memorial near Diana's burial site still attracts attention, but inside Althorp House, her portraits hang next to those of her brother and their ancestors, just one face among centuries of Spencers. There is, however, a Dianaist tone throughout the building; the rarefied environs of the aristocracy and royalty brought into contact with the outside world in the unflinching way that Diana facilitated. Amid the bottomless collection of pre-twentieth-century portraits are *Britannia* and *Rehab*, two works by the contemporary painter Mitch Griffiths. *Britannia* depicts a twenty-first-century woman, cigarette between her lips, lottery ticket by her feet, holding a CCTV camera in one hand while the other rests on the handle of a stroller that is bound up with police tape. It hangs at the end of a row of portraits of Charles II's mistresses—ironically, Althorp has a vast collection of such pictures—and is described in the explanatory text next to it as a present-day version of "a similar kind of woman." Elsewhere in the house, *Rehab* is described as a work that engages with addiction, "not only to drugs but also to salacious gossip." When the journalist Tanya Gold visited the house, she declared herself "amazed at the placing of this portrait . . . I always thought of Diana as an addict, her emotions a slipstream. She was unanchored, open to all ideas, even witchcraft. She had the self-absorption, the craftiness, the hunger for love, the fury, the mercurial kindness and the self-hatred of the addict."

On a roasting hot Sunday in August 2022, there were only a handful of visitors at Althorp. One woman was baffled that Earl Spencer could charge twenty pounds to look at hundreds of old paintings of God-knows-who, cabinets of old crockery, and just a tiny few pictures of Diana, the only reason she'd come. As she made her way into the final room on the tour, she turned to her companion and asked "Is there nothing else Diana? *Is that it?*"

ACKNOWLEDGMENTS

A large proportion of the sources cited in this book were accessed at or through the British Library. Many thanks to Madeline White and other members of the library's staff who provided guidance, clarification, and assistance.

I am also indebted to archivists at the University of Sussex, Bishopsgate Institute, the Churchill Archives Centre at Churchill College, University of Cambridge, and the Bodleian Library, University of Oxford. Thanks also to the Baring Archive, Hugo Manson at the University of Aberdeen, Jerome Farrell and Kerry Sutton Spence of the National Lesbian and Gay Survey, Kalpesh Solanki at Asian Media Group, Olivia Davies and Kate Walsh at United Agents, Lily Kovacs and Gordon Wise at Curtis Brown, and the trustees of the Mass Observation Archive.

Many other people have kindly given their time and assistance in various ways. In particular, I would like to thank Professor Akbar Ahmed, Nema Alaraby, Juliet Besly, Rachel Bowie, Grant Burnside, Ru Callender, Abdul Basit Daoud, Lesley Davies, Roberta Fiorito, Melissa Flamson at With Permission, Sir Simon Fraser, Patrick Jephson, Linus Karp, Richard Kay, Attiya Khan, Peter Lefcourt, Katharine McGee, David McGillivray, Shazia Mirza, Michael O'Mara, David Oppedisano, Erin Pizzey, Renae Plant, Donna Ranieri, Sonia Riabokin, Dr. Wendy Rickard, Pamella Roland DeVos, Kinsey Schofield, Dr. George Severs,

Ingrid Seward, Simone Simmons, Sir Roger Tomkys, Nick Todd, and Simon Watney.

For their enthusiasm, insight, patience, and advice, I owe great thanks to everyone at W. W. Norton & Company, especially John Glusman, Helen Thomaides, Wick Hallos, Anna Oler, and Susan Sanfrey; to copyeditor Ira Brodsky; and to Simon Winder at Penguin.

I am indebted to other writers whose work on Diana and the royal family has informed my own. Chief among these are Sally Bedell Smith, Sarah Bradford, Tina Brown, Professor Michael Billig, Professor Mandy Merck, Tom Nairn, and the late Dr. James Thomas.

As always, the encouragement and support of Chris Parris-Lamb has been invaluable. Thanks to Chris, Sarah Bolling, Aru Menon, and their colleagues at the Gernert Company.

Family and friends have helped in ways too numerous to list. Thank you all for everything.

NOTES

Abbreviations

BL	British Library
GDP	The Great Diary Project, Special Collections and Archives, Bishopsgate Institute.
MMB	Millennium Memory Bank, British Library.
MOA	Mass Observation Archive, Special Collections, University of Sussex.
NLGS	National Lesbian and Gay Survey, Special Collections, University of Sussex.
Scott Baker	Transcripts of the Coroner's Inquests into the Deaths of Diana, Princess of Wales and Mr. Dodi Al Fayed, 2007–08. Presided over by Lord Justice Scott Baker. See https://webarchive.nationalarchives.gov.uk/ukgwa/20090607230333/http://www.scottbaker-inquests.gov.uk/index.htm.

Undated entries have been accessed online. Unless otherwise stated, all online content was most recently accessed July 2024.

Introduction

1 **"has increasingly been . . . history"**: Ken Wharfe, *Guarding Diana: Protecting the Princess Around the World* (London: John Blake, 2017), 28.

4 **"I'm a republican . . . happens"**: "What You Think," *Liverpool Echo*, December 10, 1992, 6.

1. Blood Family

6 **"Even at the . . . brother"**: "School Friends Look Back," *Lynn News & Advertiser*, March 3, 1981, 3.

7 **"an addition to ... depends"**: "Royal Family Attend Wedding of Lovely Norfolk Bride," *Lynn News & Advertiser*, June 4, 1954, 7.

8 **According to reports ... head**: "Christening Is Royal Occasion," *Lynn News & Advertiser*, July 17, 1964, 1.

8 **However, in newspaper ... Elizabeth**: Grania Forbes, "My Hopes for the Future," *Liverpool Echo*, July 27, 1981, 3.

9 **At the outbreak ... divorce**: Gavin Thompson et al., *Olympic Britain: Social and Economic Change Since the 1908 and 1948 London Games* (London: House of Commons Library, 2012), 33.

10 **"I had to ... free"**: Sandra Paul in "The Stresses of Divorce," *Whicker's World*, BBC One, April 22, 1967.

10 **"I remember seeing ... crying"**: Andrew Morton, *Diana: Her True Story—In Her Own Words*, revised 25th ann. edition (London: Michael O'Mara, 2017), 37.

11 **In 1969, 51,000 ... 145,000**: "Divorce Rates Data, 1858 to Now: How Has It Changed?," *Guardian*, n.d., https://www.theguardian.com/news/datablog/2010/jan/28/divorce-rates-marriage-ons#data.

11 **"poor Di, so ... lovable"**: Anonymous, September 1, 1997, GDP.

11 **"Society of Deprived ... eighteen"**: Anonymous, September 3, 1997, GDP.

12 **"I was my ... that"**: Morton, *Diana: Her True Story*, 46.

12 **"terrible wrench"**: Morton, *Diana: Her True Story*, 44.

13 **"Acid Raine"**: James Whitaker and Christopher Wilson, *Diana vs. Charles: Royal Blood Feud* (Los Angeles and New York: Graymalkin Media, 2017), 66, Kindle.

13 **"good Spencers"**: Charles Spencer, *The Spencer Family* (London: Penguin, 2000), xv.

13 **"modest do-gooders"**: Spencer, xviii.

13 **"distant ... wretched ... broken"**: Margaret Douglas-Home, *A Spencer Childhood* (Great Glenham, Suffolk: John Catt Educational, 1994), 2–3.

13 **"an elderly, solitary ... between"**: Douglas-Home, 1.

14 **"the sadness of ... background"**: Douglas-Home, introduction.

14 **Diana recalled times ... bed**: Morton, *Diana: Her True Story*, 37.

14 **"I genuinely believe ... him"**: Spencer, *Spencer Family*, 319.

14 **"moved into the ... Althorp"**: Edward John Spencer, *Japan & The East* (Althorp, UK: Earl and Countess Spencer, 1986), foreword.

14 **"revenge for not ... child"**: Brett Gorvy, "A Year in the Life," *Antique Collector*, September 1993, 50.

15 **"leering little clerks ... Again"**: Robin Douglas-Home in "The Stresses of Divorce."

16 **"Lady Diana wept openly"**: Harry Arnold, "The Anguish of Charles," *Sun*, February 21, 1981, 1.

16 **"Diana probably regrets ... crying"**: Phoebe Hitchens and Rosie Oxley, *Dear Princess* (London: MacMillan, 1984), 47.

17 **"Supersloane ... cool"**: Ann Barr and Peter York, *The Official Sloane Ranger*

Handbook: The First Guide to What Really Matters in Life (London: Ebury Press, 1982), 20.

17 **"it seems as . . . Kennedys?"**: Max Riddington and Gavan Naden, *Frances: The Remarkable Story of Princess Diana's Mother* (London: Michael O'Mara, 2003), 14.

17 **"those who believed . . . write"**: Giles Kime, "Charles Spencer on History, Jane Fonda and Being 'Up to My **** in Alligators,'" *Country Life*, October 3, 2017.

17 **"born with every . . . shores"**: Catherine Ostler, "From Silver Spoon to Silver Spoon," *Tatler*, December 12, 1994, 204–5.

18 **"comfortable, ten-bedroomed . . . houses"**: Colin Campbell, *Diana in Private: The Princess Nobody Knows* (London: Smith Gryphon, 1992), 7.

18 **"brave to the . . . foolhardiness"**: Riddington and Naden, *Frances*, 19.

18 **"Burke blood"**: Campbell, *Diana in Private*, 7.

19 **"Irish temperament"**: Campbell, 9.

19 **"very difficult and . . . headstrong"**: Sarah Bradford, *Diana: 20th anniversary edition* (London: Penguin, 2017), 42, Kindle.

19 **"the blood of . . . be"**: Bradford, 42.

19 **"related by ancestry . . . destiny"**: Saul Dibb, dir., trailer for *The Duchess*, Pathé UK, 2008.

19 **"there were supposedly . . . another"**: Mary Clarke, *Diana: Once Upon a Time* (London: Pan Books, 1994), 18.

19 **"As soon as . . . qualities"**: Clarke, 146.

20 **"the advantage of . . . glare"**: Patrick Jephson, *Shadows of a Princess* (London: William Collins, 2017), 128.

20 **"Whenever things got . . . ease"**: Rosa Monckton, "Her Laughter, Her Sense of Fun," in *Requiem: Diana, Princess of Wales 1961–1997 Memories and Tributes*, ed. Brian MacArthur (London: Pavilion, 1997), 60.

20 **"When I came . . . title"**: Sally Bedell Smith, *Diana: The Life of a Troubled Princess* (London: Aurum Press, 1999), 228.

20 **"closer to people . . . top"**: Morton, *Diana: Her True Story*, 379.

21 **"They are just . . . hereditary"**: Andrew Morton, *Diana's Diary* (London: Michael O'Mara, 1990), 29.

21 **A famous example . . . peril**: Nancy Mitford, "The English Aristocracy," *Encounter*, September 1955, 5–11.

21 **"Eliza Doolittle at . . . down"**: Roy Strong, *The Roy Strong Diaries, 1967–1987* (London: Weidenfeld & Nicolson, 1997), 291.

22 **"upper-class youth . . . accent"**: Christopher South, "The Class You're in, or Want to Be," *Cambridge Daily News*, January 21, 1987, 12.

22 **"the golden age . . . A-list"**: "Sir Roy Strong Reveals All His Contradictions," *Evening Standard*, September 15, 2011.

22 **"lack of formal education"**: Morton, *Diana's Diary*, 7.

23 **"A sprig of . . . England"**: Douglas Keay, *Royal Wedding* (London: IPC Magazines, 1981), 8.

23 **"royal Stuart blood"**: Keay, 7.

24 **"Mixed blood . . . Family"**: Michael Billig, *Talking of the Royal Family* (London: Routledge, 1992), 105.

25 **"most 'British' sovereign . . . blood"**: Billig, *Talking of the Royal Family*, citing Hugh Montgomery-Massingberd, *Her Majesty the Queen* (London: Willow Books, 1986), 233.

25 **"the ancient British . . . millennium"**: Marion Bowman, "Research Note: After Diana," *Folklore* 109 (1998), 101.

25 **"dirty great foreign con"**: Julie Burchill, *Diana* (London: Orion, 1999), 7.

26 **"a beautiful Anglo-Saxon . . . Graeco-German"**: Burchill, 7.

26 **"flirtatious and gawky . . . finish"**: Burchill, 150.

26 **"power-dressed girls . . . bit"**: Burchill, 163.

26 **"surliness seemed bred . . . way"**: Burchill, 9.

26 **"The country belonged . . . commoners"**: Burchill, 7.

26 **"The Germans . . . Stavros"**: Jephson, *Shadows*, 53.

27 **"It is my . . . snobs"**: Campbell, *Diana in Private*, 221.

27 **"the man on the street"**: Morton, *Diana: Her True Story*, 116.

28 **"chinless wonders with . . . disgusting"**: "Viscount in Rumpus with DJ," *Aberdeen Evening Express*, May 23, 1984, 3.

28 **"I am not . . . me"**: Mary Fletcher, "Guess What Little Brother's Been Saying About Diana!," *Woman*, January 24, 1987, 8–10.

29 **"feel that they . . . resident"**: *Lorraine*, ITV1, June 10, 2021.

29 ***A Very Private School***: Charles Spencer, *A Very Private School: A Memoir* (London: William Collins, 2024).

29 **"the psychological trauma . . . child"**: Joy Schaverien, *Boarding School Syndrome: The Psychological Trauma of the "Privileged" Child* (London: Routledge, 2015).

30 **"natural nobility . . . family"**: Text of funeral oration published in Charles Spencer, "The Most Hunted Person of the Modern Age," *Guardian*, May 4, 2007.

30 **"It was as . . . houses"**: Anonymous, September 6, 1997, GDP.

30 **"blue blood . . . chatted"**: Prince Harry, *Spare* (London: Transworld, 2023), 303, Kindle.

30 **"The snobbery . . . nauseating"**: Prince Harry, 90.

2. The Rat Pack

32 **"It was the . . . after you"**: Morton, *Diana: Her True Story*, 50.

33 **"He was all . . . puzzling"**: Transcript of Peter Settelen tapes, published in Jack Royston, "Diana: Her True Voice," *Sun*, August 2, 2017.

33 **"close friend and confidante"**: Wensley Clarkson and Jim Newman, "Royal Love Train," *Sunday Mirror*, November 16, 1980, 5.

34 **"She holds her . . . herself"**: Michael Palin, *Halfway to Hollywood: Diaries 1980–1988* (London: Weidenfeld & Nicolson, 2009), 561.

34 **George III was . . . lives**: Linda Colley, *Britons: Forging the Nation, 1707–1837* (London: Pimlico, 2003), 197.

34 **Two hundred years . . . Palace**: Peter Tory, "Peter Tory's Diary," *Daily Mirror*, August 31, 1984, 13.

34 **In an oral history . . . garden**: Betty Judge, 2003, National Life Stories: General Interviews, BL, C464/40.

34 **Another Londoner, Ian . . . curtains**: Ian Jackman, *Flowers for Princess Diana* (Las Vegas: Interstate 15 Publishing Corp., 2002), 36.

35 **"whether he was . . . England"**: Sarah Spencer interviewed by Jeremy Slazenger, *Woman's Own*, April 8, 1978, cited in Smith, *Diana: The Life of a Troubled Princess*, 63.

35 **"You're the wicked . . . you?"**: Whitaker and Wilson, *Diana vs. Charles*, 4.

35 **he remembered the . . . her**: Smith, *Diana: The Life of a Troubled Princess*, 74.

36 **"What a cunning . . . her"**: James Whitaker, "Diana and the Tender Trap," *Daily Star*, June 29, 1981, 15.

36 **"a retired brigadier . . . daughters"**: Roy Greenslade, "James Whitaker, the Royal Reporters' Royal Reporter, Dies at 71," *Guardian*, February 15, 2012.

36 **"Nice toffs in . . . match"**: Sharon Marshall, *Tabloid Girl* (London: Hachette Digital, 2010), 86, Kindle.

36 **"One was very . . . civilized"**: "The Princess and the Press—Interview: James Whitaker," PBS online.

36 **"Admiration is no . . . be"**: Jon Akass, *Sun*, April 7, 1978, 6, cited in Adrian Bingham and Martin Conboy, *Tabloid Century: The Popular Press in Britain, 1896 to the Present* (Peter Lang: Oxford, 2015), 122.

36 **"James and I . . . Pack"**: Arthur Edwards, *I'll Tell the Jokes Arthur: Diana, the Royal Family and Me* (London: Blake Publishing, 1993), 30.

37 **"Look Diana . . . it"**: "Princess and the Press," PBS online.

37 **He named this . . . sight**: "Princess and the Press," PBS online.

37 **"He had this . . . operation"**: Peter Lefcourt in discussion with the author, July 28, 2023.

37 **"I would always . . . chase"**: James Whitaker, interviewed by Piers Brendon for *The Windsors* documentary series, ITV, 1993. The Papers of Piers Brendon, Churchill Archives Centre, Churchill College, University of Cambridge.

38 **"Tits, bums, QPR . . . fags"**: Chris Horrie and Peter Chippindale, *Stick It Up Your Punter: The Uncut Story of the* Sun *Newspaper* (London: Faber and Faber, 2013), 76, Kindle.

38 **"all the nudes . . . print"**: *Week Ending*, Radio 4, March 22, 1980.

38 **"Fuck me, Arthur . . . well"**: Greenslade, "James Whitaker, the Royal Reporters' Royal Reporter, Dies at 71," *Guardian,* February 15, 2012.

38 **"big fat tomato"**: Tina Brown, *The Diana Chronicles* (London: Arrow Books, 2017), 79, Kindle. Other sources suggest the nickname was actually "the big red tomato" or the "big, fat, red tomato."

38 **"wanted its future . . . public"**: Whitaker and Wilson, *Diana vs. Charles*, 12.

38 **"Not one . . . Simpson"**: "Let the King Make His Own Choice," *Daily Mirror*, December 5, 1936, 6, cited in Bingham and Conboy, *Tabloid Century*, 104.

39 **"well brought-up . . . evasion"**: Whitaker and Wilson, *Diana vs. Charles*, 13.

39 **"the man who . . . knew"**: Whitaker, "Diana and the Tender Trap," *Daily Star*.

39 **"wormed her way"**: James Whitaker, "Oh Joan You're Just Priceless," *Daily Mirror*, November 14, 1985, 9.

40 **When interviewed by . . . Diana**: *The 11 O'clock Show*, Channel 4, March 9, 1999.

42 **Whitaker wrote a . . . thighs**: James Whitaker, "It's Nice to See Some Things Don't Change," *Daily Mirror*, June 1, 1985, 1.

42 **"THE KISS"**: "The Kiss," *Sunday Mirror*, August 10, 1997, 1.

43 **"Don't worry if . . . true"**: Horrie and Chippindale, *Stick It Up*, 104.

43 **"the Germans . . . Germans"**: Horrie and Chippindale, 102.

43 **"sad Kate,"**: "The Sun Says," *Sun*, April 7, 1987, 2.

43 **"no-nonsense American experts . . . recovery"**: David Jones, "We're Booming Marvellous," *Sun*, April 8, 1987, 4.

43 **Diana's compassion was . . . AIDS**: Phil Dampier, "Di to Shake Hands of AIDS Victims Today," *Sun*, April 9, 1987, 11.

44 **"THE SUN INVADES . . . remember"**: "The Sun Invades Germany!," *Sun*, April 12, 1987, 1.

44 **"Dazzling Di . . . hearts"**: "Di's Right," *Sun*, April 12, 1987, 5.

44 **"republicans down the . . . back"**: Richard Stott, "By the Editor," *Daily Mirror*, June 8, 1992, 2.

45 **"Last night . . . amazed"**: "69,245 Back HRH Diana," *Daily Mirror*, July 23, 1996, 1.

45 **"this kind of . . . middle"**: John Kay, "Row Over Royal Nudes," *Sun*, April 18, 1992, 3.

46 **"Diana had a . . . day"**: Richard Kay in discussion with the author, March 4, 2023.

46 **"what's the alternative . . . you?"**: Tina Brown, "A Woman in Earnest," *New Yorker*, September 7, 1997.

46 **"profound spiritual contact . . . depths"**: Tim Graham, *Diana, H.R.H. the Princess of Wales* (London: Michael O'Mara, 1988), 9.

47 **"favourite newspaperman . . . been"**: Edwards, *I'll Tell the Jokes*, jacket cover.

47 **"Looking me straight . . . smiled"**: Edwards, 4.

47 **"Ooh. There's that . . . 'cahoots' "**: Clive James, "Mourning My Friend, Princess Diana," *New Yorker*, September 15, 1997.

48 **"The temptation would . . . again"**: Kay, discussion.

48 **she mimed vomiting . . . of**: Judy Wade, *Diana: The Intimate Portrait* (London: John Blake, 2008), 20.

48 **"hound her until . . . grave"**: *Witness*, BBC World Service, September 1, 2017.

49 **The first paparazzo . . . accidents**: Ray Bellisario, *To Tread on Royal Toes* (Aberdeen: Impulse Books, 1972).

50   **"look and sound . . . words"**: Mark Saunders and Glenn Harvey, *Dicing with Di: The Amazing Adventures of Britain's Royal Chasers* (London: Blake, 1996), 1.

50   **"While she was . . . hands!"**: Saunders and Harvey, 16.

50   **"I often felt . . . me"**: Jayne Fincher, *Diana: Portrait of a Princess* (New York: Simon & Schuster Editions, 1998), 9.

50   **"a magical human being"**: Edwards, *I'll Tell the Jokes*, 247.

50   **"the nearest thing . . . earth"**: Edwards, 240.

50   **"They gathered around . . . grace"**: Edwards, 125–26.

50   **"KEEP YOUR EYES . . . THIGHS"**: Edwards, 125–26.

51   **"Lady Diana Spencer . . . abating"**: "History in the Making," *Majesty* website.

52   **In one especially . . . friends**: "Tales from the Nursery," *Sunday Mirror*, October 21, 1984, 24–25.

52   **The morning after . . . beatifically**: Bob Williams, "Drawing by Bob Williams," *Daily Mirror*, June 22, 1982, 9.

52   **"suffering royal holy mother"**: John Pearson, *The Ultimate Family: The Making of the Royal House of Windsor* (London: Michael Joseph, 1986), 277.

52   **"'sweet babies' . . . have"**: "Our Pride That He Chose a Local Girl," *Lynn News & Advertiser*, February 27, 1981, 20.

53   **Diana's former press . . . pregnancy**: Dickie Arbiter, *On Duty with the Queen* (Dorking, UK: Blink, 2014), 221.

53   **"Happily our national . . . journalism"**: "Our Pride That He Chose," *Lynn News & Advertiser*, 20.

53   **this stunning revelation . . . page**: "I Can't Stop Biting My Nails," *Liverpool Echo*, February 15, 1985, 1.

53   **"The Princess of . . . nail-biter"**: "Hands-On Experience," *Reading Evening Post*, June 1, 1994, 8.

54   ***Newcastle Evening Chronicle* . . . teenager**: "The Best Possible Taste," *Newcastle Evening Chronicle*, April 24, 1984, 5.

54   **A paper in Dundee . . . fingers**: "Car Door Scare for Princess," *Dundee Courier*, October 22, 1986, 6.

54   **a subeditor . . . school**: "Di's Confession," *Aberdeen Evening Express*, April 16, 1984, 5.

54   **"a little bit of meaning"**: "Princes Are Being Used by Di," *Birmingham Mail*, January 13, 1996, 6.

55   **"Bloody cowing rotten . . . cow"**: Response to summer 1997 directive (Special: Death of Diana), MOA P1730, cited in James Thomas, *Diana's Mourning: A People's History* (Cardiff: University of Wales Press, 2002), 66.

3. Will the Real Diana Please Sit Down

58   **"Of course . . . means"**: "Whatever 'in Love' Means—Charles and Diana Engagement Interview," ITN Archive, 1981.

59 **"The bride's dress . . . pronounced"**: Response to 1981 directive (Special: Royal Wedding), August 12, 1981, MOA H260.

59 **"the dishevelled state . . . Dress'"**: Response to 1981 directive, n.d., MOA R470.

59 **In Rose Joseph's . . . wearing**: *The Royal Wedding*, Capital Radio, July 29, 1981.

60 **"I imagined she . . . voice"**: James Lees-Milne, *The Milk of Paradise: Diaries, 1993–1997*, ed. Michael Bloch (London: John Murray, 2005), 195.

60 **his visit to . . . evening**: James Lees-Milne, *Ceaseless Turmoil: Diaries, 1988–1992*, ed. Michael Bloch (London: John Murray, 2004), 286.

60 **"She just wouldn't . . . world"**: Anonymous source interviewed in Smith, *Diana: The Life of a Troubled Princess*, 148.

60 **Jan Ravens imitated . . . like**: Andrew Morgan, "Princess Di—as Never Before!," *Liverpool Echo*, November 12, 1985, 8.

60 **"Just make her . . . dizzy"**: Susan Henderson, "What Kate Does Best," *Aberdeen Evening Express*, December 24, 1991, 27.

61 **"I remember those . . . mischievousness"**: Colin McDowell, *Dianastyle* (London: Aurum, 2007), 8.

61 **"Can YOU Spot . . . well"**: Paul Callan, "Can You Spot Lady Di?," *Daily Mirror*, May 8, 1981, 17.

61 **Professor Therese Davis . . . cinema**: "The Face of a Saint," in *Planet Diana: Cultural Studies and Global Mourning*, ed. Ien Ang (Kingswood, New South Wales: Research Centre in Intercommunal Studies, University of Western Sydney, 1997), 95.

62 **"Dress is a . . . person"**: Cited in Philip Mansel, *Dressed to Rule: Royal and Court Costume from Louis XIV to Elizabeth II* (New Haven and London: Yale University Press, 2005), xiv.

62 **"shoulder pads and . . . star"**: Tina Brown, "The Mouse That Roared," *Vanity Fair*, October 1985.

62 **"veins along the . . . restraint"**: Joan Juliet Buck, "Di Gets Real," *Vanity Fair*, December 1989.

62 **"commanding . . . will"**: Anthony Holden, "Diana's Revenge," *Vanity Fair*, February 1993.

62 **"Diana Reborn . . . icon"**: Cathy Horyn, "Diana Reborn," *Vanity Fair*, July 1997.

63 **"A terrible thing . . . Road"**: Interview with Malcolm McLaren, n.d., YouTube video.

63 **"someone ruled by . . . middle-class"**: "Why Vivienne Westwood Wants to Dress the Princess of Wales," *Woman & Home*, August 1995, 122–23.

64 **"What the nobility . . . style"**: McDowell, *Dianastyle*, 34.

64 **"a gawky fourteen-year-old . . . thrilled"**: Felicity Clark, 2009, An Oral History of British Fashion, BL, C1046/16.

65 **"world's best-known . . . example"**: "The Englishwoman," *Vogue*, December 1984, 141, 145.

65   **"God . . . head to fit"**: Frederick Fox, 2003–2004, An Oral History of British Fashion, BL, C1046/06.

66   **"really, really sweet . . . depth"**: Fox, An Oral History of British Fashion.

67   **"captured the femininity . . . body"**: Catherine Walker, *Catherine Walker: An Autobiography by the Private Couturier to Diana, Princess of Wales* (London: HarperCollins, 1998), 27.

67   **"quirkiness and freedom . . . fussiness"**: Walker, 53.

67   **"indigo and pink . . . summer"**: Walker, 49.

67   **"English country garden colouring"**: Walker, 43.

67   **"Arthurian Princess"**: Walker, 63.

67   **It was Walker . . . Elizabeth I**: Walker, 73.

69   **JCPenney sold out . . . Virginia**: Eloise Moran, *The Lady Di Look Book: What Diana Was Trying to Tell Us Through Her Clothes* (London: Mitchell Beazley, 2022), 22, Kindle.

69   **sent sales of . . . days**: Alison Blair, "Go Vest, Young Lady," *Newcastle Evening Chronicle*, November 8, 1984, 5.

69   **"A £5,000 dress . . . good"**: "MP Wants Lady Di to Wed in Jeans," *Belfast Telegraph*, March 12, 1981, 12.

69   **For *Woman's Own* . . . silk**: The sketch was sold at auction for £5,500 via Kerry Taylor Auctions, June 17, 2019.

69   **"If the Princess . . . Collins"**: Nigel Nelson, "How I'd Dress Di for Big Night Out," *Sunday Mirror*, October 21, 1984, 24–25.

69   **Bruce Oldfield said . . . frozen out**: McDowell, *Dianastyle*, 161.

70   **"There were long . . . relieved"**: Tony Frost, "My Seven Years inside Diana's World," *Sunday Mirror*, March 2, 1985, 23.

70   **"from a shy . . . acclaim"**: Frost, 21.

71   **The glamorous West . . . Tough**: Judy Gould, "Lady Di Goes to Your Heads," *Sunday Mirror*, June 28, 1981, 4–5.

71   **"I wore Diana's . . . flats"**: Kristin Contino, "How Women Are Modeling Their Style After Diana, Princess of Wales in 2019," *Royal Central*, July 22, 2019.

72   **By one count . . . princess**: Daniel Sneider, "Charles and Diana Stop the Show in Japan," *Christian Science Monitor*, May 14, 1986.

72   **In a market . . . endorsement**: Garth Gibbs, "On the Seamy Side," *Daily Mirror*, March 15, 1985, 13.

72   **In 2010, a . . . cello**: Alison Chung, "Outrage Over 'Princess Diana' Lingerie Ad," Sky News online, September 1, 2010.

72   **Ahead of Diana's . . . thing**: "N.Y. Turns on the Glitz for Princess," *Irish Independent*, February 2, 1989, 22.

73   **To give one . . . names**: *Just Amazing*, ITV, May 5, 1984.

73   **"In a certain . . . Wales"**: "Legal Eagles," *Evening Herald*, July 5, 1996, 2.

73   **"People say you . . . first"**: "Interview: Selina Scott," *Country Life*, July 24, 2008.

73   ***Radio Times* magazine**: *Radio Times* cover, July 27, 1996.

74 **"If you look . . . it"**: "The Princess and I," *The Day That Changed My Life*, BBC Two, July 29, 1996.

74 **"a shy, unconfident . . . all"**: "The Princess and I."

74 **"Being Diana sent . . . us"**: "Stressed Lookalike Christina Gives Up the Di Job," *Daily Record*, March 20, 1997, 3.

76 **"No one plays . . . Diana"**: Caryn James, "Love-Starved Royalty, Partial to Babushkas," *New York Times*, May 15, 1996, C16.

76 **"I did it for Ireland!"**: "Student Is Jailed for Slashing Di Portrait," *Belfast Telegraph*, September 16, 1981, 4.

77 **"getting me"**: Richard Kay, "Portrait of a Princess in Pain," *Daily Mail*, February 4, 2022.

77 **"distress and neuroses . . . overdone"**: "The Art of Diana," *Omnibus*, BBC One, August 30, 1998.

77 **"If you are . . . canvas?"**: Vicki Woods, "Harpers & Queen Presents an Exclusive Preview of the New Official Portrait of HRH the Princess of Wales," *Harpers & Queen*, May 1992, 20.

78 **"all so fantastic . . . relaxed"**: Rosalind Coward, *Diana: The Portrait* (Kansas City: Andrew McMeel Publishing, 2007), 105.

78 **"Why can't she . . . diamonds"**: James Whitaker, "I'm Gonna Wash That Man Right Out of My Hair," *Daily Mirror*, January 4, 1993, 13.

79 **"Sharonisation of Diana"**: Cited in Tim Burrows, *The Invention of Essex* (London: Profile Books, 2023), 240.

79 **"Will the real . . . princess"**: Burrows, 240.

79 **"put your head . . . princess"**: Tim Clayton and Phil Craig, *Diana: Story of a Princess* (New York: Atria Books, 2001), 270.

79 **"parvenus at *Tatler* . . . not"**: Dillie Keane, "Who's the Likelier Essex Girl?," *Mail on Sunday*, March 20, 1994, 33.

79 **"trash icon for our times"**: Nigel Fountain, "A Trash Icon for Our Times," *Observer*, July 27, 1997, 21.

79 **"a talent unmatched . . . seriously"**: Rachel Tashjian, "What Does It Mean to Be the Best-Dressed Woman in the World?" *Harper's Bazaar*, November 14, 2022.

80 **"We all need . . . taste"**: Diana Vreeland, *D.V.* (Cambridge, MA: Da Capo Press, 1997), 122.

80 **"divestiture"**: Hamish Bowles, "A Royal Divestiture," *Vogue*, May 1997.

80 **Kim Kardashian paid . . . 1987**: Emily Kirkpatrick, "Kim Kardashian Buys Princess Diana's Amethyst Cross for Almost $200K," *Vanity Fair*, January 19, 2023.

80 **the original black-sheep . . . auction**: Lisa Lambert, "Million-Dollar Sweater: Bids Pour in for Diana's Sheep Jumper," *BBC News* online, September 14, 2023.

81 **"hint at a subtle rebellion"**: Moran, *Lady Di Look Book*, 34.

81 **"a bit punk"**: Moran, 63.

81   **"the biggest punk ... England"**: *Diana: Queen of Style*, Channel 4, November 15, 2021.

4. Don't Do It, Di!

85   **"clear our minds ... Queen"**: Ben Johnson, "Empire Day," Historic UK, https://www.historic-uk.com/HistoryUK/HistoryofBritain/Empire-Day.

85   **"magical feeling deep ... Prince"**: On This Day: June 21, 1982, BBC News online.

85   **"something so special ... it"**: Johnson, "Empire Day," Historic UK.

85   **"gleamed like newly ... moment"**: Paul Callan, "Diana's Nine-Month Journey to Motherhood," *Daily Mirror*, June 22, 1982, 14–15.

86   **"a strong woman ... quietly"**: "An Interview with HRH the Princess of Wales," *Panorama*, BBC One, November 20, 1995.

87   **"common touch ... Princess"**: "The People's Princess Is Fifty Tomorrow," *Dundee Courier*, December 24, 1986, 8.

87   **"memories that became ... time"**: Colleen Denney, *Representing Diana, Princess of Wales: Cultural Memory and Fairy Tales Revisited* (Madison, NJ: Fairleigh Dickinson University Press, 2005), 14.

87   **"I feel my ... wife"**: "Talking Personally: Charles and Diana Lengthy and Intimate Interview," ITN Archive, 1985.

88   **"I am the boss ... bird-brained"**: Roger Laing, "I'm the Boss in Our Marriage," *Woman*, September 12, 1987, 29.

89   **"Natural love of children"**: Audrey Whiting, "Just What Di's Doctor Ordered," *Sunday Mirror*, May 9, 1982, 11.

89   **"panel of parliamentary 'wise men'"**: Martin Philips, "Splitting Heirs," *Daily Mirror*, January 24, 1994, 7.

89   **"She's the last ... more"**: Chris Hutchins and Dominic Midgley, *Diana on the Edge: Inside the Mind of the Princess of Wales* (London: Smith Gryphon, 1996), 178.

89   **"Would any self-respecting ... happen?"**: Moreen Simpson, "Just like Dad," *Aberdeen Evening Express*, April 20, 1987, 6.

90   **Eight months into ... abortion**: Joyce Lister, letter to the editor, *Buckinghamshire Examiner*, May 14, 1982, 4.

90   **Up in Lincolnshire ... area**: "New Proposals for Midwives," *Grantham Journal*, September 28, 1984, 9.

90   **"Nappy rash and ... years"**: Angela Candlin, "Oh the Many Delights of Motherhood!," *Liverpool Echo*, May 11, 1982, 8.

91   **"It was an aristocratic curse"**: Anne Glenconner, *Lady in Waiting: My Extraordinary Life in the Shadow of the Crown* (London: Hodder & Stoughton, 2019), 178.

91   **A few days ... Camilla**: Morton, *Diana: Her True Story*, 60.

91   **"irretrievably broken down"**: *Charles: The Private Man, the Public Role*, ITV, June 29, 1994.

91 **"Affairs were expected . . . it"**: Glenconner, *Lady in Waiting*, 178.

91 **"She had everything . . . become queen"**: Brian Coombs, May 11, 1998, MMB, C900/16404.

92 **"father figure"**: Morton, *Diana: Her True Story*, 93.

93 **"sincere thanks for . . . towel"**: Letter from Buckingham Palace printed in *Spare Rib*, November 1981, 5.

93 **"People who don't . . . marriage"**: "Don't Do It!" *Spare Rib*, August 1981, 3.

93 **Fifteen years later . . . it!"**: Wade, *Diana: The Intimate Portrait*, 245.

93 **"if we are . . . sterile"**: Caroline Hearst, letter to the editor, *Spare Rib*, September 1981, 23.

94 **"small *c* conservative"**: Kay, discussion.

94 **"wander around barefoot . . . hand"**: Andrew Morton, *The Royal Yacht Britannia* (London: Oribis, 1984), 9.

95 **"*Only* a small . . . shot!"**: Michael O'Mara in discussion with the author, October 13, 2023.

95 **In the archives . . . *Mum***: Diane Stevenson, 1992, GDP.

96 **"democracy was praised . . . system"**: "Women and Love," *The Open Mind*, PBS, December 6, 1987.

96 **"Can a woman's . . . anger"**: Rebecca Walker, "Becoming the 3rd Wave," *Ms.*, spring 2002, 86–87. Originally published in *Ms.*, Jan/Feb 1992.

96 **"she had real . . . truth"**: Morton, *Diana: Her True Story*, 137.

97 **"Most people . . . scum"**: Rosalind Renshaw, "What on Earth Have They Done to Deserve This?," *Reading Evening Post*, June 15, 1992, 8.

98 **"A bit drawn . . . world"**: Joan Thwaites, February 1992, GDP.

98 **"It's lasted about . . . good"**: Thwaites, March 1992.

98 **"The Princess of . . . revealing"**: Thwaites, July 1992.

98 **"A bit chubby . . . we?"**: Morton, *Diana: Her True Story*, 93.

99 **"14-stone fatty . . . way"**: "From Porker to Corker!," *Liverpool Echo*, August 22, 1984, 3.

99 **"fastidious in her diet"**: "The Great Dieting Debate: Readers Have Their Say," *Sandwell Evening Mail*, May 26, 1986, 6.

99 **"Princess Di looks ridiculous"**: Mrs. G. Tyler quoted in "The Great Dieting Debate," *Sandwell Evening Mail*.

99 **"malnourished look"**: G. Bridges quoted in "The Great Dieting Debate," *Sandwell Evening Mail*.

99 **"unknown numbers of specialists"**: Mrs. Irene Deeley quoted in "The Great Dieting Debate," *Sandwell Evening Mail*.

100 **"Oh, my dears . . . me"**: Hutchins and Midgley, *Diana on the Edge*, 132.

100 **"conduct . . . sufficiently baffling . . . loss"**: Hutchins and Midgley, vii.

100 **"CHARLES: HIS TRUE STORY"**: Penny Junor, "Charles: His True Story," *Today*, July 6, 1992, 1.

100 **"temporarily aberrant behaviour"**: Jonathan Dimbleby, *The Prince of Wales: A Biography* (London: Little, Brown & Co., 1994), 301.